An Introduction
to the
Criminal Process
in Canada

Second Edition

Alan W. Mewett, Q.C., LL.B., B.C.L., LL.M., S.J.D.
Professor of Law
University of Toronto

CARSWELL
Thomson Professional Publishing

Canadian Cataloguing in Publication Data

Mewett, Alan W., 1930-
   An introduction to the criminal process in Canada

2nd ed.
Includes index.
ISBN 0-459-55146-9 (bound)   ISBN 0-459-55147-7 (pbk.)

1. Criminal procedure - Canada - Popular works.
I. Title.

KE9260.Z82M48   1992   345.71′05   C92-094280-6
KF9619.6.M48   1992

Typesetting: Video Text Inc., Barrie, Ontario, Canada

CARSWELL
Thomson Professional Publishing

One Corporate Plaza, 2075 Kennedy Road, Scarborough, Ontario M1T 3V4
Customer Service:
Toronto 1-416-609-3800
Elsewhere in Canada/U.S. 1-800-387-5161
Fax 1-800-298-5094

Preface

Books that purport to be introductions to technical subjects run the dual risk of either being too simple and hence inaccurate, or too complicated and thus incomprehensible. I have no doubt that such faults are present in this book.

An understanding of what the criminal process is all about is not, however, a matter that should be limited to those who have a special expertise in the subject. The criminal law affects everyone and while no one — not even the lawyer — can be expected to know all of the criminal offences that now exist, there is no reason why *how* the criminal law works should not be known to everyone who is interested. Criminal procedure embraces the whole system that starts with the commission of an offence and does not end until an acquittal or expiry of the sentence in the case of a conviction. Access to an understanding of this system, at least in its broad outline, should be available to everyone.

The Canadian Charter of Rights and Freedoms exists for the protection of everyone, and most of us are familiar with the Charter. But a knowledge of the Charter without some knowledge of how it interacts with the rules of criminal procedure gives an incomplete picture.

I have tried to make this book intelligible to the reader without a legal background. I am not sure who that reader might be, though I hope it will be anyone, from the student to the social worker, from the police recruit to the justice of the peace. The lawyer will, doubtless, find much to criticize in it. Generalities and precision go uneasily together, and I can only hope that where I have had to sacrifice detail, I have not unwittingly led the reader into error.

Preface to the Second Edition

When I wrote the first edition of this book, the Charter of Rights and Freedoms was in force, but cases were only just beginning to make their way to the Supreme Court of Canada. Now, four years later, we are seeing the enormous impact that the Charter has had on the entire criminal process in Canada. Undoubtedly, more is yet to come, but it seems appropriate to produce an updated version of the book before the present one becomes too out of date.

The reception of the first edition has been encouraging and this reinforces my belief that knowledge of the law — at least its basic principles — should be accessible to everyone interested in pursuing it. Reading this book is not going to make anyone an expert in criminal procedure, but I hope it will give him or her some understanding of how the system works.

List of Statutes

Table of Contents

1

Crime and Investigation

INTRODUCTION

Without criminal law, there could be no such thing as a crime and without a crime, no such thing as the criminal process. Criminal law must begin, therefore, with an enactment by a competent body creating a criminal offence. In Canada, this simple statement requires some elaboration. Under the Constitution Act of 1867, which is now part of the Constitution Acts, 1867 to 1982, the federal government is given jurisdiction by section 91(27) over "The Criminal Law, except the Constitution of Courts of Criminal Jurisdiction, but including the Procedure in Criminal Matters." It follows from this that only the federal Parliament is competent to legislate criminal law and criminal procedure. However, section 92 of the same Act lists those areas within the exclusive jurisdiction of the provinces and item (15) is "The Imposition of Punishment by Fine, Penalty or Imprisonment for enforcing any Law of the Province made in relation to any matter coming within any of the Classes of Subjects enumerated in this Section." Section 92 itself lists several matters within the exclusive jurisdiction of a province such as property and civil rights, shop, saloon and other licences in order to raise revenue, and all matters of a merely local or private nature. While, therefore, it is perfectly true to say that in Canada, all criminal law is federal, there is a large body of provincial legislation that imposes a penalty (either a fine or imprisonment or some lesser penalty) for its breach.

Indeed, in terms of bulk, there is probably more provincial "criminal" legislation than federal and certainly, in terms of its impact on the ordinary man in the street, provincial legislation is much more likely to intrude upon his life than is federal legislation. The reason for this is clear. Provincial legislation that merely creates a crime is invalid since it invades federal jurisdiction, but it is valid if the purpose of it is better to enforce some matter that is otherwise within the provincial jurisdiction. Since those items reserved for the provinces by section 92 are largely those governing such everyday matters as controlling traffic, regulating retail businesses, licensing alcohol and other sales, regulating municipal affairs and so on, it is not surprising to find so much provincial criminal legislation. It would be rather pointless to give the province, for example, the power to regulate speed on the highway or the sale of alcoholic beverages, if the province were not also given the power to impose a penalty to enforce its rules.

Thus Canada has two distinct branches of criminal law — that justified under section 91(27) as "criminal law" and reserved for the federal government, and that justified under section 92(15) and within the provincial jurisdiction. Section 91, however, reserves for the federal government other matters besides criminal law; banking, bankruptcy, trade and commerce, and the postal service, to name only a few (not to mention a general power to legislate for the "Peace, Order and good Government of Canada"). If, therefore, the federal government legislates over one of those particular matters and attaches a penalty to some act, that legislation may be valid criminal law, not by virtue of the criminal law power contained in section 91(27), but by virtue of powers contained in some other clause.

When one talks about the criminal law of Canada, it is therefore necessary to distinguish between criminal law that arises from section 91(27) and is within the exclusive jurisdiction of the federal government, criminal law that arises from the better enforcement of some other clause in section 91, which is also within the exclusive jurisdiction of the federal government, but which may have certain procedural differences attached to it because of its different basis, and that criminal law which is really the enforcement by way of some penal sanction of some clause of section 92 and which is within the exclusive jurisdiction of the provinces. This last is sometimes called quasi-criminal law or provincial penal law, to avoid the confusion of equating it with what is sometimes called "real" criminal law or criminal law "properly so-called."

As can be seen, the distinction between federal criminal law and provincial penal legislation may not be all that easy to draw in practice. It is possible for the two different areas of jurisdiction to overlap. For example, the regulation of traffic is within the provincial jurisdiction and hence all provinces have Highway Traffic Acts or Motor Vehicle Acts or some such named Act that creates numerous driving offences. On the other hand, if some form of driving conduct reaches such proportions as to be a danger to the public in general, it may be the subject of federal criminal legislation. Drunk driving may be seen as a matter affecting the regulation of traffic or it may be viewed as a matter of criminal law. Provincial legislation governing such conduct would be valid as being for the better enforcement of traffic regulation; federal legislation would be valid as being criminal law. In such a case both pieces of legislation would be jurisdictionally valid, but under the constitutional doctrine of paramountcy, if federal and provincial legislation (both jurisdictionally valid) cover precisely the same subject matter, the federal legislation is said to occupy the field and the provincial legislation must give way, leaving only the federal legislation in effect. This, in fact, is what has happened in the case of drunk driving and related offences.

On the other hand, if the two pieces of legislation do not cover the same subject matter, then they can co-exist and both are valid. For example, there are obvious forms of poor driving — one can drive carelessly, drive dangerously, or drive absolutely recklessly. All provinces have legislation that penalizes what is variously called careless driving or driving without due care and attention. The Criminal Code, however, creates by section 249 an offence of dangerous driving, punishment for which varies from that for merely a summary conviction offence to a maximum term of imprisonment for 14 years if death results. If these modes of driving mean the same thing, then there cannot be separate offences covering exactly the same type of act, yet provincial careless driving offences generally are punishable by a maximum of six months' imprisonment. Not without some difficulty, the Supreme Court[1] has held that both offences are valid because they do not cover the same type of act; careless driving being driving in a manner that an ordinary prudent driver would not adopt, and dangerous driving being driving that, in addition to that, has, in the circumstances, an element of danger to the public.

At the same time, one can have a situation where the province, purporting to rely on the jurisdiction given to it under section 92, of the Constitution Act, 1867 enacts penal legislation that encroaches on the federal jurisdiction over criminal law; or conversely, the federal government, purporting to enact criminal law under its section 91 power, encroaches on the jurisdiction of the provinces. In these cases, such legislation is *ultra vires*. For example, for a number of years, the Criminal Code has contained the offence of driving a motor vehicle while one's licence to drive was suspended or cancelled, on the theory that unlicensed drivers constituted a danger to all users of the highway, and thus it was properly a criminal offence within the competence of the federal gov-

---

1 In a series of cases, *O'Grady v. Sparling*, [1960] S.C.R. 804, 33 C.R. 293, 33 W.W.R. 360, 128 C.C.C. 1, 25 D.L.R. (2d) 145; *Mann v. R.*, [1966] S.C.R. 238, 47 C.R. 400, [1966] 2 C.C.C. 273, 56 D.L.R. (2d) 1; *Binus v. R.* [1967] S.C.R. 594, 2 C.R.N.S. 118, [1968] 1 C.C.C. 227; and *Peda v. R.*, [1969] S.C.R. 905, 7 C.R.N.S. 243, [1967] 4 C.C.C. 245, 6 D.L.R. (3d) 177.

ernment. However, the Supreme Court[2] has held that this was not properly criminal law, but the regulation of highway traffic since merely being unlicensed did not necessarily create any danger. It was thus properly a matter falling within provincial jurisdiction and the federal provision was held *ultra vires*. If, however, a person's licence has been suspended as part of the criminal sanction for having committed a criminal offence under the Code, then driving in violation of that criminal sanction may itself properly be a criminal offence and section 263 of the Code makes it a true criminal offence to drive in those circumstances.

It is more accurate to say, therefore, that the criminal process must begin with some valid criminal law, and that criminal law may be criminal in the real sense of the word and justified under section 91 of the Constitution Act, 1867 as being within the federal jurisdiction; or criminal in the sense of being for the enforcement of some other federal power; or criminal in the sense of being provincial penal legislation and justified under section 92 and being for the better enforcement of some power reserved for the provinces by section 92 of that Act. If must also, however, be constitutional in the sense that it does not violate the provisions of the Charter of Rights and Freedoms, which form Part I of the Constitution Act, 1982. This requirement will be dealt with in a separate chapter.

Criminal offences must also exist by virtue of an express piece of legislation. Section 9 of the Criminal Code provides that:

.... no person shall be convicted ...

    (*a*) of an offence at common law,

    (*b*) of an offence under an Act of the Parliament of England, or of Great Britain, or of the United Kingdom of Great Britain and Ireland, or

    (*c*) of an offence under an Act or ordinance in force in any province, territory or place before that province, territory or place became a province of Canada,

but nothing in this section affects the power, jurisdiction or authority that a court, judge, justice or magistrate had, immediately before the 1st day of April 1955, to impose punishment for contempt of court.

This section requires some explanation. It was not, of course, until 1867 that the power to create criminal law passed to the then newly-created federal government. Before that time, criminal law, in the various parts of what was to become Canada, consisted of that part of the English common law as had been brought into the various colonies at the time of their independent existence,[3] such imperial legislation as was applicable

---

2 *Boggs v. R.*, [1981] 1 S.C.R. 49, 19 C.R. (3d) 245, 8 M.V.R. 247, 10 M.V.R. 293, 58 C.C.C. (2d) 7, 120 D.L.R. (3d) 718, 34 N.R. 520.

3 To avoid argument, the dates were fixed at September 17, 1792 for Ontario, and October 1, 1763 for Quebec. For Nova Scotia and New Brunswick, 1758 is the generally accepted

to the colonies and any Acts of the Colonial legislatures as were criminal in nature. Indeed, section 129 of the Constitution Act of 1867 provided:

> Except as otherwise provided by this Act, all Laws in force in Canada, Nova Scotia or New Brunswick at the Union . . . shall continue in Ontario, Quebec, Nova Scotia, and New Brunswick respectively, as if the Union had not been made; subject nevertheless . . . to be repealed, abolished or altered by the Parliament of Canada, or by the Legislature of the respective Province, according to the Authority of the Parliament or that Legislature under this Act.

After the passing of the Constitution Act, 1867, the power to enact criminal law passed to the federal government and for some time therefore, criminal law in Canada was a rather confusing mixture, varying from province to province, of partly English common law, partly Imperial statutory law, partly pre-Confederation colonial legislation and partly post-Confederation federal legislation. The first codification came into force in 1892 and while it went a long way towards unifying criminal law in Canada, it was not a complete code. It not only preserved a number of criminal statutes, but also provided that the criminal law, as then existed in the various provinces, continued in force except insofar as it had been altered, varied or modified by the new Code or other legislation. Thus, criminal law in Canada might still vary from province to province. It was not until the coming into force of the Revised Code of 1955 that section 9 was finally enacted, providing, as we have seen, for the abolition of common law offences or pre-Confederation offences.

The Criminal Code of Canada, however, is certainly not a comprehensive code, by any means, of all of the criminal law of Canada at the federal level. As we have seen, many other statutes have criminal provisions making it an offence to do certain things. Such an offence may not be justified merely because it is criminal law, but because it is the only, or at least is considered to be the best way to enforce the power to regulate and control other matters within the federal competence. An incredibly large number of federal Acts of Parliament contain provisions enacting criminal offences besides the Criminal Code, such as the Income Tax Act, the Food and Drugs Act, the Narcotic Control Act and so forth. The body of federal criminal law then is the Code along with all the other federal statutes with penal provisions.

In addition, criminal law is also to be found in what is called subordinate legislation. The power to legislate criminal law must, obviously, belong to the Parliament in Ottawa in the case of federal legislation or the provincial legislature in the case of provincial legislation. But Parliament or the legislature can, in turn, delegate to someone else the power

---

date. British Columbia is fixed at November 19, 1858, and for other Provinces and Territories after the Union, the date is the date of their admission. Newfoundland continued with its own criminal law until 1949.

to legislate within the limits set out in the delegated power. An Act of Parliament may, for example, contain a section stating, "The Minister [which Minister is usually spelled out in a definition section] may make regulations governing certain matters" that are then specified, or it may state, "The Governor in Council [which, in practice, means the Cabinet] may make" such regulations. The same type of thing may occur in provincial legislation, or the Act governing municipalities may give the municipalities the power to make by-laws governing their municipal affairs. Such regulations or by-laws (assuming that they are within the terms of reference) are law and many of them contain certain penal provisions. Usually the penalties are not very serious — one tends to think of breaches of municipal by-laws as involving something like a $50 fine — but that is not always the case. For example, under the Food and Drugs Act the maximum penalty for trafficking in restricted drugs is imprisonment for 10 years, yet the Governor in Council is empowered to add any substance to the list of restricted drugs if it is deemed necessary by him to be in the public interest.

We know, then, that what is embraced in the term "criminal law" in Canada must be a statement written down somewhere — be it the Criminal Code or other federal statute or a regulation, or if it is provincial criminal law, in some piece of provincial legislation, regulation or by-law — that certain activity (or, in some cases, certain omissions) is punishable by some criminal sanction that may range from a small fine to life imprisonment.

THE INVESTIGATION

Most criminal law, unlike the Ten Commandments, for example, is not phrased in the imperative. The Criminal Code, for instance, does not say "No person shall commit murder." Rather, it defines what murder is and then states "Everyone who commits murder is guilty of an indictable offence and shall be sentenced to life imprisonment." It is a statement of an offence, and a statement of the consequences of committing that offence. Read literally, it is, of course, not true. The statement must be read in the context of the entire criminal process, with which this book is concerned.

Given that certain conduct constitutes a criminal offence, the process begins when a person engages in that conduct. From that moment, a criminal offence has been committed. But, if one asks, "what happens then?" the answer is that in many cases, absolutely nothing at all happens. Crimes can be victimless, consensual or non-consensual, although this classification is not necessarily mutually exclusive. In the case of a large number of crimes, the act is not committed against anyone else, but is merely an act declared to be a criminal offence because it is, in some way, harmful to the state. Such acts may range from minor ones such as going through a stop sign or speeding on a deserted road to very serious ones such as importing narcotics or conspiring to murder. The moment the relevant legislation has been breached it is true that an offence has been committed, but whether anything further happens depends upon someone other than the offender knowing that the offence has taken place. This may depend upon chance — upon a policeman happening to be present when a driver goes through a stop sign, or it may depend upon surveillance or investigation. As we shall see, there are legal limits to the powers of surveillance and investigation which may make the uncovering of undetected crime difficult, but, in any case, one might well ask how far society is prepared to go in committing resources and finances in the off-chance of catching a criminal. Investigating a crime that one knows has been committed may well be deserving of a higher priority than investigating to see whether any crime has been committed in the first place. Furthermore, investigating a known offence is more acceptable to most citizens than snooping about merely to see whether someone could be charged with some offence which he may or may not have committed.

Yet we do commit resources to the uncovering of undetected crime. Police set radar traps, customs officials check baggage and hundreds of inspectors of one sort or another inspect building sites, elevators, retail shops, etc., not only, of course, to catch criminals but to deter potential offenders. We try to maintain a balance between unnecessary or unacceptable interference with the daily lives of citizens and the reasonable committal of resources and manpower to deter victimless crimes and apprehend those who commit them. Even so, it is unlikely that any more than the slightest minority of speeding drivers, casual smugglers or petty income tax offenders are ever caught, much less prosecuted. For them, the criminal process begins and ends simply with the commission of the offence.

A number of crimes are consensual in nature — that is to say, while two or more people are involved, they are crimes in which those people are willing participants. Trafficking in drugs usually involves a willing seller and a willing buyer; the distribution of obscene material involves willing participants; some sexual offences such as incest and sexual intercourse with young girls or young boys may well be agreed to by both parties. In some cases, one party may be a "victim," but may also consent.

Again, whether or not the criminal process continues, will depend upon whether someone other than the consenting parties ever discovers that a crime has occurred. One party may, of course, change his mind and inform on the others, such as the young girl who later tells her mother, or the crime is discovered because she becomes pregnant. In the case of victimless crimes, the crime may be discovered as a result of investigation. Many consensual drug offences are discovered as a result of electronic surveillance — wiretapping or the installation of an eavesdropping device — or by an undercover investigating officer infiltrating a group and posing as a consensual participant. This is costly in terms of manpower and financial resources and unlikely to be utilized unless the danger is quite serious and the chances of success are reasonable. As a result, many (probably the majority) of consensual crimes remain undetected and hence the criminal process is carried no further.

Most of us, however, tend to think of crimes as those which have a victim, whether it is a homicide offence, an assault, theft, or breaking and entering. Such crimes are committed *against* someone, and, apart from homicide cases, the next step in the criminal process is usually for the victim to decide whether to complain, for if the victim chooses not to complain, the process continues no further.

There is, in Canada, no general obligation on the part of a citizen to report a crime, whether it is against himself or anyone else. It is an offence to assist another to commit an offence or to urge or incite another or to assist a person in escaping detection after he has committed an offence, but merely knowing that a crime is taking place, or has taken place, and doing nothing about it is not, in general, an offence. There are some specific exceptions to this general principle as, for example, in the case of treason or, more importantly, under various provincial Child Welfare Acts. Generally, however, the victim has a choice of whether to proceed further or not.

Surprisingly enough, a vast number of victims of crime do not complain. This may result from an attitude of "what's the use?" or "it's too much bother." It is probably true that if someone took a dollar from a table we were sitting at, it is unlikely we would call the police. If someone pushed us, but caused no injury or pain, we are not likely to invoke the criminal process even though an assault has been committed. If the harm caused is trifling, most of us choose to forget it. In fact, in the criminal process, the first step after the commission of the offence where there is a victim, is that the victim exercises his discretion in deciding what, if anything, to do next. In these examples, the discretion is exercised on logical and reasonable grounds, namely that it is just not worth pursuing.

If the victim, however, chooses not to complain for other reasons, then injustice may result. The victim of a sexual assault who has been raped and beaten, who decides not to complain because she fears the publicity of a trial and the cross-examination she may have to undergo, is not exercising her discretion freely. The victim who is threatened with further injury if he goes to the police, or who is blackmailed into remaining quiet, does not make a free choice.

Furthermore, the victim may not be able to complain. In homicide cases obviously she cannot, but concealing dead bodies is not an easy matter and the discovery of the commission of an offence comes not by means of a complaint, but by means of either the police being informed by someone else or their own investigations. The same is true, of course, in the case of those offences that are not secret or private such as arson or bombings. There may, however, be cases where the victim cannot complain. In child beating offences, often the other spouse is too intimidated and the child itself too young. A duty may therefore be imposed on someone else (a doctor, teacher or social worker) to notify the police whenever she suspects that a child has been abused. This creates one of those offences where failing to report the possible commission of an offence is, itself, an offence.

Let us assume, then, that the commission of an offence has come to the attention of the police, either because they themselves discovered it, or the victim has complained or someone else has reported it. It may happen that as a result of their investigation, the police discover that no crime has, in fact, been committed. It may happen that there is no point in embarking upon an investigation because there is no chance of solving the crime or because the cost would be totally disproportionate. For example, if one left a dollar bill on a busy downtown street and, on going back to recover it half an hour later, found that someone had taken it, a crime has been committed and one is entitled to notify the police. But to expect the police — and hence the taxpayer — to devote any time trying to locate the offender when that is a virtually impossible task and for such a trifling offence, would be quite counter-productive. The police, like everyone else, must decide how best to allocate their limited resources and they, too, must exercise their discretion in deciding whether an investigation is worth the expense and use of manpower. In all serious cases, of course, there is no doubt, and even in what are generally considered to be minor offences the police will investigate unless there is clearly no point in doing so.

When we talk about the police "solving" a crime, what we mean is the confirmation that a crime has been committed and the identification of the offender, though it is more accurate to call him, at this stage, not the offender but the person whom one believes, on reasonable and probable grounds, to have committed the offence — the "suspect" as he is sometimes called. He is not really the "offender" until a court has decided that he is and, as we shall see, locating the suspect does not necessarily mean that he will be convicted.

There are, naturally, very many offences where this sort of inves-tigation is unnecessary, where it is perfectly obvious who the offender is. A police officer who catches someone red-handed escaping from a window with a stolen stereo in his possession does not need a lengthy investigation to help him solve the crime. In other cases, a very careful and lengthy investigation may be required.

Often, the investigation is not successful. Statistics vary and are, in any case, not very reliable, but, as far as one can judge from the reported figures, in Canada about four-fifths of all murders are solved, about two-thirds of sexual offences, but only about one in 10 thefts and about one in five break and enters. However, "solving" a crime does not necessarily mean that an offender is prosecuted and convicted. For one thing, the offender may be dead, but it is perfectly clear that he is the culprit. Or he may not be amenable to jurisdiction, having fled abroad.

Quite apart from these circumstances, however, whether the person in question is actually prosecuted also depends upon the perfectly proper exercise of a discretion. If the offender is insane and has been committed to a mental institution, this does not necessarily relieve him of criminal responsibility, but it may make his prosecution rather pointless and unnecessary. If he has committed several offences and is prosecuted and convicted for one of them — murder, for example, for which he has been sentenced to life imprisonment — it may be decided that it is not worth the expense or trouble to prosecute him for other offences.

Even more important in practice is that it is a waste of money and resources to prosecute a person when there is no chance, or very little chance, of securing a conviction, even though one has a pretty good idea of who the guilty person is. Not only that, it may also be very unfair on the person prosecuted. As we shall see throughout the rest of this book, the process of the proof of guilt of an accused person is subject to numerous procedural and evidentiary rules that must be followed, all of which have the effect — quite deliberately — of making it difficult to convict an accused in the absence of a plea of Guilty, and sometimes even when there is a plea of Guilty. In our system, proof of guilt follows the adversary or accusatorial process by which the prosecution must prove beyond any reasonable doubt the guilt of an accused person according to the procedural and evidentiary rules. The accused is presumed to be innocent and has no burden of proving his innocence. If the Crown fails in its task, the accused must be acquitted — not necessarily because he is "innocent," in the sense that he did not commit the offence, but because he is "innocent" in the sense that the Crown has not proved, beyond any reasonable doubt, that he did commit the offence.

The investigative process of the police is not, however, subject to the rules of evidence. In their investigation, the police may use hearsay evidence, opinion evidence or character evidence. They may rely upon a confession improperly obtained from an accused or they may rely upon tangible evidence such as fingerprints or wire-tapped telephone conversations that have been obtained in an improper manner. None of this evidence would be admissible at the trial of the accused, but that does not mean that it is not usable by the police during their investigations. It is thus not surprising that one may have a situation where the police are satisfied in their own minds that they have identified the offender, yet be doubtful about being able to secure a conviction in a court of law.

A similar problem can arise when a vital witness for the prosecution has been available to help the police, but has died or left the country before the trial begins.

A decision must be made in these cases as to whether a prosecution is justified. Sometimes, the police will make that decision; in more complex or difficult cases, they will be advised by the prosecuting attorney or appropriate legal officer who will review the case with the police. In some cases, particularly those involving policy considerations or matters of public importance, the decision may be made at the level of the Attorney General himself. In cases which are prosecuted by the federal government,[4] it will be the appropriate federal official.

In addition to the decision whether to prosecute, a decision may have to be made as to what to prosecute for, and this may require some considerable legal expertise. It is true, of course, that in most cases, it is obvious what the charge should be. It is not very difficult to decide the charge in an obvious case of theft or of break and enter or a deliberate murder. The distinction between first degree murder and second degree murder, however, is not always easy to draw; nor between murder and manslaughter. In property offences, whether a crime amounts to theft or the different offence of obtaining by false pretences is sometimes very difficult to decide. Whether a person is an aider or abettor or is the actual perpetrator may also be a difficult question. As we shall see, if an accused is charged with an offence for which he could not, on the evidence, be convicted, he must be acquitted unless the offence for which he could be convicted is included in the offence with which he is charged.

THE DECISION TO PROSECUTE

As will be apparent, those crimes which actually result in a prosecution of someone represent only a very small fraction of crimes that are actually committed. Quite apart from all those crimes that were never detected because there was no victim to complain and no one was around to observe the offence, the process of moving towards a prosecution is essentially one of exercising a discretion — on the part of the police as to whether to investigate and, if so, for how long and at how much expense; on the part of the police or legal officials as to whether to prosecute at all and, if so, for what offence.

In the prosecutorial process, there is, however, one fundamental right that all individuals have and that is the right to initiate a prosecution against someone on his own initiative. We have assumed, hitherto, that investigation and prosecution are functions of the state in some guise or other, such as the police, or the prosecution authorities and so, in most cases, they

---

4 For this distinction, see Chapter 7, The Prosecution.

are. An aggrieved individual has neither the authority nor, in most cases, the resources to carry out his own investigation. It is far more efficient to notify the police and let them perform their duty to investigate. That is, after all, their function. But it can sometimes happen that an individual is not satisfied with what the police have done or disagrees with a decision they may have made, or, indeed, he may even decide not to go to the police and start the process himself.

The process of the criminal prosecution of anyone is started by someone laying an information[5] before a justice of the peace[6] in which he swears that someone has committed a specified offence, or that he has reasonable and probable grounds to believe and does believe that someone has committed a specified offence. We shall discuss in Chapter 8 the importance of this first step and the role of the justice of the peace in it, but it is a necessary step in the criminal process.[7] In the vast majority of cases, the person who swears out the information (the "informant," as he is called) will be a police officer, but any private person having knowledge of a criminal offence, or believing on reasonable and probable grounds that someone has committed an offence may be the informant. All that he has to do is to go to a justice of the peace with jurisdiction[8] and lay the information. This does not necessarily mean that the alleged offender will be prosecuted because the justice of the peace must first be satisfied that such a prosecution is warranted, but any person has the right to initiate this first step, and to require a justice of the peace to consider the matter.

Once the justice of the peace having jurisdiction has received the information, as he must, he must then decide whether a case has been made out for prosecuting the alleged offender. This is the first judicial determination in the prosecution process, but it is not a determination of whether the alleged offender is guilty or not, nor even whether he is probably guilty or not; it is only a determination that there are grounds that, absent any explanation or defence, would warrant the alleged offender being put on trial. Often, the only material he has before him is the information and a police officer's statement; sometimes he will require a sworn statement; sometimes he will examine the informant under oath or hear other evidence, but, in any case, he does not hear the alleged offender, nor is the alleged offender a party to the proceedings. At this stage, the justice of the peace is not concerned with any possible explanation or defence — only with whether there are grounds to support a prosecution.

---

5 For what this is, see Chapter 8, Informations and Indictments.

6 See Chapter 5, Classification of Offences and the Courts.

7 There is, for federal prosecutions, an exceptional process known as preferred indictments and many provinces have a simplified procedure for violation of some provincial laws. See Chapter 8, Informations and Indictments.

8 This normally means the place where the offence was committed.

If he is not satisfied, he will simply rule that a case has not been made out and will not authorize a prosecution. If he is satisfied, he will, as it is put, "issue process" — that is, issue a summons or even an arrest warrant, or confirm the action of the police in requiring the accused to attend for trial.[9]

Once process has been issued, or confirmed, then the first step has been taken that will, subject to the prosecution being withdrawn or terminated,[10] lead eventually to the trial of the accused.

THE POLICE

We have so far talked of "the police" and we must now consider what we mean by "the police," though we can give only a very short account of what is, in Canada, a very complex subject. Police are not mentioned in the Constitution Act of 1867, although, as we have seen, the federal government was given jurisdiction over criminal law and the provinces jurisdiction over the administration of justice. As a result, both the federal authorities and the provincial authorities have assumed, rightly or wrongly, the power to create and maintain police forces.

In Canada, there are over 400 separate police forces all of which, except for the Royal Canadian Mounted Police (R.C.M.P.), the Ontario Provincial Police (O.P.P.) and the Quebec Provincial Police (Q.P.P.), are either municipal police forces or regional police forces, ranging in size from a one-man force to a force of several thousand in Toronto or Montreal.

On the federal level, the R.C.M.P. enforce, throughout Canada, those federal criminal laws other than those contained in the Criminal Code, such as drug offences, income tax frauds and the like. On the provincial level, Ontario and Quebec have their own police forces which enforce all Criminal Code provisions and all their respective provincial penal laws throughout the two provinces except where there are local municipal or regional police forces. In the other provinces, which do not have their own provincial police forces (although some of them at one time or other in their history did), the R.C.M.P. are empowered by agreement between the province concerned and the federal government, to act as a provincial force in that it enforces, in addition to its ordinary duties, the Criminal Code and provincial penal laws throughout the province.

Historically, however, the oldest type of police force is not the R.C.M.P. or the provincial police, but a municipal police force of which there are still in Canada approximately 440 (if by "municipal" we also include "regional" — i.e., an amalgamation of adjacent municipalities). These

---

9 For the various methods of ensuring the attendance of the accused at his trial, see Chapter 4, Arrest, Summons and Compelling Attendance.

10 See Chapter 7, The Prosecution.

police forces are responsible for enforcing, within their jurisdiction, the Criminal Code, provincial offences and municipal by-laws. In some provinces, again on a contract, the R.C.M.P. may exercise the duties and functions of a municipal police force, and indeed, at least one province (Newfoundland) expressly prohibits the establishment of separate municipal police forces.

When we talk of "the police" investigating or laying an information, what police we are talking about depends very much on the province, the location within the province, and the offence in question. As complicated as the picture appears, the system, in fact, works reasonably well, given advances in communications and investigative techniques and the high degree of cooperation between the various police forces.

In addition to these "regular" police forces, there are many law enforcement officers charged with specific duties. There are, for example, on the federal level, railway police or harbour police and hundreds of inspectors and wardens of one kind or another, all of whom may have, within their limited jurisdiction, various powers and duties that may range up to those of peace officers. On the provincial level, there are again, an enormous number of law enforcement officers of one sort or another, from the traffic-warden with very narrow and defined powers to various types of inspectors and wardens with considerable powers.

In fact, as far as the Criminal Code is concerned, the special provisions relating to powers and duties of officers tend to refer not to "police" officers but to "peace" officers, a term that includes, but is not limited to, police officers, police constables, and the like. Whether, therefore, any of the persons who are not police officers — such as wardens or inspectors — may, for example, arrest someone without an arrest warrant or execute a search warrant, depends upon whether they are classified as peace officers or not. Some, such as customs or excise officers or a fisheries inspector, are; others, such as traffic wardens or municipal by-law enforcement officers, are not.

There also exist many persons who are generally, but not very accurately, called "private police." These include people like security guards, store detectives, armoured truck guards and so on. They are privately employed by a company or store to protect its property and people on the property. Generally speaking, the criminal law does not recognize the separate existence of such persons. They have, of course, all the rights and powers that any private person has, including the power to arrest in some cases, but no more rights and powers than any other citizen. They are thus no more "policemen" than anyone else. However, in a few cases, they may be sworn in as constables with limited jurisdiction (for example, campus "policemen" are often sworn in as special constables) and if so, then they become "peace officers" and have the powers and duties of any other peace officer.

For our purposes, it will be best if we assume that "policeman" means any member of a police force acting within his jurisdiction in respect of any alleged offence within his investigative competence.

2

Constitutional Guarantees

The criminal process which we are going to discuss in the subsequent chapters must be considered in the light of the Canadian Constitution, of which the Charter of Rights and Freedoms is a part. Since specific aspects will have to be examined more fully in the context of individual topics, this is merely a general chapter examining the scope of the constitution and the scheme of its enforcement.

Two "remedy" sections apply, or may apply, whenever an issue is taken as to an alleged violation of a constitutional guarantee. Section 52(1) enacts:

> The Constitution of Canada is the supreme law of Canada, and any law that is inconsistent with the provisions of the Constitution is, to the extent of the inconsistency, of no force or effect.

Section 24 of the Charter of Rights and Freedoms, which was enacted as Part I of the Constitution Act, 1982, provides:

> (1) Anyone whose rights or freedoms, as guaranteed by this Charter, have been infringed or denied may apply to a court of competent jurisdiction to obtain such remedy as the court considers appropriate and just in the circumstances.
>
> (2) Where, in proceedings under subsection (1), a court concludes that evidence was obtained in a manner that infringed or denied any rights or freedoms guaranteed by this Charter, the evidence shall be excluded if it is established that, having regard to all the circumstances, the admission of it in the proceedings would bring the administration of justice into disrepute.

Section 52 gives the courts the power to strike down legislation — federal or provincial — that is inconsistent with the Constitution, while section 24 of the Charter gives the courts wide powers to grant whatever remedy is most appropriate in the circumstances for any infringement of the Charter. Subsection (2) of section 24 is a specific evidentiary remedy providing for the exclusion of evidence obtained in some manner that infringes the Charter if its admission in evidence would tend to bring the administration of justice into disrepute.

Section 1 of the Charter guarantees the rights set out in it, but adds "subject only to such reasonable limits prescribed by law as can be demonstrably justified in a free and democratic society." The rights are, therefore, not absolute — section 1 gives the courts a very wide discretion to uphold legislation inconsistent with a right literally set out in the Charter if, in their opinion, the inconsistency is nevertheless reasonable and justifiable. One right, for example, is freedom of expression — the so-called freedom of speech clause. There are restrictions on such an absolute freedom recognized in the law concerning libel and slander, hate prop-aganda, sedition or obscenity. While these limitations are not themselves set out in the Charter, there is no doubt that section 1 would operate to justify them in a free and democratic society. Nevertheless, of course, by its very vagueness, it is clear that section 1 will remain a fruitful source of litigation as the courts interpret precisely what limitations on rights and freedoms *are* justifiable. It should, however, be noted that the courts have applied a fairly restrictive interpretation to this superficially broad proviso. It imposes on the party seeking to uphold a provision that would otherwise violate the Charter, a burden of proving that it is justified by two criteria. First, the objective desired to be achieved by the impugned legislation must be of sufficient importance to override the constitutional guarantees, and second, the means chosen by the legislation must be carefully designed to achieve those objectives, impair the constitutional guarantees as little as possible and must be no more than is necessary to achieve the objectives.[1]

Sections 7 to 14 set out what are called "Legal Rights," which are our main concern, though there are others such as equality rights under section 15 or language rights under sections 16 to 22 which could affect the criminal process.

FUNDAMENTAL JUSTICE

Section 7 enacts:

---

1 *R. v. Oakes*, [1986] 1 S.C.R. 103, 53 O.R. (2d) 719 (headnote only), 50 C.R. (3d) 1, 24 C.C.C. (3d) 321, 19 C.R.R. 308, 26 D.L.R. (4th) 200, 14 O.A.C. 335, 65 N.R. 57.

> Everyone has the right to life, liberty and security of the person and the right not to be deprived thereof except in accordance with the principles of fundamental justice.

Again, this section is not self-defining, for while it sets out the right not to be deprived of life, liberty or security, this is true only if such deprivation is not in accordance with the principles of fundamental justice — a concept that is nowhere defined. It could be argued, and indeed was forcefully argued, that the section is purely procedural in nature, that it is merely the Canadian equivalent of the American concept of "due process" and thus protects against things like arbitrary arrest, illegal detention, involuntary confessions and the like. If this were so, then section 7 would appear to be no more than a general protection of the rights that are more specifically spelled out in the succeeding sections of the Charter.

In the case of *Reference re Section 94(2) of Motor Vehicle Act (British Columbia)*,[2] the Supreme Court rejected this contention. In that case, British Columbia had imposed a mandatory term of imprisonment for the offence of driving a motor vehicle while disqualified. Furthermore, section 94(2) stated that this offence

> creates an absolute liability offence in which guilt is established by proof of driving, whether or not the defendant knew of the prohibition or suspension.

The Court held that it was contrary to the principles of fundamental justice that someone could be imprisoned for doing an act when he did not know of the facts that made that act illegal — a so-called absolute liability offence. It held that the essence of fundamental justice required some form of mental element, some form of blameworthiness, for the imposition of criminal liability resulting in the deprivation of liberty — the so-called mental element of crime. It therefore struck down the subsection.

Since then, the courts have invoked section 7 to strike down a number of sections of the Code, such as the offence of "constructive murder," wherein an accused could be convicted of murder where he caused death during the commission of a serious offence even though he had no intent to kill,[3] or that of procuring a miscarriage.[4] Furthermore, as we shall see in subsequent chapters, section 7 has been used to create a "right to silence" when the police attempt to subvert, by trickery, an accused person's desire not to make a statement to them,[5] and to limit the investigative use by

---

2 [1985] 2 S.C.R. 486, 36 M.V.R. 240, 69 B.C.L.R. 145, 48 C.R. (3d) 289, 63 N.R. 266, 23 C.C.C. (3d) 289, 24 D.L.R. (4th) 536, 18 C.R.R. 30.

3 *R. v. Vaillancourt*, [1987] 2 S.C.R. 636, 60 C.R. (3d) 289, 39 C.C.C. (3d) 118, 68 Nfld. & P.E.I.R. 281, 209 A.P.R. 281, 10 Q.A.C. 161, 47 D.L.R. (4th) 399, 32 C.R.R. 18, 81 N.R. 115.

4 *R. v. Morgentaler*, [1988] 1 S.C.R. 30, 63 O.R. (2d) 281 (note), 62 C.R. (3d) 1, 37 C.C.C. (3d) 449, 26 O.A.C. 1, 44 D.L.R. (4th) 385, 31 C.R.R. 1, 82 N.R. 1.

5 *R. v. Hebert*, [1990] 2 S.C.R. 151, 77 C.R. (3d) 145, [1990] 5 W.W.R. 1, 47 B.C.L.R. (2d) 1, 57 C.C.C. (3d) 1, 49 C.R.R. 114, 110 N.R. 1.

the police of surreptitious recordings of conversations between a suspect and a third person.[6] In fact, it is clear that section 7 has enormous potential in enabling the courts to control not only the substance of criminal legislation but also many aspects of investigation and procedure beyond those specifically set out in the Charter.

UNREASONABLE SEARCH OR SEIZURE

Section 8 enacts:

Everyone has the right to be secure against unreasonable search or seizure.

We shall discuss in some detail later on the limits of legal searches and seizures. Obviously, if someone is subject to an illegal search, or has property illegally seized, he may seek redress in the form of compensation or damages from the person who acts illegally. But section 8 prohibits unreasonable searches or seizures, not illegal searches or seizures, which are already prohibited by the ordinary law. Section 8 thus adds something more to the ordinary law regarding search and seizure. If the search or seizure is not only illegal, but also unreasonable, then section 24(1) and (2) may come into play, so as to give the affected person not only the right to damages (which he would have any way), but also any other remedy that may be considered appropriate, including the remedy of having any evidence obtained thereby excluded as evidence. As we shall see, evidence that is merely illegally obtained is not inadmissible for that reason alone, but evidence that is unconstitutionally obtained must be excluded if its admission would bring the administration of justice into disrepute.

In practice, of course, a search that is illegal would most often also violate section 8 since the illegality of the search would also be unreasonable. But one can think of situations where this would not necessarily be so. A search warrant that is void because of some technicality may make the search illegal, but not necessarily unreasonable; an honest mistake as to the identity of the premises to be searched may, in the circumstances, be reasonable. Whether, conversely, it is possible to have a legal search that is nevertheless unreasonable, is doubtful. A legal search must necessarily be premised upon its reasonableness — if without a warrant or authorization, because the officer so acting believed, upon reasonable and probable grounds, that it was reasonable; if with a warrant or some prior authorization, because the justice or other person issuing the warrant was satisfied as to the reasonable and probable grounds for issuing it.

---

6 *R. v. Sanelli, (sub nom. R. v. Duarte)* [1990] 1 S.C.R. 30, 71 O.R. (2d) 575, 74 C.R. (3d) 281, 53 C.C.C. (3d) 1, 65 D.L.R. (4th) 240, 37 O.A.C. 322, 45 C.R.R. 278, 103 N.R. 86.

ARBITRARY DETENTION OR IMPRISONMENT

Section 9 enacts:

Everyone has the right not to be arbitrarily detained or imprisoned.

The word "arbitrary" is not free from difficulty, but it must be read in conjunction with section 7 dealing with the right not to be deprived of liberty except in accordance with the principles of fundamental justice. Section 9 clearly guarantees a right against arbitrary detention — that is to say, a detention with no pretext of justification or lawfulness, a detention made without basis. Section 7, however, is more general in that if the reason or justification for the deprivation of liberty exists in law, but that law itself violates the principles of fundamental justice, then there is an infringement of section 7. In other words, section 9 protects against unjustified detention, but section 7 enables the court to examine any purportedly justified detention.

ARREST OR DETENTION

Section 10 enacts:

Everyone has the right on arrest or detention
  (a) to be informed promptly of the reasons therefore;
  (b) to retain and instruct counsel without delay and to be informed of that right; and
  (c) to have the validity of the detention determined by way of *habeas corpus* and to be released if the detention is not lawful.

These rights only arise upon arrest or detention. We shall be dealing in a later chapter with arrest, but "detention" is not a word that has much legal precedent. The Charter envisages a difference between "arrested" and being "detained." Clearly, false imprisonment or wrongful incarceration could be "detention" without necessarily being "arrest" — at least in the sense that it is understood. But to detain someone may, in common parlance, mean merely to stop someone, even for a brief period of time. The police can, of course, stop someone merely to ask him a question. Has that person been "detained" so as to bring section 10 into effect? More importantly, the police are often given power to stop a person for various reasons without arresting him. For example, where they have reasonable grounds to believe that a driver has been drinking, they may stop him and require him to take a road-side breathalyzer test. That person has not been arrested since the test is for the purpose of discovering whether he has committed an offence, but has he been "detained?"

The courts have interpreted the word "detention" fairly widely. Merely stopping a person even for the purpose of asking him his name and address, or for the purpose of requiring a road-side screening test, may be detention within section 10. "Detention" connotes some form of compulsory restraint upon a person's liberty.[7] Thus section 10 operates only once a person has been arrested or has been subject to restraint other than by an arrest. At this time the rights set out in section 10 come into play.

To be Informed Promptly of the Reasons

Unless a person knows why he is being arrested, it is difficult for him to be able to exculpate himself, but conversely and just as importantly, it is easy for him to inculpate himself. Unless person knows what is alleged against him, he cannot make a sensible reply to the charge and, of course, if an arrested person does have an explanation, he must be given the opportunity to give that explanation at the first available time. Equally, however, if a person is guilty, but does not know what he is charged with, he may say something in an attempt to explain away what he thinks he is charged with and, in so doing, only succeed in incriminating himself further for the offence with which the police are actually charging him. This is why it is essential for reasons of justice and fair play that an arrested person be informed as to why he is being arrested.

To Retain and Instruct Counsel

The right to receive legal advice and assistance is fundamental to our concept of fairness in criminal proceedings. However, the best legal counsel in the world is not going to be of much help if he only enters the picture at the trial stage when all the damage may be done at the pre-trial stage. An arrested person who does not know his legal rights may, at the police station, make a confession or other incriminating statement, or may be tricked or manoeuvred into providing evidence against himself. As we shall see, the rules of evidence do provide protection against the use of confessions that are involuntary or not the result of the operating, conscious mind of the accused, but, in general, they do not provide such protection if the police merely trick or manoeuvre the accused into making a statement. In many cases, the harm is done to the accused's defence long before the trial takes place.

The Charter, therefore, now provides that the arrested person must, without delay, be informed that he has the right to consult a lawyer and to be allowed to exercise that right. Failure to so inform him or, once he has been informed, failing to allow him to exercise that right (for example, by continuing to question him before counsel arrives, or by moving him to another police station where the lawyer cannot find him), will be

---

7 *R. v. Therens*, [1985] 1 S.C.R. 613, 38 Alta. L.R. (2d) 99, 45 C.R. (3d) 97, 32 M.V.R. 153, [1985] 4 W.W.R. 286, 18 C.C.C. (3d) 481, 13 C.R.R. 193, 18 D.L.R. (4th) 655, 59 N.R. 122, 40 Sask. R. 122.

an infringement of the Charter, though whether it will result in any remedy will depend upon what is appropriate and just in the circumstances or whether the use of any evidence obtained thereby would result in the administration of justice being brought into disrepute.

The Remedy of Habeas Corpus

One of the most cherished rights that exists in common law jurisdictions is the remedy of *habeas corpus.* Whenever a person is detained in custody against his will, he has the right to have the legality of that detention tested by bringing an application for the writ of *habeas corpus.*[8] If the applicant, or someone acting on his behalf, shows cause (that is to say makes out a *prima facie* case), the court will order the person detaining him to appear and justify, in law, the detention. If the detention is found to be unlawful, then the court will order the release of the applicant. It is a simple and effective way of determining the legality of a person's continued detention after arrest, or his incarceration, or detention pending extradition and so forth. It is this right to have the validity of detention determined by way of *habeas corpus* that is now guaranteed in the Charter.

CRIMINAL AND PENAL PROCEEDINGS

Section 11 enacts:

Any person charged with an offence has the right
(*a*) to be informed without unreasonable delay of the specific offence;
(*b*) to be tried within a reasonable time:
(*c*) not to be compelled to be a witness in proceedings against that person in respect of the offence;
(*d*) to be presumed innocent until proven guilty according to law in a fair and public hearing by an independent and impartial tribunal;
(*e*) not to be denied reasonable bail without just cause;
(*f*) except in the case of an offence under military law tried before a military tribunal, to the benefit of trial by jury where the maximum punishment for the offence is imprisonment for five years or a more severe punishment;
(*g*) not to be found guilty on account of any act or omission unless, at the time of the act or omission, it constituted an offence under Canadian or international law or was criminal according to the general principles of law recognized by the community of nations;
(*h*) if finally acquitted of the offence, not to be tried for it again, if finally found guilty and punished for the offence, not to be tried or punished for it again; and
(*i*) if found guilty of the offence and if the punishment for the offence has been varied between the time of commission and the time of sentencing, to the benefit of the lesser punishment.

These rights arise only when a person has been charged with an offence.

---

8 The scope of *habeas corpus* is discussed in Chapter 19, Appeals and Other Remedies.

The word "charge" does not have any precise meaning in law, but merely means that steps have been taken that will, in the normal course of things, lead to criminal prosecution. As we have seen, the beginning of the prosecution process is the swearing out of an information against a person and certainly, once this has been done, that person has been "charged" with the offence set out in the information, but it is not clear whether a person may be "charged" even at some stage before the information is laid. As we shall discuss, the criminal process may be brought to bear upon an accused person before the actual prosecution process begins — a person may be arrested without a warrant, or given an appearance notice or be required to enter into a promise to appear, and these are steps that are taken before any information is laid. Whether a person subject to one of these steps but in respect of whom an information has not yet been laid is a person "charged" with an offence was the subject of some disagreement in the Supreme Court,[9] but the majority would limit the operation of section 11 to the time when the information has been laid.[10]

To be Informed of the Specific Offence

This is merely a more precise requirement than a person's right to be informed of the reasons for his arrest. For example, a person may be arrested for the unlawful killing of someone, but at that time it may not be known whether the charge will be first degree murder, second degree murder or manslaughter. It may not be clear, until after examination of the evidence, whether a person should be charged with theft or being in possession of stolen property, or with fraud, or obtaining by false pretences. The Charter now requires that, once the specific offence has been charged, the accused must be informed of it without unreasonable delay. Similarly, of course, a person can be charged without being arrested — he may have no idea that an information has been laid against him until he is informed of it. Again, this must be without unreasonable delay.

To be Tried Within a Reasonable Time

This is a new, and exceedingly complicated right provided for by the Charter. Canada has, in general, no so-called Statute of Limitations for criminal offences. A person may be tried for an offence no matter how long ago it was committed — one year, five years or 10 years ago — although, from a practical point of view, it is desirable to prosecute an offender while the facts are still fresh in the minds of witnesses, and indeed,

---

9 *R. v. Kalanj*, [1989] 1 S.C.R. 1594, 70 C.R. (3d) 260, [1989] 6 W.W.R. 577, 48 C.C.C. (3d) 459, 40 C.R.R. 50, 96 N.R. 191.

10 Or a direct indictment has been preferred. See Chapter 8.

if some essential witnesses for the prosecution have disappeared or have died since the commission of the offence, a successful prosecution may be impossible.

Nevertheless, in law, mere passage of time from the commission of an offence does not prevent a prosecution. There are exceptions to this; some specific offences have a limitation period — certain cases of treason, for example. In addition, there is a six-month limitation period in the case of summary conviction offences and most provincial offences. That is to say, criminal proceedings must be commenced (by the laying of the information or other necessary step) within six months of the commission of the summary conviction offence or provincial offence, or else the offender cannot be prosecuted. But, in virtually all indictable offences, there is no such rule.

The *words* of the Charter say that a person charged with an offence has the right to be tried within a reasonable time. All this would seem to mean, at least on the surface, is that once an information has been laid, the accused must be tried within a reasonable time from then. That, as a concept, is not difficult to accept, although in practice it may be difficult to apply. There are all sorts of reasons why an accused may not be able to be tried immediately. The defence counsel may need time to prepare, witnesses may have to be found, courtroom facilities may be lacking and so on. In fact, except in the simplest case, it is probably not in the interest of the defence nor the prosecution for a trial to take place "immediately," so there are often remands or adjournments until the actual trial. Whether that delay is reasonable will depend upon all the circumstances. At the one extreme, if it is the accused's own fault that the trial has been delayed (for example, by leaving the jurisdiction and then only returning some time later), he can hardly complain that the delay is unreasonable. At the other extreme, if the prosecution has deliberately stalled as long as possible in the expectation that some crucial defence witness will die or otherwise become unavailable, it is not difficult to characterize such a tactic as unfair and contrary to the Charter. In between these two extremes, the court will have to determine whether, taking into account all the circumstances, the delay is reasonable.

In the case of *R. v. Askov*,[11] the Supreme Court listed four factors that should be considered in determining whether a delay has been unreasonable. These are (a) the length of the delay, (b) any explanation that may be given for the delay, (c) any waiver that the accused may have given and (d) whether there has been any resulting prejudice to the accused. As the Court pointed out, the very concept of *unreasonable* delay depends very much on taking the circumstances of each individual case into account.

---

11 [1990] 2 S.C.R. 1199, 75 O.R. (2d) 673, 79 C.R. (3d) 273, 59 C.C.C. (3d) 449, 74 D.L.R. (4th) 355, 49 C.R.R. 1, 42 O.A.C. 81, 113 N.R. 241.

The longer the delay, the more difficult it will be to justify it, and if the reason for the delay is imputed to the prosecution this will weigh in favour of the accused. On the other hand, the more complex a case is, the more tolerable may be a delay.

What complicated that case was the factor of what might be called institutional or systemic delays caused, for example, by shortage of courtroom facilities or lack of court reporters or pressure of work on judges or counsel. These, the Court stated, in general, also weigh against the prosecution. While there is no necessity for precise comparisons, nevertheless one can get a good idea of roughly what is reasonable by seeing how long cases took to come to trial in various parts of the country and if it appeared that one particular jurisdiction was grossly behind others then this, in itself, would violate the right of the accused.

Askov, of course, is not easy to apply in practice, given the enormous variations that can occur in individual cases and circumstances, but it has fleshed out the bare words of the provision and given some guidance to lower courts on its application.

Suppose, however, that the police have all the evidence to support a successful prosecution and that the accused is available in the jurisdiction, but they merely delay the laying of the information so as to embarrass the accused in his defence. The accused is not yet "charged," so section 11(*b*) does not, on its wording, apply. In such a case, if there is no unreasonable delay between the laying of the information and the trial, then there has been no infringement of section 11(*b*). However, it may be that if the pre-trial delay results from some oblique motive on the part of the prosecuting authorities, then section 7, guaranteeing the right not to be deprived of life, liberty or security of the person, except in accordance with the principles of fundamental justice, may be invoked enabling the court to apply such remedy as is appropriate and just in the circumstances.[12]

Not to be Compelled to be a Witness

Another fundamental principle of the law is that while an accused person may, if he wishes, testify in his own defence at his trial, he cannot be compelled to testify. In other words, he cannot be forced to help incriminate himself at his trial by being compelled to be a witness if he does not wish to. If the prosecution cannot succeed in proving the guilt of the accused beyond reasonable doubt by all the other evidence that they may have, then an accused is entitled to be acquitted.

The right of the accused not to be forced to testify also generally applies to the accused's wife or husband, as the case may be. A spouse

---

12 *Carter v. R.*, [1986] 1 S.C.R. 981, 52 C.R. (3d) 100, [1986] 4 W.W.R. 673, 26 C.C.C. (3d) 572, 21 C.R.R. 170, 29 D.L.R. (4th) 309.

may, indeed probably must, testify for the accused if he or she is called as a witness, but cannot be called as a witness for the prosecution. In the case of spouses, there are, however, certain exceptions. In a number of sexual offences, and offences involving a victim under the age of 14, a spouse can be compelled to testify for the prosecution whether he or she wishes to or not and whether or not the accused wishes it. In any offence committed against the person or liberty of the spouse, he or she is also a compellable witness.

The right not to be compelled to testify is testimonial in nature — that is to say, it is only the right not to be forced to be a witness in *proceedings against* that person. There is no similar right when the proceedings are not *against him* — for example, a coroner's inquest or a Royal Commission Inquiry — nor when the proceedings are against someone else — for example, an accomplice or some person charged with some other offence. Nor is there such a right when there are no "proceedings" — for example, when a person is compelled to give a statement to a police officer following an automobile accident or when the police trick a person into making a confession that he did not want to make. In these cases, however, a different right may have been infringed and that is the privilege against self-incrimination. Since this is a somewhat complex topic, it will be more fully discussed in Chapter 14, Self Incrimination.

To be Presumed Innocent

The normal method of solving abstract problems is to start with no preconceived notions and then conduct an inquiry in the attempt to reach a solution. At the end of the inquiry one may be no better off than at the beginning and have to conclude that an answer has not been found. Another method, however, is to begin with a positive assertion and then require the person making the assertion to prove that it is correct.

In legal terminology, the former type of method is called the inquisitorial process and the latter the adversarial or, in criminal law, the accusatorial process. While we do use the inquisitorial process in some proceedings such as a coroner's inquest or a Royal Commission Inquiry, in both civil and criminal trials we adopt the adversarial process. In a civil case, the plaintiff alleges that the defendant has committed some wrong against him, such as a breach of contract or negligent damages; in a criminal case, the prosecution alleges that the accused has committed a criminal offence.

Once the allegation is made, it is presumed that the opposite is true unless the person making the allegation succeeds in proving that the allegation is true. In a civil case, it is presumed that the defendant is not liable, while in a criminal case it is presumed that the accused is not guilty. Whereas, in the inquisitorial process, it is possible to reach a conclusion of saying "we do not know what the answer is," in the adversarial process, either the person making the allegation succeeds in proving it, or he does not. If he does not, then an accused is entitled to be found not guilty — not because he is "innocent" in the sense that he did not, objectively speaking, commit the offence, but because he is "innocent" in the sense that the prosecution has not proved that he did commit the offence.

However, nothing in human conduct can be "proved" with mathematical certainty. The best that we can expect is to be satisfied to some extent that a person did act in the way it is alleged, but to what extent? How "satisfied" must the person having to make the decision be? This is called the burden of proof. In civil law, the person making the allegation (the plaintiff) has to prove that the allegation is true on the balance of probabilities. That is to say, the fact-finder must be satisfied that the allegation is more likely to be true than the opposite. In criminal law, this is not sufficient. There, the fact-finder must be satisfied beyond any reasonable doubt that the allegation that the accused has committed a criminal offence is true. This does not mean beyond any doubt (which is another impossibility), but only beyond any reasonable doubt. Even so, it places a heavy burden on the prosecution and it is not one that is easily discharged. If there exists in the mind of the fact-finder any reasonable doubt as to the guilt of the accused, then he must find him not guilty — not because he is convinced that he is innocent, but because the prosecution had not proved to the requisite degree that he is guilty.

This principle is the one that is now enshrined in the Charter as the presumption of innocence. Any law that violates this presumption of innocence is therefore invalid. For example, if a law states that where a person is proved to be in possession of narcotics, he shall be presumed to be in possession for the purpose of trafficking in narcotics unless he proves that he did not have the purpose of trafficking, there is, in effect, a presumption that such a person is guilty unless he proves that he is not guilty and such a provision offends against the Charter.[13] This does lead to difficulties in construing various provisions. If they merely require the accused to introduce or point to some evidence in order to rebut the presumption, then there is no reversal of the onus of proof and they would be valid; if, on the other hand, they require the accused to establish or prove something in order to escape liability, then they are inconsistent with the presumption of innocence.[14]

The section also requires that this proof be in a fair and public hearing

---

13 See *R. v. Oakes, supra*, note 1.
14 See, for example, *R. v. Whyte*, [1988] 2 S.C.R. 3, 64 C.R. (3d) 123, [1988] 5 W.W.R. 26, 29 B.C.L.R. (2d) 273, 6 M.V.R. (2d) 138, 42 C.C.C. (3d) 97, 51 D.L.R. (4th) 481, 35 C.R.R. 1, 86 N.R. 328; and *R. v. Holmes*, [1988] 1 S.C.R. 914, 65 O.R. (2d) 639 (note), 64 C.R. (3d) 97, 41 C.C.C. (3d) 497, 50 D.L.R. (4th) 680, 27 O.A.C. 321, 34 C.R.R. 193, 85 N.R. 21. See Chapter 12, Proof of Guilt.

by an independent and impartial tribunal. These requirements are pretty self-explanatory, though their interpretation is not easy. Fairness will have to be judged in the light of the past 400 years or so of the development of the common law in England, and, subsequently, in Canada. It embraces many principles which, in general, are familiar but which, in detail, will need further refinement. The right to be represented by counsel, the right to make full defence, the right to cross-examine witnesses for the other side, the right to speak to sentence are only a few rights, the exact scope of which is still not clear. Do these rights include, for example, the right to have counsel appointed and paid for by the state if the accused cannot afford one himself? Do they include the right to know the details of the case for the prosecution before an accused is called on to plead? Must the Crown disclose the existence of a witness who may have important evidence for the defence? There is no definite answer to any of these questions at the moment, nor to many similar questions, but one assumes that, in the course of time, the courts will be called upon to resolve them.

A public hearing is one to which the public has access as of right within the limits of the accommodation that can reasonably be provided. "Secret" trials are anathema in any democratic society. The presence of the public protects the accused in many ways. It prevents, or at least minimizes, the arbitrary abuse of power by state officials such as judges, prosecutors or police; it opens the testimony of witnesses to public scrutiny and this, in effect, is a check on perjury; it ensures that the accused's rights are respected and so on. Of course, the public nature of a trial is not absolute. Sometimes, the public may be excluded where it is necessary in the interests of the administration of justice, such as to maintain order or protect public morals or where there is some public policy involved as, for example, where the trial involves state secrets.

Furthermore, the right to be tried in public does not necessarily mean that the trial, in all its phases, has to be subject to newspaper or other news media coverage. In general, it is true that reporters, as members of the public, have the right to attend trials and to report on what takes place, but the courts have the power in some circumstances to make an order that there is no report of certain matters. This may arise when such a report would prejudice the trial — for example, a report on the evidence given at a preliminary hearing[15] or on a voir dire[16] when the jury is absent; or when it would unfairly reflect upon a witness — for example, the evidence of the victim of a sexual assault. The right of the public to be present at a trial, is not the same as the right of all members of the public to read edited versions of what goes on in the courtroom in newspapers or to see it on television.

---

15 See Chapter 6, The Accused's Appearance in Court.
16 See Chapter 13, Interrogation and Confessions.

The impartiality and independence of our judges are things which have been fought for over many hundreds of years. Somebody must appoint and pay our judges and that somebody is the state, in some form or other — i.e., the "government" or the cabinet. But, once appointed, judges must be free to render their decisions honestly and impartially without fear of being fired or having their salaries reduced if they give judgments unfavourable to the state. Thus, once appointed, our judges cannot be dismissed in the ordinary course of things by the government in power. As far as federally appointed judges are concerned, they can only be dismissed for cause (such as scandalous conduct or gross dereliction of duty) and then only after an inquiry and only upon resolution of both houses of Parliament. Provincially appointed judges enjoy a similar protection, although the machinery for their removal is slightly less complicated.

The Right to Bail

In fact, section 11(*e*) is expressed in rather awkward terms. As we shall see,[17] every effort is made under the Code (and, even more so, under provincial penal statutes) to avoid the actual arrest of a person charged with an offence. Rather, some other machinery (such as a summons or an order requiring her to appear) is adopted to ensure that the accused will appear for her trial. Actual arrest of an accused usually only occurs if she is charged with one of the more serious offences or if she refuses to identify herself, or for some other sufficient reason, such as believing she will not appear for trial or will attempt to destroy evidence or intimidate witnesses. Once arrested, an accused person may spend several weeks or months in custody pending her trial unless she is released by some procedure even though she has not yet been convicted of any offence and, indeed, may ultimately be acquitted.

When we examine bail and release, we shall discuss the various mechanisms for releasing an accused person pending her trial and, as we shall see, there are many ways of doing this, quite apart from any bail provisions. Bail, essentially, is the release of an accused person into the custody of someone else who undertakes to the court that the accused will appear for her trial on penalty of forfeiting a sum of money which she is required to post, or of having to pay a sum of money which she is required to promise in the event of the accused's failure to appear. In the course of time, the practice emerged that in appropriate cases, rather than a third person having to deposit the money or enter into the promise (or recognizance, as it is called), the accused herself could deposit the money or make the promise to pay (or enter into her own recognizance, as it is expressed in law).

---

17 Chapter 4, Arrest, Summons and Compelling Attendance.

While section 11(*e*) is, on its face, limited to merely establishing that an accused should not be denied reasonable bail, that is to say, that the amount of money required to be deposited or the sum stipulated in the recognizance shall not be unreasonable (having regard to the seriousness of the offence, the likelihood of the accused's appearing and her financial means), the spirit of the section probably demands that an accused shall be released pending his trial by whatever mechanism is most appropriate (including, but not limited to, bail) unless there is just cause why she should remain in detention. We will look later on at what a "just cause" might be.

The Right to Trial by Jury

The right to a trial by jury is only guaranteed where the offence charged is punishable by five years' imprisonment or more and thus is limited to the more serious offences. We shall discuss the difference between summary conviction offences and indictable offences in Chapter 9, but, at the moment, it is sufficient to state that indictable offences are those that *may* (not must) be tried by a judge and jury, unless they are at the lower end of the scale when the accused does not have the right to trial by jury, while charges for summary conviction offences cannot be tried by judge and jury, under any circumstances. Under the Code, then, there is no right to trial by jury if the accused is charged with a summary conviction offence (generally speaking, punishable by a maximum of no more than six months' imprisonment and a fine of $2,000) or one of those indictable offences listed in section 553, which, generally speaking, carry a maximum penalty of two years' imprisonment. Nor, of course, is there a right to a jury trial when the offence is one under provincial legislation since these are all summary conviction offences. In practice, therefore, this section will have little effect on the present system of the Code, as its provisions already provide for the right to a jury trial in all serious offences.

What is not yet clear is precisely what a trial by a "jury" entails. We are used to thinking of a jury as being a panel of 12 impartial persons who must deliver a unanimous verdict, if they deliver any verdict at all. In fact, in the Territories, juries consist only of six members. It has been held that such a six-member jury is unconstitutional (although on the ground that it is a discrimination against equality rights[18]). Suppose, as has happened in a number of other jurisdictions, that the Code were changed to provide for majority verdicts. Would this violate the accused's right to a "jury" trial? The answers to these and similar questions will have to wait until the courts have decided what a "jury" trial actually embraces.

18 *R. v. Punch*, 48 C.R. (3d) 374, [1985] N.W.T.R. 373, [1986] 1 W.W.R. 592, 22 C.C.C. (3d) 289, [1986] 2 C.N.L.R. 114, 18 C.R.R. 74 (S.C.).

Non-retroactivity of Criminal Law

A person may commit an act today which is not a criminal offence and Parliament enact a law tomorrow that says that act is a criminal offence. To punish that person for committing an act which was perfectly lawful when he did it would be to apply that criminal legislation retroactively. This provision therefore enacts that, generally speaking, criminal law is not to have this retroactive effect. It is not, however, quite that simple. While this principle is true as a general proposition, the Charter does provide for some degree of retroactivity in limited circumstances — namely if the act, while not an offence under actual Canadian criminal legislation, was an offence under international law or was regarded as criminal under general principles of world opinion. This is unlikely to happen very often, but it can occur. Until recently, for example, Canada had no provision relating to the hijacking of airplanes beyond its borders, nor did it have any provision relating to terrorist activities directed toward Canadian diplomats abroad. Yet, from an international point of view, most people would regard those acts as "criminal" in the generally accepted sense of the word. The Charter would permit that type of criminal legislation to have retroactive effect.

Double Jeopardy

The concept of double jeopardy, which is a phrase with which most people are familiar, is actually very complex and difficult to apply and a more detailed discussion of it will be better postponed until Chapter 9, but the general principle is fairly clear and is now incorporated into the Charter. Once a person has finally been acquitted of an offence ("finally" means that the appeal process has been satisfied), he cannot again be prosecuted for that same offence. He can, however, be prosecuted for a different offence, even if it arises out of the same set of circumstances, unless that offence is one for which he could have been found guilty at his first trial. Conversely, if he has been found guilty (again, assuming that the appeal process has been exhausted) and punished, then he cannot be tried again for the same offence.

The Benefit of the Lesser Punishment

It happens that from time to time Parliament changes the maximum penalty for various offences either up or down. This section provides that where the punishment has been altered between the time of the commission of the offence and the time the sentence is imposed after a finding of guilt, the convicted person is liable only to the lesser of the penalties. Thus, if the penalty has been increased, he is liable only to the maximum provided under the old law; if the penalty has been decreased, he is liable only to the maximum provided under the new law.

CRUEL AND UNUSUAL TREATMENT OR PUNISHMENT

Section 12 of the Charter enacts:

Everyone has the right not to be subjected to any cruel and unusual treatment or punishment.

One would, of course, hope that torture and physical abuse is no longer part of the criminal process in any democratic society, however common it might have been a few hundred years ago. But people's conception of what is cruel varies according to the times they live in. What would have been acceptable penitentiary treatment only last century — maintaining absolute silence, the treadmill, or, even more recently, the chain gang or floggings — would not be acceptable to most people today. No one needs to be reminded of the controversy that still surrounds the issue of capital punishment. Cruelty simply is not an absolute term any more than "usual" is, and can only be interpreted in the light of current standards.

We still have many forms of punishment and treatment about which reasonable people may differ. Certainly, the death penalty is one, but we also have solitary confinement, deprivation of various advantages that people not in prison take for granted, such as sexual intercourse or family visits, preventive detention, life imprisonment, and even things like compulsory electric shock treatment or other medical treatment. Attempts have been made already to have the courts declare some of these to be "cruel and unusual" although so far without much success. At least, however, the section opens up all forms of punishment and treatment to the scrutiny of the courts and enables them to strike down any provision that is seen, by contemporary standards, to be unacceptable. In particular, it has enabled the courts to strike down a number of provisions (many of them in provincial legislation) purporting to impose mandatory minimum terms of imprisonment upon conviction without regard to the individual circumstances of the case.

SELF-INCRIMINATION

Section 13 enacts:

A witness who testifies in any proceedings has the right not to have any incriminating evidence so given used to incriminate that witness in any other proceedings, except in a prosecution for perjury or for the giving of contradictory evidence.

This is called the privilege against self-incrimination and has a history stretching back to the mid 1600s. We shall examine its scope in more detail in Chapter 14, but the essential problem is easy enough to state. Suppose that a person called X is on trial for murder and Y is called as a witness. Y is a compellable witness and must testify whether he wants to or not, or else be committed for contempt. When he takes the witness stand, he is asked questions, the answers to which will be evidence that he himself is guilty of a crime. If there were no protection for him, he would be compelled to answer the questions and then he could be later prosecuted for the crime to which he has been forced to admit and those answers would be practically conclusive evidence against him. In this way it would be possible to manoeuvre a person into being forced to provide the very evidence that would secure his own conviction.

The original solution to this problem (and one that still exists in most jurisdictions apart from Canada) is to give a person who is compelled to testify the right to refuse to answer any question that incriminates himself — hence the name "privilege against self-incrimination." There is a defect to this solution, however, and that is that the evidence may not only be incriminatory of the witness, but crucial for the conviction of the person on trial. To give the witness the right to refuse to answer the question, not only protects him, but it also has the effect of perhaps preventing the conviction of a guilty person. To meet that objection, Canada, in 1893, abolished the privilege against self-incrimination and, in its place, enacted that the witness must answer the question, but that answer was not admissible in evidence against him if he were subsequently prosecuted. He does not, however, have any right to lie on the witness stand so that if he does answer and his answer is untrue, he may still be prosecuted for perjury even though that would entail the use of his answer to prove the perjury.[19]

INTERPRETER

Section 14 provides:

A party or witness in any proceedings who does not understand or speak the language in which the proceedings are conducted or who is deaf has the right to the assistance of an interpreter.

The right of an accused to a fair trial must, of course, include his being able to defend himself and follow the proceedings. Clearly, if an accused does not understand the language being used, he must be entitled

---

19 On a perjury charge, the prosecution must prove that the statement made under oath was false. Where a witness says two different things under oath on two different occasions, it may be difficult for the prosecution to prove which is false and which is true or whether both are false. To meet this difficulty, there is the offence of giving contradictory evidence under oath, where the prosecution does not have to prove which is false, only that the two answers are contradictory.

to the services of an interpreter in order to understand what is being said. Section 14 goes further than that, however, and also gives the same right to witnesses. If a witness is unable to understand questions or he makes his answers unintelligible, it is unfair both to the witness and to the accused. Presumably, where a witness has been denied an interpreter, not only is his right infringed, but also that of the accused, if not under section 14, then under section 11(*d*), guaranteeing a fair trial, so that even if the witness himself does not object, the accused may still do so.

3

Search, Seizure and Surveillance

SEARCH AND SEIZURE

As we have seen, section 8 of the Charter provides:

Everyone has the right to be secure against unreasonable search or seizure.

This is fine as a general statement[1] but it does not really tell us very much about the differences between lawful searches and unlawful searches.

It is first necessary to distinguish between the searching of places and the searching of persons because whereas the Criminal Code has some specific provisions regarding the former, it is largely silent regarding

---

1 The Supreme Court of Canada has set out the general principles determining the reasonableness of searches in the case of *Hunter (Director of Investigation & Research) v. Southam Inc.*, [1984] 2 S.C.R. 145, 33 Alta. L.R. (2d) 193, 27 B.L.R. 297, 41 C.R. (3d) 97, [1984] 6 W.W.R. 577, 55 A.R. 291, 14 C.C.C. (3d) 97, 2 C.P.R. (3d) 1, 9 C.R.R. 355, 11 D.L.R. (4th) 641, 84 D.T.C. 6467, 55 N.R. 241. While there may be exceptional cases in which different criteria may be justified, normally a valid search requires (i) a prior authorization, (ii) granted by an independent person acting judicially, (iii) based upon reasonable and probable grounds for believing in the prior existence of facts justifying the search, (iv) sworn to under oath by the person seeking the authorization. The case did not strike down all searches not conforming to these minimum standards, but would require that any departure from them be demonstrably justified in the circumstances. See also *Collins v. R.*, [1987] 1 S.C.R. 265, 13 B.C.L.R. (2d) 1, 56 C.R. (3d) 193, [1987] 3 W.W.R. 699, 33 C.C.C. (3d) 1, 74 N.R. 276.

Specimen Search Warrant

CANADA	)	To the peace officers in the
PROVINCE OF ONTARIO	)	Judicial District of York,
JUDICIAL DISTRICT	)	Province of Ontario
OF YORK	)	

WHEREAS it appears on the oath of John Smith, police officer, of Court Bureau, City Hall, Metropolitan Toronto in the Judicial District of York that there are reasonable grounds for believing that three television sets, the property of Henry Jones, stolen from the said Henry Jones, contrary to section 334 of the Criminal Code are in Apt. 204 at 179 Blank Street, Toronto, in the Judicial District of York, Province of Ontario, hereinafter called the premises.

THIS is, therefore, to authorize and require you between the hours of 9 a.m. and 9 p.m. to enter into the said premises and to search for the said things and to bring them before me or some other justice.

DATED this 15th day of May,	)	
19__ A.D. at the Municipality	)	
of Metropolitan Toronto in	)	Peter Brown
the Judicial District of York.	)	_____

A Justice of the Peace in and for the Province of Ontario

the latter. In the second place, it will simplify matters if first we look at the federal criminal law and then deal with various provincial provisions.

As a general proposition, unless the police act under the justification of some previously issued authorization, their entry upon any premises for the purposes of a search constitutes a trespass and is therefore unlawful. To this general proposition there are several exceptions.

The object of a search is not to see whether a crime has been committed. It is not designed to enable the police to go poking about in the hope of finding something they can charge someone with. It is essential to realize this basic fact of the search process. It is, rather, a technique for securing evidence which will help prove the commission of a crime that is already believed to have taken place.

The most common method of securing an authorization to search is by way of search warrant. This is an authorization granted by a justice of the peace to police officers to search any "building receptacle or place" named in the warrant. The justice will only issue such warrant if he is satisfied, after the police officer has sworn an information, that there is reasonable ground to believe that in that building, receptacle or place there is:

1. anything upon or in respect of which an offence has been committed or is suspected to have been committed; or
2. anything that there is reasonable ground to believe will be evidence of an offence having been committed; or
3. anything that there is reasonable ground to believe is intended to be used in the commission of an indictable offence.

The issuing of a search warrant is not, therefore, automatic. The justice must make the determination that there are reasonable grounds to believe that one of the three items are on the premises, and the police officer must swear under oath that he so believes.

The search warrant can only be issued to search a building, receptacle or place, and while this expression is very wide, the one thing it does not cover is the body of a person. A search warrant cannot be issued to search a person. The warrant must name both the building, receptacle or place and what it is that the police are to search for, but once the warrant is lawfully being executed (that is, when the police actually conduct the search pursuant to the warrant) they may seize, not only what is named in the warrant, but also anything else that they believe on reasonable grounds has been obtained by the commission of an offence, or used in the commission of an offence.

The warrant, then, not only authorizes the search, but it also authorizes the police to seize such items as are named in the warrant (or anything else that they may lawfully seize) and take it before the justice of the peace.[2] The justice of the peace will order it detained in safekeeping pending trial, though there are provisions for returning it to its rightful owner if the trial is unduly delayed or if it appears that the object will not be needed.

A warrant may also be issued where the police officer merely makes a report in writing, rather than under oath by way of information, in connection with gaming and betting offences, and certain bawdy house offences. While the scope of these warrants is limited, in practice they are very useful. Unlike the ordinary search warrant, they not only authorize a search and seizure of anything that might be evidence of a gaming or bawdy house offence, but they also authorize the taking into custody of any person found on such premises. Unlike an ordinary search warrant that must normally be executed by day, a gaming house warrant may be executed by day or night.[3]

Under section 101 of the Code, a police officer may search a person, vehicle or place without a warrant where he believes on reasonable grounds that a weapons offence is being or has been committed and that evidence of this is likely to be found "where the conditions for obtaining a warrant exist but, by reason of exigent circumstances, it would not be practicable to obtain a warrant." This section was enacted only recently, after *Hunter v. Southam Inc.*, and presumably represents an attempt to preserve the legality of some form of warrantless search within the constitutional constraints laid down in that case. It remains to be seen whether the courts will hold that the attempt has been successful, but, at least on the surface, it would seem to conform to the *Hunter v. Southam Inc.* requirements.

These Criminal Code provisions apply to the enforcement not only of the Criminal Code itself, but also to any other federal criminal provisions, unless the Act creating those federal criminal offences provides its own search and seizure machinery. In fact, a large number of federal statutes do have specific provisions relating to searches in the enforcement of the particular Act in question. Thus, Acts such as the Food and Drugs Act, Narcotic Control Act, Official Secrets Act, Excise Act and so on, have their own provisions relating to the search of various premises and persons.

A search without a warrant, unless specifically authorized by the Code or some other statute, is illegal, unless the person in possession of the premises consents to the search, save for two exceptions which are preserved from the common law. The first of these is where an officer is proceeding lawfully to arrest a person when he may, as an incidence

---

2 If this is practicable. If it is not, as for instance after a stolen truck is seized, the object may be detained and a report in respect thereof made to the justice.

3 Since these warrants, issued under s. 199 of the Code, do not conform to all the minimum requirements set out in *Hunter v. Southam Inc., supra*, note 1, they may, in fact, be unconstitutional. See *Vella v. R.* (1984), 14 C.C.C. (3d) 513, 12 C.R.R. 293 (Ont. H.C.).

of that arrest, search that person and the immediate surroundings in order to protect himself while effecting the arrest — e.g., to seize any hidden weapon — and to prevent the destruction of evidence — e.g., to prevent the arrested person from swallowing drugs or the like). The legality of such searches depends upon the legality of the arrest, but a lawful search of premises in the immediate vicinity is limited to the place where the arrest takes place — e.g., the chair upon which the accused was sitting, or the room in which he was found. It cannot be used as an excuse to conduct a search of his whole apartment or house.

The second exception is in cases of emergency. A police officer may enter premises without a warrant if he believes on reasonable and probable grounds that an offence is being committed or is about to be committed, that is causing or would cause serious injury to some person therein, for the purpose of preventing or terminating that injury. Similarly, though the position is not quite so clear, it would appear that where a police officer is proceeding lawfully to execute an arrest, or is in hot pursuit of an offender where he could arrest without a warrant, he may enter on to premises (even those of a third person) in order to effect the arrest. But merely having the right to arrest a person does not, in its absence of a warrant or hot pursuit, entitle a police officer to enter in order to effect the arrest.

Apart from a few specific provisions such as in the Narcotic Control Act, there is no statutory provision for the search of a *person*, as opposed to the search of *premises*, in federal criminal law. The search of a person is only justified as an incidence to a lawful arrest. In other words, the arrest must be lawful *first*, in order to justify the search, since the search cannot be a pretext used in order subsequently to justify the arrest.

Several provincial statutes have provisions relating to search and seizure covering matters within the provincial jurisdiction. There are so many of these provisions that here we can only look at the type of situations that are most common. Most provincial Highway Traffic Acts enable the police to stop motor vehicles in order to check on their brakes and other safety devices and all provinces have special provisions relating to the control of liquor sales which give the police, in certain circumstances, the power to enter premises in which they reasonably suspect a violation of the Act is taking place. Various Game and Fish Acts under a variety of titles authorize game wardens or conservation officers to stop and search vehicles and aircraft where they believe, on reasonable and probable grounds, that a breach of the Act is taking place or has taken place.

Finally, there is a myriad of specific legislation dealing with the inspection of various activities that fall within the provinces' regulatory powers. These frequently give designated officials ("inspectors" of one sort or another) the authority to enter and inspect to ensure that the appropriate Act is being complied with. These cover, for example, such areas as construction safety (to ensure that workers are protected), weights and measures (to protect the consumer), elevators in public buildings (to protect the user) and so on.

In short, therefore, while dwelling houses do enjoy a certain measure of protection from search in the absence of a duly authorized search warrant, even this protection is not absolute and there are occasions when the police may enter even in the absence of a search warrant. In the case of other premises (or "places"), while the same general proposition holds true, there are so many exceptions under both federal and provincial legislation, that the same measure of protection by no means applies. Whether, in the absence of a warrant, an entry upon, for example, one's place of business or one's car is justified and legal without the consent of the owner, will depend upon finding somewhere in the applicable legislation a provision authorizing such an entry. Frequently, in view of the vast amount of legislation, this is not a difficult task.

These provisions tell us when a search (and any subsequent seizure) is legal, but section 8 of the Charter guarantees a right, not against illegal search or seizure, but against unreasonable search or seizure. The difference is important because, as we shall see, while the mere illegality of a search does not generally affect the admissibility of any evidence obtained as a result of the search, if the search is unreasonable, then evidence so obtained must be excluded if to admit it would bring the administration of justice into disrepute.

There is not much difficulty in the obvious cases in holding that a search is both illegal and unreasonable where, for example, a person is stopped on the street and is searched without any justification whatsoever. Even what purports to be a legal search, in that there is some statutory authorization for it, may be unconstitutional if the courts find that the statutory provision violates the Charter. For example, the Narcotic Control Act contains a provision enabling a police officer to search any premises, except a dwelling house, whenever he has reasonable grounds to believe that narcotics may be on those premises. A search warrant is not required. It is not entirely clear yet from the cases, but probably such a provision violates section 8 of the Charter, at least insofar as it purports to give a blanket right to search in all cases.[4]

Conversely, however, just because the search is illegal, it does not necessarily follow that it is also unreasonable or, even if it is, that the administration of justice would be brought into disrepute if the evidence

---

4 *R. v. Rao* (1984), 46 O.R. (2d) 80, 40 C.R. (3d) 1, 12 C.C.C. (3d) 97, 4 O.A.C. 162, 9 D.L.R. (4th) 542, 10 C.R.R. 275 (C.A.), leave to appeal to S.C.C. refused (1989), 40 C.R. (3d) xxvin, 4 O.A.C. 241n, 10 C.R.R. 275n, 57 N.R. 238 (S.C.C.); *R. v. Debot* (1986), 54 C.R. (3d) 120, 30 C.C.C. (3d) 207, 26 C.R.R. 275, 17 O.A.C. 141 (C.A.), aff'd [1989] 2 S.C.R. 1140, 73 C.R. (3d) 129, 52 C.C.C. (3d) 193, 37 O.A.C. 1, 45 C.R.R. 49, 102 N.R. 161.

were admitted, but further discussion on this would be better postponed until Chapter 15 when we examine illegally obtained evidence.

ELECTRONIC SURVEILLANCE

Modern advances in technology have added a new weapon to the arsenal of police investigation techniques — the ability to intercept telephonic communications and to eavesdrop on private conversations. The surreptitious recording of telephone conversations or the surreptitious installation of a microphone to enable the recording of private conversations frequently enables the police to obtain evidence of criminal activities, particularly in the case of crimes such as conspiracies, gambling offences and any offence relating to organized crime where the parties must meet or speak together in order to plan their activities.

The Code now makes it an offence to intercept a private communication by means of any "electromagnetic, acoustic, mechanical or other device" — private communication being defined as any oral communication or telecommunication made under circumstances in which it is reasonable for the originator to expect that it will not be intercepted by any person other than the one he intends to receive it. To this basic rule there are, however (apart from certain technical exceptions), two circumstances where the interception is lawful. The first is where it is intercepted by someone who has the consent of either the originator or the person intended by the originator to receive the communication. The second is where it is intercepted in accordance with a prior authorization.

In each province and, where appropriate, in the federal government, several senior policemen have been designated agents of the Attorney General (or Solicitor General of Canada) for the purposes of making application for an authorization to intercept. The application must be made to a judge of the superior or county or district court (but not to a provincial court judge or a justice of the peace) and be accompanied by a sworn statement attested by a police officer. The application must:

1. Ensure that the offence being investigated is one for which an authorization is available. These offences are listed in the Code and are generally all the more serious offences punishable by imprisonment for five years or more, or that are believed to be part of organized crime or that are specifically listed, such as drug offences, sexual offences, murder or gaming offences.
2. Set out the factors justifying the belief that an authorization ought to be given.
3. List the names, addresses and occupations of the persons, if known, whose communications are to be intercepted, together with a description of the place and manner of interception.

4. Disclose whether there have been other applications.
5. Set out the period for which the authorization is requested.
6. State whether other investigative techniques have been tried and failed or why other methods would not likely succeed or why the urgency of the situation requires an intercept authorization.

The judge may then grant the authorization if he is satisfied that it would be in the best interests of the administration of justice to do so and that investigative procedures short of interception have been tried and failed or are unlikely to succeed or that the situation is urgent. The authorization itself permits an interception for a maximum period of 60 days (though there are provisions for an extension) and it sets out the offence in question, the type of communication that may be intercepted (e.g., a phone conversation or a face to face conversation), the persons whose communications are being intercepted and any other terms or conditions that the judge thinks advisable.

Obviously, if the subjects know that their communications are being intercepted, there would not be much point in engaging in the exercise, so there are provisions regarding the secrecy of the application, though the subjects must eventually be informed that their communications were intercepted once the investigation is over. There are also special provisions for emergency applications where there is not the time for the normal procedure.

If the interception is unlawful (that is, not made under an authorization or with the consent of one of the parties), then not only is the interceptor guilty of a criminal offence, but evidence of the communication is inadmissible against either the person originating the communication or the person intended by the originator to receive it, unless either of those persons consents to its admission. It is not, however, inadmissible as against third persons, though in practice this is unlikely to arise after since it is only in exceptional cases that a statement made by one person is admissible as evidence against a different person (a conspiracy charge is one case where it might be admissible); nor is evidence obtained as a result of the illegal interception itself inadmissible. For example, if, as a result of an illegally intercepted telephone call, the police locate a cache of drugs, the telephone call would be inadmissible, but evidence of the drugs themselves would admissible. There is, however, a discretion on the part of the trial judge to exclude even this indirect evidence where its admission would bring the administration of justice into disrepute.

That, at least, is what the Code provides, but in the case of *Duarte*[5] the Supreme Court added another dimension to the problem. There, a police informer had worn a "body-pack" at the instigation of the police and had

---

5 *R. v. Sanelli*, (*sub nom. R. v. Duarte*) [1990] 1 S.C.R. 30, 71 O.R. (2d) 575, 74 C.R. (3d) 281, 53 C.C.C. (3d) 1, 65 D.L.R. (4th) 240, 37 O.A.C. 322, 45 C.R.R. 278, 103 N.R. 86.

taped incriminating statements made by the accused. The informer had obviously consented to the interception, but the Court held that the surreptitious interception of the accused's conversation with someone he thought was a fellow criminal by the police or one of their agents in the course of police investigations violated the accused's rights under section 8 of the Charter. In its view, it is unacceptable in a free and democratic society that the state or its agents should use modern technology to record and transmit our words and conversations in its unfettered discretion by means that thwart the protections envisaged by the authorization sections set out in the Code. Such undercover investigative techniques were unreasonable searches. Thus, in spite of the wording of the Code, it would appear that when one of the consenting parties to the interception is the "state" or one of its agents engaged in investigation, the consent of that party is not, in itself, sufficient to render the interception admissible. Rather, an authorization will be required in accordance with the provisions of the Code.

Finally, it should be noted that some communications, even if lawfully intercepted, are not admissible if they involve what is called a "privileged communication." The two most commonly encountered in this context are a communication between a lawyer and client and a communication between a husband and wife. Indeed, usually an authorization cannot be obtained to intercept communications in a lawyer's office or residence unless it is reasonable to believe that the lawyer himself (or an employee or member of his household) is a party to the offence in question. But the interception may be made at the client's house and involve a conversation he has with his lawyer or his wife. In such a case, the conversation remains privileged and inadmissible unless the client, in the first case, or the wife, in the second case, waives the privilege and consents to its admission.

Mention should also be made of the provisions regarding breathalyzers and blood tests. Sections 254-258 of the Code set out the powers of the police to demand breath samples (or, in some cases, blood samples) from drivers of motor vehicles, vessels, aircraft and railway equipment. A "roadside" screening test may be required where the driver is "reasonably suspected" of driving while alcohol is present in his body, but the results of such a test merely furnish the grounds for a more complete and accurate "breathalyzer" test, which may also be demanded where a police officer "believes on reasonable and probable grounds" that the driver is committing or has, within two hours, committed the offence of impaired driving or driving with more than .08 per cent blood alcohol concentration. A blood sample may be required (subject to several medical safeguards) where a breath sample would be impracticable or where the driver is incapable of providing one or under the authority of a warrant issued by a justice of the peace.

The constitutional validity of these provisions has been upheld on numerous occasions, on the grounds that they do not violate the right to life, liberty or security of the person in section 7 of the Charter or on the ground that if they do violate section 8 (unreasonable search and seizure), they are a reasonable limit justified under section 1. On the other hand, being detained in order to comply with the demand for a breath or blood sample is a detention within section 10 so as to give rise to all the safeguards under that section. It has also been held on a number of occasions that the *random* stopping of motorists for the purposes of spot checks, permitted under provincial legislation, does violate section 9 as an arbitrary detention but is again a reasonable limit under section 1. Stopping when there are pre-existing reasonable and probable grounds is not arbitrary and does not violate section 9.

4

Arrest, Summons and Compelling Attendance

If it is decided that a person should be charged with an offence, the obvious first consideration is to ensure that he shows up for his trial. Fundamentally, this can be achieved either by seizing him and forcing him to appear, or by asking him to appear and threatening him with various unpleasant consequences if he does not show up. This basic distinction becomes, in the first case, arrest, detention before trial and compulsory appearance at trial. In the second case it becomes the issuing of a summons (or some other order to appear) and the expectation that the accused will appear at trial.

The only absolute, certain way of ensuring attendance is the first method. If the accused is physically restrained and forced to appear, one can be certain that he will do so. Under the second method, there is always the risk that the accused will not appear. Arrest and pre-trial detention is, therefore, certain but it is also expensive. The time between arrest and trial may be a matter of months, and incarceration of an accused person which costs over $100 a day is not cheap.

More importantly, however, that person is only accused, not convicted, and if he is ultimately acquitted he will have spent perhaps months in jail as an innocent person. In addition, whether ultimately found guilty or not, he is kept in detention and unable to work, thus depriving his family of his support; he is not at liberty to find witnesses and prepare his case to help in his defence; while he may consult with his lawyer, consulting a legal adviser in the environment of a prison is not as convenient as being free to consult him at will; his mail is subject to various restrictions; and his visiting rights are limited. For these, and probably several other similar reasons, it can be seen that arrest and detention, while certain, are also in many ways unfair and unjust. Fortunately, the law recognizes this and thus we have a basic proposition that arrest and detention before trial, while legal in some circumstances, should be employed only as a last resort and only if justified in view of all the facts.

At this point we must again distinguish between the position in federal criminal law and the position under provincial law in regard to provincial offences and it will be less complicated if we deal with the position under federal law first.

Given that arrest and detention are undesirable for the reasons outlined above, it will be seen that, when it has been decided to charge a person with an offence and one is concerned with ensuring that he will appear for trial, in descending order of both certainty and unfairness, one could (i) arrest that person and detain him until his trial, (ii) arrest that person, but then release him if one could be fairly sure that he will appear for trial, or (iii) never arrest him in the first place, but merely require him by some means or other to appear at a certain date in order to be tried. What the Code tries to do is to ensure that the least unfair method is tried first before resorting to the most unfair, but at the same time most certain method of arrest and pre-trial detention.[1]

Before we examine the process in more detail, however, it will be as well to set the scene. One can have the situation where the fact that a crime has been committed comes to the attention of the police who then embark upon an investigation and finally locate the person who should be charged. They can then go to a justice of the peace and lay an information against that person. If the justice is satisfied that a case has been made out, he will, as we saw in Chapter 1, issue a process against the accused. That process may either be an arrest warrant — that is, an authorization to the police to arrest the person in question — or it may be a summons — that is, an order directed to the accused requiring him to appear on a set date at a set court. Whichever of the two processes is issued, the laying of the information comes first, before there is any procedural contact with the accused.

On the other hand, one can have the situation where the police encounter a person in the course of committing an offence, or who has just committed an offence. Here, there is no time to go to a justice of the peace first, nor, indeed, would it be much use to do so, if the police did not know the identity of the person involved. Here the policeman must

---

1 The relevant sections of the Criminal Code, ss. 493-525.

act on his own initiative and only after he has started the process does he then have time to go to a justice of the peace and lay the information. In this case, the laying of the information comes after the first procedural contact with the accused.

Which of these two methods is used depends, of course, upon the circumstances of each case, but let us start with the simpler of the two — that is, where the information is laid first and a justice of the peace issues process.

INFORMATION FIRST

Where the information is laid first, a justice of the peace will have to have been satisfied that a case has been made out against the accused, or else no process is issued. There is, therefore, a protection for an accused person — a judicial officer has determined that the facts justify proceeding further.

The information may be laid before any justice of the peace who has jurisdiction to receive it.[2] Jurisdiction may be based upon one of two principles — either the commission of the offence or the presence of the accused. The information may allege that the accused has committed an offence within the county or district in which the justice sits regardless of where the accused is at the time of the information, or it may allege that the accused has committed, anywhere in the province (but not outside the province), an offence and the accused is, or is believed to be, or resides, or is believed to reside, in the county or district in which the justice sits. (There is a slightly wider jurisdiction in the case of receiving or being in possession of stolen property which need not concern us here.) Since, as we shall see, all trials normally take place in the place where the offence was committed, it is the former basis of jurisdiction that is most commonly relied upon.

A justice who is so satisfied may issue either an arrest warrant or a summons. She must, however, issue a summons rather than an arrest warrant unless the allegations of the informant (that is, what the police officer tells her), or the evidence of any witnesses she hears, discloses reasonable and probable ground for her to believe that it is necessary in the public interest to issue an arrest warrant.[3]

What would be necessary in the public interest cannot be stated with any certainty, but if the offence were serious — e.g., murder or sexual assault — or if the accused were unlikely to show up for trial or might destroy evidence or tamper with witnesses or commit other offences, an arrest warrant would be justified. At the other extreme, if the offence is

---

2 Section 504.
3 Section 507.

Form of the Information

CANADA	)	INFORMATION of John Smith of Court
PROVINCE OF	)	Bureau, City Hall, Police Officer
ONTARIO JUDICIAL	)	(occupation). The informant says that he
DISTRICT OF YORK	)	has reasonable and probable grounds to
	)	believe and does believe.

That Henry Jones on or about the _____ 10th day _____ of ___ May ___, 19__, at the Municipality of _____ Metropolitan Toronto in the _____ Judicial District of __ York __ unlawfully did

Steal an automobile, the property of William Black, at the value of more than $1,000.00 and did thereby commit theft contrary to the Criminal Code.

SWORN before me, ___ Peter Brown,	)	
this ___ 15th ___ day of __ May __	)	
19__ at the ___ Municipality ___	) _____ John Smith _____	
of Metropolitan Toronto in the	) (signature of	
Judicial District of York	) informant)	

_____
Peter Brown
A Justice of the Peace in and
for the Province of Ontario.

[The Information will, in practice, also contain, on the back, various blank spaces and check boxes which will detail the history of the case as it moves through the court system until final disposition.]

relatively minor and if the accused is a settled and stable member of the community, clearly a summons would be appropriate.

A summons is addressed to the person accused and recites that he has been charged with the offence in question. It then commands him, in Her Majesty's name, to attend court at a specified time and place to appear before a justice. He is then warned that if he fails to do so, he will be guilty of the offence of ignoring a summons. In addition, a warrant may be issued for his arrest so that he may be found guilty not only of the original offence, but also of the offence of failing to appear.

A warrant to arrest is addressed to the police of a particular jurisdiction authorizing them to arrest the person named therein for the offence specified and to bring him before the court to be dealt with.

Once the summons is issued it must then be "served" on the accused so that he will know what his obligations are. Once the arrest warrant is issued, it must then be "executed" by actually arresting the named person.

Service of Summons

The summons must then be delivered to the accused personally by a police officer (or other officer). However, if the accused cannot be found, it is sufficient if it is left at his last or usual place of residence with someone living there who appears to be at least 16 years of age or older. If the accused disputes that he ever received the summons, the officer who delivered it may testify orally that it was delivered or, more commonly, swear an affidavit attesting to its delivery.[4]

Execution of Warrant

The normal arrest warrant is addressed, as we have seen, to the police officers of a particular locality — e.g., Metropolitan Toronto, or such and such a county — and is authority for them to arrest the named person. But it is authority for them to arrest him not only within the limits of the place for which they have jurisdiction, but to arrest him anywhere in the province in which the warrant was issued. The warrant may therefore be "executed" anywhere in the province. It may not, however, be executed outside the province unless it is a specific type of warrant known as a "Canada-wide warrant" which can be executed anywhere in Canada. Such warrants are only of limited availability and are exceptions to the general rule. They can only be issued in respect, for example, of an accused person who attends for trial but then absconds half way through, or who fails to appear after a bail hearing.

---

4 Section 509.

The general rule is that a warrant issued, for example, in Toronto, may be executed in Toronto or anywhere in Ontario but it may not be executed in Vancouver or Winnipeg. This would be rather awkward if an accused committed an offence in Toronto and then fled to Vancouver. To obviate this difficulty, there is a procedure whereby such a warrant may be "endorsed" (that is, signed on the back) by a justice of the peace in British Columbia. This then becomes authorization for not only the Metropolitan Toronto Police, but also for any police officer in British Columbia to arrest the accused and, of course, cause him to be transported back to Toronto for his court appearance.[5]

The limits of Canadian jurisdiction, however, stop at the Canadian border. If an accused flees to a foreign jurisdiction, then none of this procedure is available and if the prosecution is to continue it must be preceded by recovering the accused by means of extradition proceedings from that foreign jurisdiction.

When the warrant is executed, the accused is arrested and taken into custody in a police station. Since what happens to him then is paralleled by what happens to a person arrested without a warrant, let us leave him there for the moment, and turn our attention to the other process.

INFORMATION SECOND

Where someone is "caught in the act," there is, as we have seen, no opportunity for the information to be sworn out first and the process of compelling the appearance of the accused starts before the information is laid. Let us look first at the *powers* to arrest without a warrant — that is, when an arrest without a warrant would be lawful. As we shall see, merely because a person *may* arrest without a warrant does not necessarily mean that he *should* arrest without a warrant.[6]

Arrest Without Warrant

Anyone, whether a police officer or a private citizen, has the power to arrest without warrant anyone whom he finds committing an indictable offence,[7] or anyone whom he believes to have committed any offence (indictable or summary conviction) and to be escaping from and being freshly pursued by a person having the authority to arrest him (in practice,

---

5 Section 528.

6 Sections 494, 495.

7 The difference between an "indictable offence" and a "summary conviction offence" will be discussed in Chapter 5, Classification of Offences and the Courts. There are crucial procedural differences between the two but, at the moment, it is sufficient to note that indictable offences are the more serious offences and summary conviction offences the less serious ones.

of course, being pursued by a police officer). In addition, any owner or lawful possessor of property (or an agent of such person) may arrest without warrant anyone he finds committing an offence in relation to that property.

Arrest by a private person (the so-called citizen's arrest) is possible, but of limited scope. Where such an arrest does take place, the citizen must forthwith deliver the arrested person to a police officer to be dealt with in accordance with the procedures we shall discuss shortly.

A police officer's power to arrest without warrant is considerably wider than that of a private person. He may arrest:

1. Anyone whom he finds committing any criminal offence (not merely an indictable offence, as is the case with a citizen's arrest);
2. Anyone who *has* committed an indictable offence;
3. Anyone whom he believes, on reasonable and probable grounds, has committed or is about to commit an indictable offence;
4. Anyone in respect of whom he believes that there is an arrest warrant outstanding that is in force in the jurisdiction.

Leaving aside the rare cases of fresh pursuit, outstanding warrants and the special position of owners of property, a private citizen cannot arrest for a summary conviction offence and, in the case of an indictable offence, only if the person is actually committing it in his presence. If he is wrong, and the person is not committing the offence, then the arrest is unlawful, however reasonable it may have been to think otherwise.

Not only may a police officer arrest whenever he finds a person actually committing an offence, but he may also arrest if that person *has* committed an indictable offence or if he believes that he has committed an indictable offence, or is about to commit such an offence. The police officer is therefore protected from honest and reasonable mistakes. In the case of summary conviction offences he may arrest only if he finds a person committing an offence; he may not arrest where that offence *has* been committed or where he thinks it has been committed or is about to be committed.

However, while these are the *powers* that a police officer has, the Code then goes on to state that a police officer shall not arrest, even though he has the power to do so where the offence that is being committed is a summary conviction offence; where the offence in question is listed in the relevant Act as either a summary conviction offence or an indictable offence;[8] or where the offence, although indictable in nature, is so minor compared to other indictable offences that the accused does not have the

---

8 This "hybrid" offence will be explained in Chapter 5, Classification of Offences and the Courts.

right to a jury trial,[9] in any case where the officer has reasonable and probable grounds to believe that the public interest may be satisfied without arresting that person,[10] and he has no grounds to believe that that person will fail to attend court as required.

Appearance Notice

In the case of these offences, instead of arresting the person in question, the police officer may issue to him what is called an "appearance notice." This is a document which set out the name of the accused, the substance of the offence alleged to have been committed and the time and place where the accused must attend court. It also contains a statement that it is an offence to fail to appear as required and describes the consequences of failing to appear.

It will be observed that this mechanism gives the police officer the power to initiate the proceedings by enabling him to require the accused to appear in court — a power that is traditionally reserved for a judicial officer. As we have seen, the essence of the criminal process is that it is not started until a justice of the peace has been satisfied that a case has been made out against the accused. Yet, in the case where a police officer issues an appearance notice, there has been no prior intervention by a justice of the peace and this flies in the face of our traditional guarantees. To meet this objection, the Code requires any police officer who issues an appearance notice to lay the information as soon as practicable afterwards, but in any case, before the time set out in the appearance notice for the accused's first court appearance.[11] The justice of the peace shall then proceed to consider the matter in the same way as if the information were an ordinary one, but at the conclusion, if he is satisfied that a case has been made out against the accused, he shall confirm the appearance notice; if he is not so satisfied he shall cancel the appearance notice and cause the accused to be notified that it has been cancelled and that he is no longer required to attend court as specified in it. In other words, if he hears nothing the accused must show up; if he is notified that the appearance notice is cancelled, then the accused need not show up. In this way, the accused's right to have a judicial officer determine whether he should appear for trial or not is preserved, even though the actual order was issued by a police officer without prior judicial authorization.

The only people who should actually be arrested, therefore, in spite

---

9 Again, this will be explained, but this category of offence includes crimes such as gaming and betting offences.

10 Such interest would not be satisfied where, for example, the suspect refuses to identify himself, or there is some reason to believe he may destroy evidence or continue the offence.

11 Section 505.

of the wide *powers* of arrest that a police officer has, are those charged with the more serious indictable offence or those charged with some lesser offence, but in respect of where there is some reason to think he will not appear for trial unless arrested, or in respect of whom there is some public interest to be served by the arrest — as, for example, if the accused will not identify himself, or where the offence is continuing, such as impaired driving, or where there is danger that he will destroy evidence. But in these latter cases, the public interest may be satisfied as soon as the arrest has been effected. For example, an accused person who refuses to identify himself, may, after he has been arrested, identify himself. In such a case, the police officer, although he has effected an arrest, may, if the public interest justifying the arrest in the first place disappears, then release the accused and give him an appearance notice, or may simply release him and proceed by way of laying an information and having a summons issued against the accused.

Accordingly, persons actually arrested and taken to the police station are only those charged with the more serious offences or those whose arrest and custody are justified on the grounds of public interest, or in respect of whom it is believed that they will not appear for trial unless arrested. But, at this stage, it is the policy of the Code to get as many people as possible out of the police station as soon as one can.[12] It therefore provides that the officer in charge (e.g., the senior officer on duty at the time) of the station to which the accused is brought, shall release the arrested person as soon as practicable, if the offence is one of the less serious ones we have described above, or if it is any indictable offence punishable by imprisonment for five years or less (unless, again, he believes it is in the public interest to keep the accused in custody), or if he has reasonable and probable grounds to believe that the accused will not show up for trial if released.

Release from Custody by Officer in Charge

The officer in charge has a number of options open to him when releasing the accused. He may just tell the accused to go and then lay an information and have a summons issued against him; or he may require the accused to sign a written promise to appear in court at a specified time and place; or he may require the accused not only to promise to appear, but also to enter into a recognizance (that is, an acknowledgement that he will be liable to have a sum of money forfeited to the state) up to maximum of $500, but he cannot require any deposit of actual cash or valuables, nor can he require securities (that is, someone else also to render himself liable to forfeiture of money if the accused fails to appear).

---

12 Section 497.

In the single case where the accused is not ordinarily a resident in the province or does not ordinarily reside within 200 kilometres of the police station, the officer in charge may require the accused to deposit a sum not exceeding $500 (or its equivalent in valuables).

Here, again, in all of these cases, there has as yet been no judicial intervention, so the information must be laid as soon as practicable and in any case before the time specified for the accused's appearance in court, so that a justice of the peace can examine the matter and, if he is not satisfied that there is a case against the accused, cancel what the officer in charge has done.

This machinery applies whenever a person is, or could be, arrested without a warrant. Where there is a warrant, that is, as we have seen, sufficient authority for the police to arrest the accused and keep him in custody until he is brought before the court. However, an arrest warrant, when issued by a justice of the peace after the information, may itself contain an endorsement if the offence is one of the less serious ones or if it is an indictable offence punishable by imprisonment for five years or less. That endorsement may authorize the officer in charge of the police station to which the accused is brought, to release him, in spite of the arrest warrant, on similar terms as if he had been arrested without a warrant.

The result of this apparently rather complicated machinery is that the only persons who are actually arrested and detained in custody should be those charged with indictable offences punishable by more than five years' imprisonment; or those charged with lesser offences who, for some reason of public interest, or by reason of the fact that it is reasonably believed they will not appear for trial, should not be released from custody; or those arrested under the authority of an arrest warrant which has not been endorsed so as to authorize their prior release. The next question, therefore, is what happens to these people who are now in custody in a police station or some other holding facility?

Release from Custody by Justice of the Peace

The Code requires that all such persons are to be brought before a justice of the peace,

1. where a justice is available within a period of 24 hours after the arrest, without unreasonable delay and, in any event, within that 24-hour period, or
2. where a justice is not available within a 24-hour period, as soon as possible.[13]

The purpose of these provisions is to attempt to ensure that an accused

---

13 Section 503.

person remains in police custody for as short a time as possible before his detention is reviewed by a justice of the peace. Of course, justices of the peace are not constantly available 24 hours a day, particularly in other than metropolitan areas and particularly over weekends and holidays. There is, therefore, no absolute maximum period in which an accused can be detained in police custody, save that it must be within 24 hours if a justice is available. In other cases, it is merely as soon as possible. This does mean that it is still possible for an accused to remain in police custody for some substantial period of time (a fact that we will examine further when we discuss interrogation and confessions in Chapter 13).

"Show-cause"

The duty of the justice of the peace is to determine whether the accused should be released pending his trial — a process colloquially known as the "bail hearing," but in fact, "judicial interim release hearing" is a more accurate term. He must order the accused to be detained in custody where he is charged with treason, hijacking (and related offences) and first or second degree murder (in these offences only a superior court judge may authorize the release of the accused), but in all other cases, the justice must consider releasing the accused pending trial.

Generally speaking, the justice *shall* order the release unless the prosecutor shows cause why detention is justified and, furthermore, *shall* release merely upon the accused undertaking to appear for trial, without any conditions attached, unless the prosecutor shows cause why the release should not be unconditional. Hence, these hearings are called "show-cause" hearings.[14]

If the prosecutor does show cause why the release should not be unconditional or why the accused should not be released at all, there is then an ascending order of options open to the justice who shall not impose any more rigorous control over the accused unless he is satisfied that any less rigorous control is not appropriate. He starts from the proposition that the accused should be released without conditions merely upon his undertaking to appear for trial.

The next more rigorous step is to accept his undertaking, while at the same time imposing certain conditions — for example, to report to a police officer periodically, not to leave the province, to surrender his passport and the like. Next, he may require the accused to enter into a recognizance to forfeit a sum of money if he does not appear, but without requiring any actual deposit of cash or any third party sureties to guarantee his appearance. The next most rigorous step is the same, but with one or more sureties who agree that they will forfeit a sum of money if the

---

14 Sections 515, 525.

accused fails to appear. This is, of course, a considerable step up since it does require the accused to be able to find someone who is willing to face the prospect of losing what might be a considerable sum of money if he does not honour his commitment to appear for trial.

Next, the justice may, if the prosecutor consents, instead of requiring sureties, release the accused on his own recognizance if the accused actually deposits the sum of money (or its equivalent) with the court. This ensures that if the accused fails to appear, there will be no problem collecting the amount that may be forfeited, but, of course, it is not much use to an accused who does not have the means to put up the requisite amount of cash or valuable security.

In only one case may the justice require *both* sureties and a cash deposit and that is if the accused is not ordinarily resident in the province or does not ordinarily reside within 200 kilometres of the place where he is in custody.

If none of these methods is fitting, then, and only then, may the justice order the accused to be detained in custody and, upon making such order, he must state, in the record, his reasons for so ruling.

As can be seen, the presumption is that an accused must be released, and released upon as less rigorous terms as possible. The onus of showing why more rigorous terms should be imposed or, ultimately, why the accused should not be released at all, is on the prosecutor. In some cases, however, this normal process is reversed. If the accused is charged with an indictable offence alleged to have been committed while he was on release awaiting trial for a previous offence; if he is charged with an indictable offence and is not ordinarily resident in Canada; if he is charged with failing to appear while on release for a previous offence; or if he is charged with drug trafficking or drug importing or conspiracy under the Narcotic Control Act,[15] then the justice shall order him detained in custody unless the *accused* shows cause why he should *not* be detained in custody. If the justice agrees to his release, he shall state his reasons and impose any of the conditions we have discussed above unless the accused shows why such conditions should not be imposed.[16]

Bail hearing

There are several procedural matters connected to a show cause

---

15 In *R. c. Pearson*, 79 C.R. (3d) 90, 59 C.C.C. (3d) 406, 5 C.R.R. (2d) 164, [1990] R.J.Q. 2438, the Québec Court of Appeal held that this reverse onus contravened both s. 11(*d*) and s. 11(*e*) of the Charter.

16 We should note that where an accused is charged with murder only a Superior Court judge may order his release and release is not ordered unless the accused shows cause why he should be released. It is difficult, but not impossible, to be released pending trial for murder.

hearing that are of importance. For example, the justice has the power, during the hearing, to remand the accused to custody in prison for a period of up to three days (or longer with the consent of the accused). During such period he is not in the custody of the police, but of the prison officials, and, in some jurisdictions, may be able to undergo psychiatric assessment.[17]

At the bail hearing, the justice may hear any relevant evidence and may question the accused, save that the accused shall not be questioned by either the justice or the prosecutor or anyone else as to the offence with which he is charged. Where it is intended to show cause (either by the prosecutor in the normal case or by the accused in those cases where the burden is on him) the justice must be informed of what is about to happen and *may*, or *shall* if the accused so applies, make an order, either at the beginning or anytime during the hearing, directing that no evidence or information or representations or reasons shall be published in any newspaper or broadcast until the accused is discharged or the trial of the accused is over.

The actual mechanics of a bail hearing of this nature are fairly straightforward. In the vast majority of cases, they are of a routine nature. As we have seen, there is a legal obligation on the part of the detaining police officers to bring an accused before a justice of the peace within the specified time limit, whether or not the accused has asked or demanded that this be done. Since it is, in the usual case, up to the "prosecutor" to show cause why the accused should not be released without conditions, the prosecutor, at this stage, is usually the police officer who swears out the information. It is unlikely that this early in the proceedings, the Attorney General will have intervened. Unless he needs more time to assemble his material, in which case he may ask for an adjournment under section 516 of the Criminal Code, he will usually know whether he is going to oppose unconditional release or not, based on the accused's record (which by now he will have), the seriousness of the offence, and the attitude and circumstances of the accused. Not infrequently, the bail hearing will be little more than a formality. In other cases, it may develop into a full-scale hearing. Most often, it is somewhere in between with the real dispute not being as to release or detention, but as to the conditions to be imposed or whether to require securities for the release of the accused.

Bail review

There are a number of provisions relating to a review of the order made by the justice of the peace, either by the accused where he has not been released unconditionally, or by the prosecutor where the accused has not ordered detained in custody. The review is held by a superior court

---

17 Section 516.

judge or, depending upon the province, by a county or district court judge, or, in Quebec, by a panel of three judges of the session of the peace or the provincial court. Such judge may consider all the relevant material and hear any additional evidence and then either uphold the justice's decision or vary his order.

It may sometimes happen that after an accused has been released pending trial (either with or without various terms and conditions) it appears that he has violated one or more of the conditions of his release, or is about to violate them, or it appears that he has committed an indictable offence while at large. In such instances, if a justice is satisfied that there are reasonable and probable grounds to believe that this is the case he may issue a warrant for the arrest of the accused. The accused is then brought before the justice (or judge where the offence is one or murder, etc.) for a hearing to determine that this is actually the case. If so, the release mechanism is cancelled and the accused is ordered to be detained in custody unless he shows cause why he should not be detained.

All this means is that it is really only in the more extreme cases that the accused is detained in custody prior to his trial — either the offence is very serious or it has been shown that the accused cannot be trusted if he is released (that is to say, he is likely to flee or not show up, or continue to commit offences or something of that sort), or that the accused cannot meet the conditions imposed for his release. All other persons should be out of custody on some form of pre-trial release, ranging from merely having an appearance notice or receiving a summons, all the way up to being released after entering into a recognizance for a substantial sum of money and depositing cash or valuable security. Of course, that still leaves a significant number of people in custody pending their trial. But here again the Code might come to their rescue.

Apart from the case of murder, for which, as we have seen, along with treason and hijacking, there are specific provisions, where an accused has been in custody for 90 days in the case of indictable offences and 30 days in the case of summary conviction offences, the person having custody of him (the warden or superintendent of the detention facility) shall apply to a judge to have a date fixed for a hearing to determine whether or not the accused should be released. At that hearing he may take into consideration whether the prosecutor or the accused has been responsible for the delay and may order the accused released (imposing various terms and conditions) if he is not satisfied that the continued detention of the accused is justified. An accused cannot, therefore, be held indefinitely in custody prior to his trial and, in any case, as we have seen, if he is not tried within a reasonable time after he has been charged with an offence, his constitutional rights have been infringed and he is entitled to any appropriate and just remedy.

This is the scheme adopted under federal criminal law. It applies whenever the accused is charged with a federal criminal offence. The position where the accused is charged with a provincial offence is, in essence, no different, but for a number of reasons, much less complicated. Provincial offences are all of the less serious summary conviction nature and, even if an arrest is possible, it is not likely that one could justify the detention of an accused in custody pending trial for a relatively minor offence. The time lag between charge and trial is likely, in any case, to be quite short. But, most of all, the actual arrest of a person for a summary conviction provincial offence is not likely to be a frequent occurrence, and in some provinces, notably Ontario, it is not even possible, save for certain specified offences or where the accused has failed to appear for his trial the first time. In other provinces, the power to arrest for a provincial offence is limited by the Criminal Code provisions relating to summary conviction offences which have been incorporated into the provincial offence procedure.

PROVINCIAL OFFENCES

Without examining each province separately (which is not possible in a book of this nature) it is impossible to make a general statement about the actual procedure in each of them, except to say that it is only in the most exceptional case that an accused would be arrested and taken into custody, and even more exceptional that he would not then be released upon some form of pre-trial release pending his trial. It *is* possible, under some situations, for a recalcitrant accused to be detained in custody charged with a provincial offence pending his trial, but it is such an unusual occurrence that, generally speaking, the problems we have discussed in connection with federal criminal offences do not arise. Normally after the laying of the information, the accused will merely be served with a summons and will appear at the place and time specified. A more informal method may apply in the case of parking infractions or minor traffic offences, permitting the accused to pay a set fine without any court appearance at all.

Ontario has, however, adopted its own code of procedure[18] for provincial offences which does preserve the process of information, summons, appearance and trial as in any ordinary conviction prosecution, but it also adopts a more informal method of proceeding in less serious offences by way of what is known as a "certificate of offence." This is issued by a police officer (or other official designated a provincial offences officer) to someone he believes has committed an offence, informing him that an offence has been committed and specifying what it is. Unlike the federal appearance notice, it does not inform that person that he must

18 Provincial Offences Act.

appear in a specified court at a particular date and time. Rather, it merely makes the allegation and is accompanied by, or is followed within 30 days by what is called an "offence notice." The offence notice gives the offender three options: (i) he may sign the plea of guilty provided in the notice and remit or deliver it to the court office together with the amount specified as the fine for that offence; (ii) he may sign the not guilty portion of the offence notice and deliver it to the court offence, in which case a time and date for trial is set and the offender notified (failure to attend may result in a conviction in absentia); or (iii) the offender may attend at a justice's of the peace office to plead Guilty, but to offer some explanation why the set fine should not be imposed or some other sentence variation be adopted. The justice cannot find the accused not guilty (though he may, in practice, advise the offender that he does have a defence and rather than enter a guilty plea, he should sign the not guilty portion of the offence notice), but may accept the explanation and reduce the penalty. Generally, there is no term of imprisonment for the offence notice procedure and the maximum fine is $300 (or whatever lesser amount the specific statute that has been violated may provide).

If the offender fails to do any of these three things within 15 days, it is assumed that he does not wish to dispute the charge and a conviction may be entered, though there is a provision for the convicted offender re-opening the matter where, for example, he alleges that the offence notice never reached him, or reached him too late.

To sum up, then, what we see is that an accused, against whom an information has been laid, is required to appear in a specified court on a certain day at a specified time. This may be because a police officer has issued him an appearance notice setting out the time and place and that has been confirmed by a justice. It may be because an information has been laid and he has received a summons. It may be because he has been arrested, but has been released by the senior officer on duty in the police station and he has promised to appear, or entered into a recognizance and that officer's action has also been confirmed by a justice. It may be because he was arrested and taken into custody, but has been released by a justice (or a judge in the case of murder), on various terms and conditions, upon his giving an undertaking that he will appear at the place and time specified in the undertaking. Finally, it may be because he has been detained in custody or, having been released, has been retaken into custody, and is taken involuntarily to court on the time specified. In any of these cases, apart from the last, should the accused not show up as required, a warrant for his arrest may be issued and he may be brought before the court involuntarily.

At any rate, one way or another, the time will come when the accused makes his first court appearance and we must now turn to a consideration of what happens next.

Compelling the Appearance of the Accused

Commission of Offence and Investigation

Either — Or — Or

Either: Appearance Notice Issued by Police Officer → Release of Accused by Officer in Charge → Laying of Information Before J.P. to Cancel or Confirm

Or: Accused Arrested Without Warrant → Laying of Information Before J.P. → Bail Hearing

Or: Laying of Information Before J.P. → Issuing of Summons to Accused

Warrant for Arrest of Accused → Release by Officer in charge if Warrant Endorsed

Bail Hearing → Detention Before Trial

Bail Hearing → Judicial Interim Release

First Court Appearance by Accused

5

Classification of Offences and the Courts

Crime, to use the word in its broadest sense, can range in gravity from the trivial to the heinous, from littering a sidewalk to multiple first degree murder. The procedure for trying an offence largely depends upon the type of offence we are dealing with and our first task is to sort out how all offences are classified. If we start with the classification used in the Code, we will then easily be able to see how other offences and provincial offences fit into the scheme. But in order to understand the classification system, some understanding of the structure of trial courts will first be necessary.

TRIAL COURTS

Under the Code, there are three levels of trial court — not three courts but three levels. These are known as the superior court of criminal jurisdiction, the court of criminal jurisdiction and the summary conviction court.

The superior court of criminal jurisdiction is the highest level of trial court in each province and its actual designation varies from province to province. Often it is called the Supreme Court of the Province, or the Court of Queen's Bench. It may also be called the Superior Court of the Province, while in Ontario it is called the Ontario Court of Justice (General Division). It is always presided over by a federally appointed judge, designated Mr.

Justice X (or, of course, Madam Justice X), and addressed as either My Lord (or Lady) or as Your Honour. The superior court of criminal jurisdiction has jurisdiction to try all indictable offences, although in practice, as we shall see in a moment, it does not actually exercise such wide jurisdiction. In criminal cases it sits with a jury, although it is possible for the jury to be dispensed with, but only with the consent of both the accused and the Attorney General.

The court of criminal jurisdiction is more complicated. It has jurisdiction to try all indictable offences except those (of which murder is the most important) that *must* be tried in a superior court of criminal jurisdiction. But the court of criminal jurisdiction appears in three different guises, each of them having equal jurisdiction. First, it may consist of a court composed of a judge and jury, usually known as a court of general sessions or sessions of the peace. This judge will in most cases be a judge of the superior court of the province — that is to say, the same person who presides over the superior court of criminal jurisdiction, but this time sitting, not as a superior court of criminal jurisdiction, but merely as a court of criminal jurisdiction.[1] He will, as we shall see, normally be the judge presiding at the trial when the accused elects to be tried by "judge and jury."

Second, it may consist of precisely the same judge who presides at the first type of court of criminal jurisdiction, but this time sitting without a jury. That is to say, it will consist of a superior court judge of the province (except Nova Scotia, where it will be a county court judge), however he or she is designated, but no jury. This is the judge who will preside when the accused elects to be tried by "judge without a jury."

Third, it may consist of a judge sitting without a jury, but this time a different judge from that defined as a judge for the purpose of the first two forms of court of criminal jurisdiction. When an accused elects[2] to be tried by a judge without a jury, he is given a choice between being tried by "a provincial court judge" or simply by "a judge." If he chooses the latter then he will be tried by a judge as we have discussed in relation to the second type of court of criminal jurisdiction, but if he chooses the former, he will be tried by a judge appointed by the province and designated, under the Code, as a provincial court judge, although the provincial legislation under which he is appointed may utilize some other title. While this may not, superficially, appear to make all that much difference, there are, as we shall see, crucial differences in the following processes, depending

---

1 In Nova Scotia, this court of criminal jurisdiction is presided over by a federally appointed judge called a county court judge who is one level down from the superior court judge. This was, at one time, true in all other provinces too but superior court judges and county (or district) court judges have been amalgamated into one in all provinces except Nova Scotia.

2 We shall see in a moment what this entails.

upon whether the accused elects trial by a "judge" or trial by a "provincial court judge."

In sum, the court of criminal jurisdiction has three different forms. It may be a court composed of judge and jury; it may be a court composed of a judge sitting without a jury; lastly, it may be a court composed of a provincial court judge sitting without a jury.

The third, and lowest, level of criminal trial court is the summary conviction court. This is a court with limited territorial jurisdiction presided over, in practice, by a provincial court judge with jurisdiction to try only summary conviction (i.e., minor) offences. In some cases, the summary conviction court may be presided over by a justice of the peace who is provincially appointed and normally addressed as Your Worship. She is of considerably more importance in the trial of provincial offences than in the trial of federal offences and we will discuss that role a little later. As far as federal criminal offences are concerned, she is of the utmost importance on many procedural matters, but although the Code gives her some trial jurisdiction, in practice, she is not often utilized as a trial judge in federal offences.[3] Procedurally, however, she is the person before whom informations are laid and who must be satisfied that a case is made out against the accused before process is issued; she is the person to whom the police must go to obtain search warrants; and she will often be the person presiding at "show cause hearings" to determine whether the accused should be released from custody pending trial. She may sit under the direction of a provincially appointed judge for the limited purpose of adjourning cases or remanding accused persons, but not actually trying them, except in one or two very minor cases. While the Code does give her jurisdiction to sit as a summary conviction court and to preside over a preliminary inquiry,[4] she is not, in general, utilized for these purposes. From the point of view of the *trial* of federal offences (as opposed to other procedural matters) it is not likely therefore that the accused will appear before a justice of the peace, but it is not impossible.

CLASSIFICATION OF OFFENCES

All offences in Canada are divided into either indictable offences or summary conviction offences.[5] Summary conviction offences are those that must be tried by a summary conviction court (as discussed above) and generally are punishable by a maximum term of six months' imprisonment and a fine of not more than $2,000, though there are exceptions. Generally,

---

3 In some provinces the functions of the justices of the peace are performed by provincially appointed judges all of whom are *ex officio* justices of the peace for the purposes of their functions under the Code.

4 This will be discussed in the next chapter.

5 *Not* felonies and misdemeanours — a division Canada has not had for 100 years.

they can only be tried in the county or locality in which the offence was committed and the proceedings against the offender must commence within six months of the offence being committed. All provisions creating the offence will state whether the offence is a summary conviction offence.

Indictable offences are not, however, that easily disposed of, and are further sub-divided. There is a group of offences that are so serious that the accused must be tried by a superior court of criminal jurisdiction sitting with a jury (unless both he and the Attorney General consent to trial without a jury). He has no choice in the matter. The most important offence in this category is murder (either first or second degree), but it also includes a few others such as treason and piracy. These are called "supreme court exclusive" offences, or some such title.

At the other end of the scale, there is a group of indictable offences that are not considered serious enough to require a trial by judge and jury or a trial by a federally appointed judge. Here again, the accused has no choice in the matter and must be tried by a provincial court judge unless, for some exceptional reason, the judge decides otherwise. These include theft under $1,000 when prosecuted as an indictable offence, most gaming and betting offences and some other fraud and property offences of a relatively minor nature. These are called "absolute jurisdiction" offences.[6]

In all other indictable offences, the accused has a choice as to how he wishes to be tried because while he must be tried by a court of criminal jurisdiction, that court, as we have seen, appears in three different guises, so it is up to the accused to choose in which of these three different courts he wishes to be tried. As soon as he has been arraigned,[7] he must be addressed by the presiding judge as follows:

> You have the option to elect to be tried by a provincial court judge without a jury and without having had a preliminary inquiry; or you may elect to have a preliminary inquiry and to be tried by a judge without a jury; or you may elect to have a preliminary inquiry and to be tried by a court composed of a judge and jury. If you do not elect now, you shall be deemed to have elected to have a preliminary inquiry and to be tried by a court composed of a judge and jury. How do you elect to be tried?

This is known as "putting the accused to his election," and is a necessary first step in the trial of the bulk of most indictable offences. We shall consider a little later on what happens after the accused makes his election.

Finally, there is one other category of offence known as a hybrid or ambivalent offence which complicates the picture even further. For example, section 3(1) of the Narcotic Control Act makes it an offence to be in possession of a narcotic and subsection (2) then says:

---

6 They are set out in the Criminal Code, s. 553.

7 That is, the information is read out to him and the formal proceedings are ready to begin.

Every person who violates subsection (1) is guilty of an offence and is liable

(*a*) upon summary conviction for a first offence, to a fine of one thousand dollars or to imprisonment for six months or to both fine and imprisonment . . . or

(*b*) upon conviction on indictment, to imprisonment for seven years.

It was said earlier that the section creating the offence will always state whether the offence is an indictable offence or a summary conviction offence, yet section 3 of the Narcotic Control Act (and there are several other similar sections)[8] states that the offence can be either. In such offences it is the prosecuting official who has the first choice — he may choose to proceed by way of summary conviction or he may choose to proceed on indictment. If he chooses the former, then the trial proceeds in every way as though the offence were a summary conviction offence; if he chooses the latter, then the trial proceeds in every way as if the offence were an indictable offence — the accused must be put to his election and may elect one of the three modes of trial.

There are thus, under the federal system, five categories of offences. They are:

1. The summary conviction offence — minor offences usually carrying a maximum penalty of a $2,000 fine and six months' imprisonment, tried by a provincially appointed judge and subject, generally, to a limitation period of six months from the date of the commission of the offence.
2. The absolute jurisdiction indictable offence — at the lower end of the scale of gravity of indictable offences. The accused has no election and will normally be tried by a provincially appointed judge without jury.
3. The election indictable offences — the bulk of indictable offences, tried by one of the three courts of criminal jurisdiction. The accused has the option of being tried by a provincially appointed judge without a jury, a federally appointed judge without a jury, or a federally appointed judge with a jury.
4. The supreme court exclusive indictable offences — in practice, first or second degree murder. The accused must be tried not only by a federally appointed judge and jury (except where there is consent to dispense with the jury), but by a judge appointed to the Superior Court, Supreme Court, or Court of Queen's Bench (or some equivalent designation).
5. A number of hybrid or ambivalent offences where the Crown first has the choice of whether it wishes to proceed by way of indictment or by way of summary conviction proceedings. Once that choice has been made, the trial proceeds accordingly.

---

6 For example, see s. 271 of the Code (sexual assault).

PROVINCIAL OFFENCES

The classification of provincial offences is an easy matter. All provincial offences are summary conviction offences. Provincial offences, it will be recalled, are only constitutionally valid if their objective is the better enforcement of some other power within the jurisdiction of the province. An offence that is, of its nature, so serious as to warrant trial upon indictment is, of necessity, going to be inherently criminal and hence within the criminal law powers of the federal government, or so concerned with a Canadian as opposed to merely a provincial matter as to be within some other power within the federal jurisdiction. There is no actual legislation that forbids a province from creating an indictable offence, but it is most unlikely that it would be held to be constitutionally valid.

An easy way for a province to legislate what procedure it should adopt for the prosecution of provincial summary conviction offences is merely to copy the federal legislation in the Code dealing with the prosecution of summary conviction offences. This can be done by a provincial Act merely repeating the Code provisions or, even more simply, by merely enacting that the relevant sections of the Code apply, making the necessary technical changes, to provincial prosecution. Where this is done, what we have said about federal summary conviction procedure applies to provincial offence procedure.

On the other hand, the province may choose to adopt its own code of procedure for the prosecution of its own provincial offences. Ontario, for example, has its own Provincial Offences Act. It establishes a Provincial Offences Court presided over either by a justice of the peace or by a provincial court judge. The actual trial of provincial offences in Ontario does not differ greatly from trials for provincial offences in other provinces, though there are some significant pre-trial differences.

Canadian Criminal Courts (Simplified)

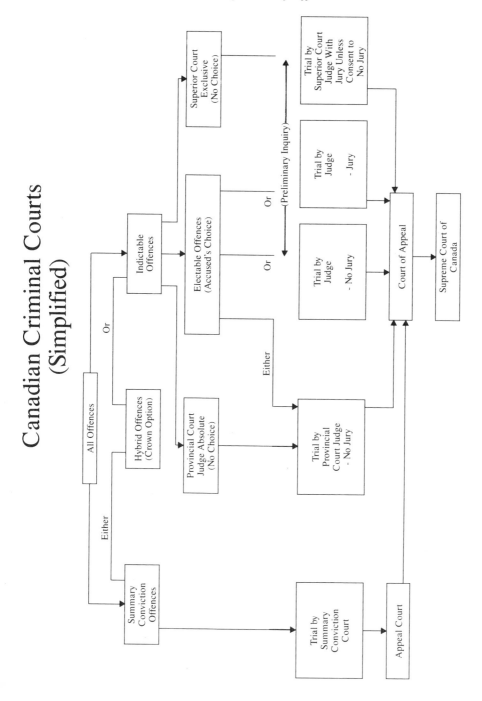

6

The Accused's Appearance in Court

As we have seen, the time will arrive for the accused's first court appearance so that the trial process may begin. He may have been issued a summons or appearance notice; he may have given a promise to appear or some undertaking; he may be at liberty under conditions, with or without his recognizance and without sureties; or he may have been detained in custody. When his name is called, what happens next depends very much on the type of offence he is charged with, and, indeed, where the courtroom is located.

Once the charge has been read out to the accused in open court by the court clerk, the trial process is under way and from that moment on there are very important statutory procedural rights that the accused has and procedural limitations on the powers of the presiding judge that must be observed and we shall discuss these in a moment. But it very often happens that neither the Crown nor the accused is actually ready to proceed at the time specified for his first appearance. This is particularly true in more serious or more complex cases when both sides may need more time to interview potential witnesses, go over the files and prepare their case. In such cases, the actual first court appearance is for little more than setting a future date and time that will be acceptable to both the Crown and the accused. Indeed, this may happen more than once when, even at that future date, neither side is ready. Where both sides are agreeable, usually there is little difficulty in this process being repeated, though there may come a time when the presiding judge will refuse a further remand, even if both sides want one, and will insist upon the proceedings getting under way.

Where the Crown and the defence disagree, either as to any postponement at all or as to the date until when the proceedings are to commence, the judge will exercise his discretion as to whether to grant the adjournment, bearing in mind the rights of the accused as well as the rights of the Crown and considering whether the request is legitimate or is merely a delaying tactic.

If the request for a delay is granted, then a new court date is set and, generally speaking, the accused will be released on the same terms and conditions as he had been released on pending his first appearance. That is to say, the order made as to his pre-trial release, if any, continues in force, though there is power to vary or modify it as the need arises.

Let us assume, therefore, the time has now come when the process really gets under way. The accused's name is called, he stands up, and the clerk reads out the information to him. The judge who is presiding at this appearance will be a provincially appointed judge and what happens next will depend upon whether the accused is charged with an indictable offence and, if so, what kind of indictable offence, a hybrid offence, or a summary conviction offence.

We know that if it is a summary conviction offence the trial must take place before the summary conviction court (which the provincially appointed judge is) so that nothing is left to be done before the trial can proceed by asking the accused whether he pleads Guilty or Not Guilty. We also know that if the offence is within the absolute jurisdiction of the provincially appointed judge, even though it is an indictable offence (such as a gaming offence), the accused has no choice in the matter so, again, the trial may proceed. We also know that, at the other end of the scale, if the accused is charged with a supreme court exclusive offence (such as first degree murder), the presiding provincial court judge has no jurisdiction to try the accused, so that the one thing that cannot happen is for the trial to proceed. We will see in a moment what does happen.

In the case of hybrid offences, before we know what can happen next, the Crown must decide whether it is going to proceed by way of indictment or summary conviction. Usually the Crown will announce that on this charge it is proceeding by way of, for example, summary conviction. Sometimes the judge will ask the Crown how it is proceeding. Very occasionally, through an oversight, there will be no indication at all and the trial will proceed without any formal announcement. Clearly this is undesirable, but it will appear immediately from the next step how, in fact, the Crown is proceeding — so it is not likely that anyone will actually be misled.

INDICTABLE OFFENCES

Election by Accused

In the case of all election indictable offences, until we know how the accused elects to be tried, we simply do not know what the next step is going to be. So the first thing that must happen in such a case, after the information has been read out, is that the accused must be "put to his election," in the manner discussed in the previous chapter. The judge must explain to him that since he has been charged with, for example, break and enter, he has the option of being tried by a judge and jury, a judge without a jury, or a provincial court judge, and will then ask him, "How do you elect to be tried?"

If the accused elects to be tried by a provincial court judge since he is before a provincial court judge, the accused can be called upon to plead and the trial can proceed. At least this is so in theory, and in practice in some cases. But in the larger centres, if the accused pleads Not Guilty, it is unlikely that the judge in question will be prepared to proceed with the trial since, more likely than not, the court docket will be taken up that morning with other accused persons' appearances and elections. Indeed, it is most likely in such instances that the plea will be taken and a date will be fixed for the accused to appear for trial before the same or a different provincial court judge. If the accused pleads guilty, so that no trial on the merits is necessary, again, the accused may be sentenced immediately or remanded until the judge has had a chance to hear submissions as to sentence and to consider the matter.

If the accused fails or refuses to make an election then he is deemed to have elected trial by jury and the proceedings continue as though he had so elected. Furthermore, if the case is particularly serious or complex, the presiding judge may refuse to accept the election of the accused to be tried by him and inform the accused that, regardless of his wishes, he is going to proceed as if he had elected trial by a judge and jury.[1] In addition, if the accused is charged with an offence punishable by more than five years' imprisonment, the Attorney General may require the accused to be tried by a judge and jury even though he has elected trial by a judge without a jury or trial by a provincial court.[2]

Preliminary Inquiry

Where the accused is charged with an offence that must be tried by a judge and jury, or where he elects trial by a judge and jury, or where the provincial court judge refuses his election and requires him to be tried

---

1 Criminal Code, s. 555.
2 Section 568.

by a judge and jury, or where the Attorney General requires him to be tried by a judge and jury, or lastly, where the accused elects to be tried by a judge without a jury, a vital step in the process arises. In all of these cases, the next step is the holding of what is called a "preliminary inquiry." Although the provincial court judge before whom the accused is appearing cannot proceed to try him, once he knows that the accused is going to be tried either by a judge and jury, or by a judge without a jury, he must proceed to hold this preliminary inquiry (or, more commonly, fix a date for the preliminary inquiry to commence).

The purpose of the preliminary inquiry is to determine whether, on the evidence that is adduced by the Crown (and by the defence if it wishes), a reasonable jury (or judge where there is no jury) could — not would — find the accused guilty. It is not the provincial court judge's function to determine whether the accused *is* guilty or not guilty, but only to determine that on all the evidence he has heard (and only upon that evidence) it would be possible for a reasonable jury to be satisfied, beyond any reasonable doubt, that the accused was guilty. His function is not to determine whether he himself would actually convict or not; the burden on the Crown is not, at this stage, therefore actually to *prove* the guilt of the accused beyond any reasonable doubt, but only to introduce sufficient evidence to make his guilt a reasonable possibility.

This burden on the Crown is not, in consequence, as high or as difficult as the burden that is on it at the actual trial. It may be, therefore, that the Crown will decide not to call *all* of the evidence that it has available. This is all right so long as it calls sufficient evidence to persuade a judge that it has a reasonable case against the accused.

After all the evidence for the Crown is in the presiding judge must then address the accused, informing him that he has heard the evidence against him and ask him if he wishes to say anything in answer to the charge. The accused is not obliged to say anything, but if he does, it is taken down and may be used in evidence against him at his trial. It is not often, of course, that an accused will respond to such an invitation. Once that formality has been observed, the accused is then entitled to call any witnesses for the defence or to testify himself.

At the conclusion of all of the evidence, the presiding judge must then decide whether, in his opinion, the evidence is sufficient to put the accused on trial in the sense we have discussed. If it is, he will, as it is said, "order the accused to stand trial"; if it is not, he will "discharge the accused." We shall examine, in a moment, what these two phrases mean and what the effect is.

It will be seen that the onus on the Crown is not a particularly difficult one — certainly not as difficult as proving guilt beyond a reasonable doubt. So long as the Crown introduces sufficient incriminating evidence to get past the judge, there is no obligation on its part to introduce all of the available evidence it has. Conversely, it is not easy for an accused to succeed in having the judge discharge him at the preliminary inquiry stage and, as a result, he will often not put in all or even any of his defence at that stage, since, in many cases, he will merely be disclosing to the prosecution the strengths of his defence and afford it an opportunity to prepare a rebuttal to it when the trial actually comes on. Indeed, an accused may, and often does, waive the preliminary inquiry with the consent of the prosecution or, more accurately, waive the necessity for calling any evidence or any further evidence.[3] If he already knows the gist of the case for the prosecution and knows that he does not stand much chance of succeeding at the preliminary inquiry stage, it is somewhat pointless to prolong the procedure.

On the other hand, there are some occasions when the accused will wish to put in a defence even at the preliminary inquiry stage, or, if not to put in a full defence, at least to call defence witnesses. In the first place, if he can succeed in getting a discharge at that stage, it saves the necessity of a trial, and hence saves money, time and publicity. So, if he has a good defence, he may well be advised to go all out for a discharge at the preliminary inquiry. In the second place, there are occasions when he may wish to get the testimony of witnesses on the record as soon as possible. An obvious instance would be if a defence witness is very ill and may not be alive at the time of the trial. If the evidence provided by that witness can be taken at the preliminary inquiry, he may be able to read it in at the trial. Or one may have a forgetful witness or a witness who is not too reliable and it is as well to strike while the iron is hot. Or perhaps the accused has an alibi defence that will be strengthened if it is advanced at the earliest time.

All of these considerations lead to the danger of the preliminary inquiry being viewed, if not as a game, then at least as a process of jockeying for position. The Crown will disclose enough, but not too much; the defence will disclose only what suits it without it being too helpful to the prosecution. The Crown, however, is not only governed by what is strictly legally required; it is also subject to ethical considerations of fair play. It should not deliberately hold back important evidence that it has merely because it may be helpful to the accused. Rather, it may be obliged to inform the accused or his counsel of evidence that it has that the defence should know about. Just how far these ethical considerations should go tends to vary from prosecutor to prosecutor. Some will be highly cooperative; some less so. But, in the same way, while there is no obligation on the defence to introduce evidence helpful to the prosecution or to inform the prosecution of any evidence it has that may help convict the accused, the preliminary inquiry may be balanced very much against the prosecution in requiring

---

3 Section 549.

it to disclose its case, while the defence does not have to disclose any of its case.

In fact, it may well be that as the Charter is interpreted and as the cases develop, the courts will use either section 7 or section 11(*d*) to impose some constitutional duty on the Crown to disclose to an accused at least the main thrust of its case against him before trial. There are already signs[4] that there is indeed some *legal* duty to disclose, but no cases have yet discussed precisely what that duty is and how far it may extend.

For these reasons there is some dissatisfaction with the preliminary inquiry as it now exists, yet it does serve the vital function of ensuring that an accused shall not be tried upon indictment unless the judge is satisfied that there is sufficient prosecution evidence to warrant it. Various proposals and experiments have been suggested, ranging from the abolition of the preliminary inquiry (generally this has not received much support), to preserving the preliminary inquiry (or at least the right to one), but augmenting it by some form of pre-trial disclosure of the case for the prosecution and for the defence, with variations in between. It remains to be seen what reforms will eventually be effected.

At the moment then, we still have the preliminary inquiry with all its shortcomings. It will be seen that as a result of its purpose and function, it can result in some very bad publicity for the accused. The evidence tends to be very one-sided (that is, prosecution oriented) since there is usually little, if any, rebutting defence evidence. Accordingly, a person reading reports of it in a newspaper may be unduly persuaded of the guilt of the accused. This may be particularly true if the prosecution introduces in evidence a confession of the accused which the defence does not choose to rebut at that time.

There are provisions to counter this adverse publicity. If the prosecution introduces in evidence at the preliminary inquiry any confession of the accused, no report shall be made of this fact (or of the contents of such confession) in any newspaper or broadcast unless the accused has been discharged, or, if ordered to stand trial, the trial has ended.[5] Further, any accused may request the judge to make an order (and if requested, the order must be made) prohibiting any evidence given at the preliminary inquiry from being published in any newspaper or broadcast until such time as the accused is discharged, or, if ordered to stand trial, the trial has ended.[6]

Once the preliminary inquiry has commenced, it must continue without interruption until its termination, but the presiding judge does have

---

4 See *R. v. Ertel* (1987), 58 C.R. (3d) 252, 35 C.C.C. (3d) 398, 20 O.A.C. 257, 30 C.R.R. 209 (C.A.), leave to appeal to S.C.C. refused (1987), 61 C.R. (3d) xxix (note), 24 O.A.C. 320 (note), 30 C.R.R. 209n, 86 N.R. 266 (note) (S.C.C.).

5 Section 542.

6 Section 539.

power to adjourn the inquiry for up to eight days. He may adjourn for a longer period, only if the accused and the prosecution consent to the longer adjournment. He also has the power (extremely important in practice) to remand the accused for a psychiatric examination for a period of time, but we will deal in Chapter 19 with the whole question of the mentally disturbed offender and this power will be better examined at that time.

If, after all the evidence has been received, the presiding judge discharges the accused on the ground that there is insufficient evidence to put him on trial, it is important to understand that the accused has not been found not guilty. There is no acquittal — only the finding that the evidence is insufficient for the the accused to stand trial. This means that the accused cannot be tried *on that information* and that the proceedings *on that information* are terminated. There is nothing expressed in the Code that prevents the prosecution from laying a new information and trying again before the same, or, more likely, a different, provincial judge, particularly if additional evidence comes to light that makes a committal for trial a more likely prospect the second time around. However, while there is nothing in the Code expressly forbidding this practice, if it is done merely to harass the accused, or for some improper motive (where, for example, the prosecution had negligently failed to prepare its case properly the first time), there is little doubt that the courts would prevent it from happening by ruling that it would be unfair to the accused and an abuse of process. Where there is no improper motive or harassment (for example, where an important Crown witness only came forward after the first preliminary inquiry was ended), it is not so clear that the prosecution would be stopped from laying a new information identical to the first. The accused has not been acquitted and hence no real problem of double jeopardy arises, but the Crown does have an alternative avenue along which to proceed known as a "preferred indictment," and it may be that the courts will insist upon the prosecution taking that route rather than the route of merely laying a second information. The preferred indictment is, in effect, a way of by-passing the requirements of a preliminary inquiry by the Crown proceeding directly to the trial level rather than first going through the preliminary inquiry. It will be discussed in more detail in Chapter 8 dealing with informations and indictments.

To understand what will happen if the accused is ordered to stand trial, let us go back to the commencement of the preliminary inquiry. The accused will have been read the information alleging that he committed a specified offence and will have elected (or have been required to stand) trial by a superior court judge and jury, trial by a district (or similar) court judge and jury, or trial by a judge alone. The judge presiding at the preliminary inquiry will have the information before him. He then proceeds to hear all the evidence, for and against the accused, and must make his decision based on this evidence. He must decide whether the evidence warrants the trial of the accused for the offence with which he is charged. He may then commit the accused. But for what? The information will charge the accused with a specific offence and all the evidence led by the Crown will be directed towards proof of the commission of that offence. Indeed, evidence would not be admissible if it were not relevant to prove the commission of the offence specifically charged. But that evidence may also tend to prove that the accused committed some other offence either instead of the one charged or in addition to the one charged. For example, if the information charged the accused with committing break and enter of a dwelling house with intent to commit an indictable offence, the evidence relevant to that may also show that the accused was armed with a weapon at the time and assaulted a resident during the break and enter.

Section 535 provides that where an accused is before a judge for the preliminary inquiry regarding the offence set out in the information, the judge may inquire not only into that charge but also into any other indictable offence in respect of the same transaction founded on the facts disclosed by the evidence. Consequently, under section 548, at the conclusion of the preliminary inquiry, the judge may order the accused to stand trial (if, of course, satisfied that the evidence warrants it) not only for the offence charged in the information, but for any other indictable offence contemplated in section 535, and make a note on the back of the information that he is doing so.

Where the accused is ordered to stand trial, all the documentation (the evidence, the information, the accused's statement) is then sent to the clerk of the court by which the accused has elected (or is required) to stand trial. The file thus ends up in the office of the Crown attorney, Crown prosecutor or appropriate official, however he is designated, and it is then his task to prepare, on the basis of that file, the formal indictment. This will be examined in Chapter 8.

Re-Election by Accused

Before we get to the consideration of the indictment, however, there is a practical matter of some importance to examine. If one understands that a finding of Guilty means that the prosecution has proved its case beyond any reasonable doubt and that a finding of Not Guilty means that the prosecution has not succeeded in this proof, it will also be understood that when an accused is asked whether he pleads Guilty or Not Guilty, the most honest answer he could give would be: "I don't know, until I see how strong the case for the prosecution is. If it is so strong that there is no point in contesting it, then I shall plead Guilty; if, on the other and, it is not very strong, then I shall plead Not Guilty." All accused persons are perfectly justified in pleading Not Guilty, not only when "they didn't do it," but also when they did do it, but they do not think the prosecution can prove it. This fundamental principle pervades the whole criminal process from arrest and the right to remain silent and the privilege against self-incrimination, up to the trial and the non-compellability of the accused to be a witness.

The accused who is charged with a summary conviction offence or who elects trial by a provincial court judge when charged with an indictable offence (or who must be tried by a provincial court judge even though charged with an indictable offence) is called upon to plead before he knows how strong the case for the prosecution against him is. Usually, of course, he has a pretty good idea and will often be advised by his counsel that there is no point in pleading Not Guilty and that he may derive some benefit in pleading Guilty when it comes to sentencing by showing remorse, sparing the victim the embarrassment of testifying or saving the state the costs of the trial. This is why there are, in fact, many pleas of Guilty, which is just as well since the system would be clogged if everyone pleaded Not Guilty.

If, however, there is some process whereby an accused can see how strong the case against him is, *before* he is called upon to plead, he will be in a better position to decide whether to plead Guilty or Not Guilty. In fact, the preliminary inquiry can be used as an assessment of the case for the prosecution — not a perfect one, as we have seen, but at any rate, better than nothing.

In all election indictable offences, one might well ask what motivates an accused to choose one way rather than another. In fact, in most cases (across Canada some 75 or 80 percent) the accused elects trial by provincial court judge. That is to say, he gives up his right to a preliminary inquiry and proceeds directly to trial, and about 80 percent of those plead Guilty. These are, of course, the more or less open and shut cases where there is no point in pleading Not Guilty and perhaps something to gain by pleading Guilty. But, even in the case where the accused pleads Not Guilty, there are valid reasons why he should choose trial by a provincial court judge. The process, for one, is likely to be much quicker (indeed, it is certain to be quicker); it is also likely to be less expensive (where the accused is paying for counsel); there is less likelihood of any notorious publicity; the provincial court judge may have considerably more day-to-day experience in criminal matters than a superior court judge, he may have demonstrated some sympathetic understanding in past cases of a similar matter; or, probably more often than not, the accused merely wants to see the trial over with a minimum of formalities.

Where the accused elects to be tried other than by a provincial court judge, he may do so, again for a number of valid reasons. A jury may be more sympathetic to some factual defence that he has; he may be relying on some important legal defence that he wants decided by a higher court;

but, most of all, he may want to see what sort of case the prosecution has before he decides on his plea.

Section 561 provides for fairly straightforward methods of enabling an accused to change his mind after he has elected by a process known as re-election. If the accused has first elected trial by a provincial court judge, but later decides that he wishes to be tried by a federally appointed judge and jury, he may do so simply by notifying the provincial court judge (or, more likely in practice, the clerk of the court) in writing, so long as he does so not later than 14 days before the date set for the trial. He may be permitted to do so even later than that, but he then requires the consent of the prosecution to do so.

If he originally chose to be tried by a federally appointed judge or a judge and jury, he may re-elect to be tried by a provincial court judge at any time before or after the completion of the preliminary inquiry, if he has the written consent of the prosecutor. If he wishes to change from trial by a federally appointed judge and jury to federally appointed judge without a jury or vice-versa, he may do so, as of right, so long as he gives written notice before completion of the preliminary inquiry or less than 15 days after completion of the preliminary inquiry. After that time he may still do so, but only with the written consent of the prosecutor. In practice, the most common change is for trial by judge and jury to trial by federally appointed judge, since this is a case where, if he does it within the time limit, the accused needs no one's consent and may do so as of right. Thus, an accused may initially keep all his options open by electing trial by judge and jury, see how strong the case for the prosecution against him is at the preliminary inquiry, and then realize that nothing is to be gained by going to trial and pleading Not Guilty and inevitably being found Guilty, so he re-elects trial by federally appointed judge and actually ends up pleading Guilty.

In other words, the preliminary inquiry is very often used merely as a technical (and administratively cumbersome) method of determining whether to plead Guilty or Not Guilty. Again, it goes without saying, that if, in fact, this is how it is being used, some form of pre-trial disclosure and pre-trial conference would probably be a simpler and more satisfactory way of accomplishing the same ends.

SUMMARY CONVICTION OFFENCES

The procedure at the first court appearance of an accused charged with a summary conviction offence or a provincial offence is much simpler. There is, of course, no election and no problem about a preliminary inquiry or committal for trial. The information will be read to the accused and he will be asked to plead Guilty or Not Guilty. The trial will then proceed, subject to any adjournments of up to eight days unless both parties consent.

The summary conviction court has the power to remand the accused for a psychiatric assessment but, again, this is best left until we discuss the mentally disordered offender.

CO-ACCUSED AND MULTIPLE COUNTS

We have hitherto assumed, for the sake of simplicity, that there is one accused charged with one offence. In fact, the situation may also involve one accused charged with two or more different offences, two or more accused charged with one offence, or two or more accused charged with two or more offences.

When the information is originally laid before the justice of the peace, it may allege that the accused person committed offence A and offence B. The justice will have to inquire into each offence and issue process in respect of one or both of them (or, of course, neither). Each offence will be listed separately in what is called a separate count. These offences may be connected in the sense that they are all part of the same transaction (for example, break and enter, theft and use of a firearm involving the same break and enter), or they may be totally unrelated (for example, theft on one day, sexual assault two weeks later and uttering counterfeit currency three weeks after that). As we shall see, so long as *each count* is in proper form, there is no limit on the number and variety of separate counts (with the single exception of murder). The accused may be tried on all the counts in a single trial or he may be tried on each count in separate trials. Initially, this will depend upon how the prosecution chooses to proceed, though the accused may apply to the court to order the prosecution to proceed separately on each count (or combination of them) where it would be unfair to the accused to proceed with them all at the same time.

It may also happen that the information, instead of charging one person, X, with an offence, alleges that three persons, X, Y and Z, committed the offence. Again, the justice will have to be satisfied that a case is made out against X, Y and Z before issuing process against all three. Of course, if he does so at the time of the first court appearance, instead of there being only one accused, the three of them will be present and will have the charge read out to them. In fact, for reasons that will become apparent when we consider the course of the actual trial, the police may choose, instead of laying one information against X, Y and Z, to lay three different informations against each of them separately. Let us assume, however, that at the moment there is one information and three accused.

If the offence is a summary conviction offence, or an indictable offence where the accused have no choice as to how they will be tried, the procedure is no different from that where there is only one accused, except that in those cases where there is a preliminary inquiry, the provincial court judge may be satisfied as to the case against, say X and Y, and hence commit them for trial, but not satisfied as to the case against Z, and hence discharge Z. Basically though, X, Y and Z will be tried jointly, subject, as we shall see, to their right to apply to the trial judge to order that they be tried separately, if it would be unfair to try them all at the same time, or, if for example, a complication arises where X and Y plead Not Guilty but Z pleads Guilty. However, these are matters best left for a later discussion.

One initial problem that can arise where the three are charged with an electable indictable offence arises because each of them must be put to their election. If all three elect the same way, then matters proceed just as if there were only one accused. But what happens if they all elect differently — one electing trial by provincial court judge, one electing trial by judge without a jury and one electing trial by judge and jury? There is nothing, legally, to prevent them from so doing, but it is easy to see how undesirable it would be. There would then have to be three different trials with perhaps three different results and almost certainly with three different, and disparate, sentences passed in the event of convictions. Each accused would then be a compellable witness at the trials of the other two, whereas if all three are tried together, none of them can be forced to testify.

Of course, if one or more of them are going to plead Guilty anyway, then the problem is not so significant; but if all are going to plead Not Guilty, then there can be serious difficulties. These are resolved by provisions that may — not must — result in requiring all the accused to be tried in the same manner, regardless of how they may have elected. The provisions are not mandatory, because there may be exceptional cases where different modes of trial are justified, but generally speaking, unless one accused is going to plead Guilty, it is unlikely that different accused, charged in the same information, will be permitted to elect different modes of trial.

7

The Prosecution

Up to this point, reference has been made, somewhat vaguely, to the "prosecution," but it is now time to look more closely at this crucial aspect of the criminal process.

It will be recalled that in an overwhelmingly large number of cases, it is the police who will swear out the information alleging that the accused has committed a criminal offence. That person is known as the "informant." But we have also seen that any private person has the right to go to a justice of the peace and also swear out an information. It is common to call such a person a "private informant." Thus, any person who starts the whole process is the informant.

At common law (and still in some jurisdictions, though not in Canada), there used to be criminal proceedings known as "private prosecutions." In a private prosecution, a private person swore out the information, bore the expense of investigation, conducted the prosecution in his name, instructed counsel to act for him and received, for his own pocket, any fines or forfeits that might be levied against the accused in the event of conviction. In a somewhat less developed society, before the organization of police forces and a state prosecution machinery, such private prosecutions may be justified as a legitimate method of law enforcement. Private prosecutions in this sense have long been abolished in Canada.

We have adopted the view that a crime is necessarily an offence against the state (whether or not the act itself is directed against a victim), and whether the informant is the state itself (in the guise of a police officer) or a private person, what is being alleged is that the accused has committed an offence against the state. For that reason, all criminal trials are conducted in the name of the state, as it is the state that is the aggrieved party. In the Canadian monarchical system this is the Queen, and this is the reason why all criminal prosecutions are styled *R. v. X.*[1]

But the Queen, obviously, is not involved in the actual litigation and someone must conduct the prosecution in her name. When a police officer swears out an information, he does so because he is acting in the interests of the Queen or the state; similarly, while a private person who swears out an information may do so (in fact, usually does so) because he is a victim or an aggrieved person, he too does so as a method of initiating *state* proceedings, not private proceedings, against the accused. But, at this stage, it is the informant who is the "prosecutor" — he is the one prosecuting, in the sense of initiating the process, even though the prosecution itself is in the name of the Queen. Thus, at this stage, the prosecutor means the informant and while that is usually a police officer, it may be a private person. Since there can be a private prosecutor, a practice has thereby arisen of referring to those as "private prosecutions."

The Code, however, enacts that if the Attorney General intervenes, then prosecutor means the Attorney General or counsel acting on his behalf. This requires some explanation.

THE ROLE OF THE ATTORNEY GENERAL

In all provinces of Canada, there is an organized state prosecution machinery under the control of the provincial Attorney General, while, for those offences that are prosecuted by the federal government,[2] there is a similar federal prosecution machinery under the control of the Minister of Justice and Attorney General for Canada. Part of this machinery consists of staff members (lawyers) who are assigned to various localities (counties, districts or cities) and have various titles, but it is usually something like Crown Attorneys, Crown Prosecutors, City Prosecutors, Federal Prosecutors, and so on (some may be part-time and called "agents"). They have many duties and functions, but the one we are concerned with here is

---

1 *Regina* is Latin for The Queen (frequently shortened to *R.*) and *v.* is the Latin abbreviation for *versus*, against.

2 The provinces are responsible for the administration of justice and hence the Attorney General, or his agents, prosecute all criminal offences that are made such by virtue of the criminal law powers of the federal government. But where there are criminal offences made such by virtue of some other provision dealing with the federal powers (called non-criminal code offences), they are prosecuted by the federal Department of Justice, not the provincial Attorney General. This includes drug offences, customs and excise offences, income tax offences and the like.

that of prosecuting criminal offences on behalf of the Queen. All of these lawyers are agents of the Attorney General of the Province, or of Canada, as the case may be, and if they intervene in a prosecution, then, as the Code tells us, the prosecutor becomes the Attorney General. The informant is the prosecutor only up to the time when the Crown attorney or other official intervenes, if he does intervene. If he does not, then an informant will remain the prosecutor.

In all provinces (and in the federal jurisdiction) the Attorney General has the *power* to intervene in all prosecutions, whether the informant wishes him to or not. Once the Attorney General (through, of course, his agent) has intervened, then the informant ceases to be one of the *dramatis personae* in the prosecution of the case. This can have very important consequences since, in the adversary system, the conduct of the case for the prosecution is in the hands of the prosecutor, subject to the overriding control of the court. He is the one who decides which witnesses to call or not call, how to present the case or, indeed, whether to present any evidence at all. The case is, in effect, taken out of the hands of the informant. Suppose, for example, that a private person swears out an information against his neighbour charging him with assault. So long as he remains the prosecutor, that person will have the control of the prosecution and decide how to conduct the case. He may even offer no evidence against the neighbour at trial with the resultant acquittal; he may, subject to some court control which will be discussed shortly, withdraw the information if he decides not to go ahead. Once the agent of the Attorney General intervenes, however, the informant has no control over any of these matters. The agent is the one who makes these decisions, even to the point of withdrawing the information when the informant does not wish to or, conversely, of insisting on a prosecution and, if necessary, calling the informant as a compellable, though reluctant, witness even in the face of his objections.[3]

Obviously these difficulties are not likely to arise where the information is sworn by a police officer, since the agent of the Attorney General and the police usually have identical interests and there is not likely to be any conflict between the two. Indeed, the police would, in any case, usually defer to the judgment of the agent of the Attorney General. But intervening in a private prosecution is no light matter. On the one hand, it does relieve the private citizen of the trouble and costs of privately pursuing the prosecution, but, on the other hand, it removes from him the control of the conduct of the prosecution.

To say, then, that the Attorney General has the power to intervene

---

3 It should be noticed that a "victim" as such has no particular standing in the criminal process. If the victim is the one who lays the information, then he becomes the informant; if the information is laid by someone else, then the victim is merely in the legal position of any other witness and may be compelled to testify even if he changes his mind and does not wish the prosecution to continue — that is not his decision to make.

in all prosecutions does not necessarily mean that he should, or would, intervene in all cases. The actual practice varies from province to province and in a general book of this nature we can only give the broad picture rather than the details.

Indictable offences, being the more serious offences, are obviously more likely to be those where the interests of the community at large are involved rather than the interests of private individuals. Sexual assault or theft, for example, do have identifiable victims, but it is in the interest of everyone that rapists and thieves be prosecuted and convicted. In practice, therefore, it would be unlikely that process for this sort of offence would be started by way of a private information, although it could happen. If the Attorney General did not intervene, one would then have the situation where, at the accused's court appearance, the prosecution would be represented, not by some official of the state, but by the informant personally, or his counsel. The same process would be followed that we discussed in the previous chapter — a preliminary inquiry where the accused must be tried by a superior court of criminal jurisdiction, or where he elects to be tried by a judge or judge and jury, or a trial where he must be tried by the provincial court judge or elects to be so tried.

If the accused elects to be tried by a provincial court judge or must be so tried, there is no reason why the private informant could not continue as the prosecutor. If, on the other hand, the accused elects some other mode, while the informant could continue as the prosecutor at the preliminary inquiry, if the accused is committed for trial, a complication arises. If the accused elects trial by a judge alone or a judge without a jury, and, after the preliminary inquiry, the accused has been ordered to stand trial, the prosecutor may prefer[4] an indictment against that accused in respect of any charge on which he was ordered to stand trial.[5] However, if the prosecutor is anyone other than the Attorney General, then that person needs the written order of a judge of the court before he may prefer such indictment.

So, while a private person may prosecute an accused, even upon indictment, he, unlike the Attorney General (or his agent) can only do so with the written order of a judge of the court before which the trial is to take place.

In practice, this is all rather academic anyway. In some provinces it is the duty of the agent for the Attorney General to intervene in the prosecution of *all* indictable offences, regardless of who the informant is, and to conduct the prosecution in all preliminary inquiries. In other

---

4 We shall discuss what this means in the next chapter, but it is sufficient at the moment to state that in this context it means merely the formal presenting of the charge in the trial court.

5 Or certain other charges, discussed in the next chapter.

provinces, there is no duty spelled out in the statute, but it would only be in the most exceptional case that there would not be such intervention. In effect, one can say that, in practice, the prosecutor in indictable offences will be, by the time that the trial process has got under way, the Crown attorney, Crown prosecutor or some similarly designated official, at least in the vast majority of cases.

Perhaps, somewhat paradoxically, the position with regard to summary conviction offences is rather more complicated. There are two factors that are relevant. First, summary conviction offences are considerably more numerous than indictable offences and range from the trivial to the relatively serious (though not, of course, as serious as indictable offences). Second, summary conviction offences are more likely to be the subject of private informations than are indictable offences since, in the case of the latter, the police are much more likely to carry out the investigation and be responsible for the laying of the information, whereas there may be many summary conviction offences such as disputes between neighbours or family squabbles where the police, having investigated, do not feel that a prosecution is warranted but the aggrieved person does.

Whether the Attorney General will intervene in the prosecution of Criminal Code summary conviction offences depends upon a consideration of all the factors in each individual case. Since it is only in the most exceptional case that there will have been a private informant in the first place, all that we can say as a general proposition is that it is more likely that in such cases the Attorney General will not interfere, thus permitting a private person to remain the prosecutor.

WITHDRAWING A CHARGE

As we have seen, the prosecutor is fundamental to the criminal process since he is the person who has control of the conduct of the prosecution. Obviously, in most cases, his duty is to present the facts and arguments as honestly and fairly as possible, subject to all procedural and evidentiary rules, towards the conviction of the accused. But, in some cases, factors will emerge after the laying of the information, that may make the continued prosecution of the accused impracticable or undesirable. For example, there may be new evidence that clearly indicates the innocence of the accused; or it may be that a reassessment of the admissible evidence against the accused shows that it would not support a conviction.

One case where it not infrequently arises is where the victim changes his mind. Suppose, for example, a woman complains to the police that her male friend has beaten her and, after an investigation, the police lay an information against him charging assault. A few days later, the two are reconciled and the woman tells the police she "wishes to withdraw the charge." This, as we have seen, is not her decision to make, but that of the prosecutor, who, by this time may, in effect, be the Crown attorney or Crown prosecutor.

One can also have situations where it appears, after the information has been laid, that it would not be in the best public interest to continue the prosecution. For example, the accused, charged with some relatively minor offence, may be committed to a mental institution and there may be no point in continuing to prosecute. It may, of course, arise because of some political pressure, though one would hope that this would be political pressure in the positive sense of the word (e.g., to preserve some secret of international or national importance), rather than some petty partisan reason.

No matter what the reason, the prosecutor now has a decision to make — whether or not the prosecution should continue. If he decides that it should not (or is instructed by his superior that it should not), then there are three ways in which this objective may be achieved, all of them having different consequences.

In the first place, the prosecutor can continue with the process, but when the time comes for him to present the case for the prosecution, he may offer no evidence against the accused. If this occurs, the accused must be found Not Guilty (or, as it is phrased in the case of summary convictions, the information must be dismissed). The result of this is that because of the doctrine of double jeopardy the accused can never be prosecuted for that same offence again.[6]

Alternatively, the prosecutor may withdraw the information, but this is not as simple a process as one might think. All the cases talk about the *Crown's* right to withdraw charges, but it does not seem in principle that the situation would be any different if it were a private prosecutor seeking to withdraw the information. It is clear, that if we are dealing with an indictable offence where the accused has elected trial by judge or trial by judge and jury, and the matter has proceeded to the stage of the presenting of the indictment, there can be no such thing as withdrawing the information since, as we shall see, it is the indictment that becomes the prosecuting instrument, not the information. We are therefore talking only of summary conviction offences, or indictable offences at a stage before the preferring of the indictment.

While the principles are not quite as clear as one might wish, it would appear that the prosecutor may withdraw the information as of right at any time before the accused has been called on to plead and evidence has commenced to be taken in the case of summary conviction offences, or indictable offences where the accused has elected to be tried or must be tried by a provincial court judge; he may, in other cases, withdraw the information as of right, at any time before the commencement of the

---

6 Discussed in Chapter 9, The Plea and the Verdict.

preliminary inquiry. In all other cases, the prosecutor may withdraw the information, but only with the consent of the presiding judge.

There are valid reasons for the distinction. If the information is withdrawn before the proceedings actually get under way, then the information is nullified and consequently there is nothing giving the judge jurisdiction to embark on the criminal process — the trial or the preliminary inquiry, as the case may be. But once the process has started, then it is within the jurisdiction of the presiding judge and is under his control. Whether, in such circumstances, the judge should consent to the withdrawal of the information depends upon a consideration of a number of factors. If a withdrawal is made before the process has started, then the accused has never been in jeopardy of being convicted and hence, at least as far as the basic criminal process is concerned, there is nothing to prevent the prosecutor from laying a new information charging the identical offence, though this may, in some circumstances, amount to an abuse of process and would be stopped by the court.

If the process has started, then the accused is in danger of being convicted since the case against him has begun. Whether the prosecutor should be permitted to withdraw may well depend upon the reason why it wishes the withdrawal. If, for example, it is because a vital witness for the prosecution is missing and the prosecutor has had ample time to secure his attendance, it may be fairer to the accused to force the prosecutor to continue with an inadequate case and acquit the accused for lack of evidence, thus preventing any further proceedings for the same offence. If it is, on the other hand, because the victim has changed his mind, the presiding judge will have to consider whether it is in the better interests of the general public that the prosecution should go ahead in spite of the victim's reluctance (because, for instance, there is some reason to believe that the accused represents a danger not only to the victim but to other people as well), or whether it is primarily a private matter between two people in which the general public has some, but not very great interest, in which case, he may permit the withdrawal.

What is not yet clear from the cases is what the effect of a withdrawal after the taking of the evidence against the accused is. If it is at or during a preliminary inquiry, then clearly the accused has never been in jeopardy of being convicted of any offence, since the preliminary inquiry is not a trial and, subject to any argument on abuse of process, it seems clear that the prosecutor could relay the information and try again. But, if it is during the course of a trial, one could well argue that whether the information is withdrawn or whether the trial is required to continue to a verdict, the accused has been in jeopardy and therefore a subsequent information alleging the same offence ought not to be permitted. However, it cannot be stated that this is the law with any certainty and it may be that where a withdrawal is permitted, the information becomes, *ex post facto*, a nullity and therefore the accused, retroactively, was never in jeopardy.

STAY OF PROCEEDINGS

Another important procedural device which is available to the Attorney General or counsel instructed by him is a procedure known as a stay of proceedings. It is available in respect of both indictable offences and summary conviction offences. It is important to note that this procedure is available only to the Attorney General (or counsel); it is not available to a private prosecutor. Furthermore it is available to the Attorney General whether he is also the prosecutor or whether a private person is the prosecutor.

Section 579(1), regarding stay of proceedings, reads as follows:

> The Attorney General or counsel instructed by him for that purpose may, at any time after any proceedings in relation to an accused or a defendant are commenced and before judgment, direct the clerk or other proper officer of the court to make an entry on the record that the proceedings are stayed by his direction, and such entry shall be made forthwith thereafter, whereupon the proceedings shall be stayed accordingly and any recognizance relating to the proceedings is vacated.

This is the Attorney General's right and is not subject to the consent of the trial judge. The right may be exercised at any time between the commencement of proceedings (that is to say, the laying of the information) and before the judgment. This may be before the trial has commenced, during the trial itself, and, indeed, after the trial, but before the judgment is entered. It pertains to both summary conviction proceedings as well as to proceedings for indictable offences.

The effect of the directing of a stay is not to nullify the process but to stay it. The information or the indictment remains valid to form the basis of a subsequent prosecution, subject to the provisions of section 579(2), merely by the Attorney General (or counsel) notifying the clerk that the proceedings are to be recommenced. If, however, such notice is not given within one year after the directing of the stay or such shorter time within which the proceedings would have had to have been commenced for those offences with a specific limitation period, then the original proceedings are deemed never to have commenced and the original indictment or information becomes a nullity.

It is important to understand the raison d'être of the stay. The Attorney General is the Chief Law Officer of the Crown and as such has supervision over the prosecutorial process. It is ultimately within his discretion to decide who should be prosecuted for what and it is not the function of the courts to interfere with his duty. He is, of course, politically accountable and may have to answer in the legislature or in Parliament for his decisions. As we have seen, he may intervene and take over all prosecutions, but conversely, he may intervene and stop all prosecutions or intervene and stay a prosecution. His reasons for deciding upon one course or the other may be as varied as the factual circumstances of each case, but whatever the reasons, it is his decision and his alone.

To this absolute proposition, there has recently developed an important gloss. It is true that the courts cannot direct that a person be prosecuted — that is not their function — but it is not the case that the courts cannot stop a person being prosecuted. Even before the Charter of Rights gave the courts very wide powers to grant whatever remedy is appropriate in the circumstances where a constitutional right has been infringed, the courts themselves had developed a technique for preventing the conviction of a person where to do so would be an abuse of the judicial process and this technique was nothing less than the court itself ordering a stay of proceedings. This power is nowhere to be found in the Code, but has developed into an inherent right of the courts to safeguard the integrity of their own process.

With the introduction of the Charter of Rights, of course, it cannot be doubted that the courts now have such a power where a Charter right has been infringed, but the power extends beyond this. To take one example that is not infrequent, consider the problem of entrapment, as it is called. A person, not previously disposed to commit an offence is enticed, inveigled, entrapped or pressured into committing an offence by an undercover police officer for the sole purpose of then arresting that person. It usually arises in drug trafficking cases, where an undercover police officer or agent pretends to be a drug addict and deliberately persuades another person to supply him with drugs. As soon as he does so, he is arrested. It may be considered very unfair that the police, of all people, should instigate an offence by someone who, apart from the instigation, would never have committed the offence. One solution, possibly, would be to convict the accused and impose some minimum penalty, but the accused would still have a criminal conviction. Another solution would be to acquit the accused, but it is difficult in principle to argue that the accused is not guilty since he has committed the offence, and if the pressure applied by the police falls short of what is required for the affirmative defence of duress (which generally requires threats of death or bodily harm, among other things, to be a valid defence), he does not appear to have any legally applicable defence.

However, what the courts have done[7] is to label such conduct an abuse of the process of the court and direct that the prosecution be stayed, thus neither acquitting nor convicting the accused but merely, in effect, directing

---

7 See *R. v. Mack*, [1988] 2 S.C.R. 903, 67 C.R. (3d) 1, [1989] 1 W.W.R. 577, 44 C.C.C. (3d) 513, 37 C.R.R. 277, 90 N.R. 173, and *R. v. Barnes*, [1991] 1 S.C.R. 449, 3 C.R. (4th) 1, [1991] 2 W.W.R. 673, 53 B.C.L.R. (2d) 129, 63 C.C.C. (3d) 1, 121 N.R. 267.

that he not be prosecuted. It now seems beyond doubt that, in proper circumstances, the courts do have this power, quite apart from the provisions of the Charter, but it is far from clear under what circumstances they will exercise the power. The courts are concerned that they not be made vehicles for the improper prosecution of an accused person, but, as might be expected, there is considerable disagreement as to precisely when conduct on the part of officials will amount to an abuse of process, though there appears to be a doctrine developing that if the prosecution of the accused would, in all the circumstances, bring the administration of justice into disrepute,[8] a stay will be directed. It is clear that it will be exercised only sparingly and only in cases of flagrant misconduct, but that, of course, does not detract from its importance.

What, therefore, we have said about the importance of the prosecutor in the criminal process and about the discretion of the Attorney General and his agents in the prosecutorial process, is subject to this overriding control by the courts to prevent abuses of *its* process.

Generally, what we have said about the role of the prosecutor in the federal criminal justice system applies equally well to the prosecution of provincial offences. As we have seen, many provinces simply incorporate Part XXIV of the Criminal Code (dealing with summary convictions) into their procedure for the prosecution of provincial offences, and what we have said about the process with regard to summary conviction federal offences applies equally to the process in provincial offences. Even in Ontario, where there is a separate Provincial Offences Act, the same principles apply save that the Act defines prosecutor as (i) the Attorney General, or, where he does not intervene, as (ii) "the person who issues a certificate or lays an information," to take into account the special procedure by way of certificate of offence. It also makes it quite clear that the right to withdraw a charge is quite distinct from the right to order a stay — which is probably true under the Code as well, although it is not expressly made absolutely certain.

---

8 A phrase found in s. 24(2) of the Canadian Charter of Rights and Freedoms.

8

Informations and Indictments

When an accused appears for trial, he is faced with a written allegation of what it is that he is charged with. This is then read out to him by the clerk of the court and he is asked to plead. We must now look more closely at this written allegation.

THE INFORMATION

As we have seen, all criminal prosecutions[1] begin with the information which, in fact, has two aspects. It is the document which is the basis of compelling the appearance of the accused in court, upon which is based the summons, the arrest warrant or the confirmation of some other process such as the promise to appear or appearance notice. As such, it is an essential part of the process for getting the accused to court. Its other aspect is that it is also the written basis of the charge for which the accused is prosecuted once he gets to court. This dual aspect is important because one can have a situation where an information may be void as to one aspect, but still perfectly valid as to another. For example, where an appearance notice has been issued, the information has to be laid "as soon as practicable."[2] But suppose it is not so laid and, in fact, is not laid until

---

1 Except those provincial offences for which some informal method is provided and those indictments that by-pass the normal process.

2 Criminal Code, s. 505.

some later time that is convenient for the police, as is often the case. Is the information void? The answer is that it is void as a mechanism for compelling the appearance of the accused — so that if he does not appear as required in the appearance notice, no action can be taken against him on that notice. However, if he does appear at the time and place specified (which will actually be the case since he will not normally know until the event that the information was laid out of time), then the information is still valid as a mechanism for initiating the trial process.[3]

If the accused is charged with a summary conviction offence, or an indictable offence that is triable by a provincial court judge without any election on the part of the accused, or an indictable offence where the accused elects trial by a provincial court judge, then the information is the only written allegation of the offence there is and it is on this document that he will be tried. Where the accused elects trial by a judge and jury or must be tried by a judge and jury, or where he elects trial by a judge without a jury, the information is the written allegation that provides the basis of the preliminary inquiry, but if he is ordered to stand trial, he is tried not on the information, but on a new document known as an indictment. Since much of what we are going to discuss in relation to the form and content of the indictment applies equally well to the form and content of the information, it will be more convenient if we deal with indictments first and then return to the informations.

THE INDICTMENT

When an accused is ordered to stand trial after a preliminary inquiry, or is ordered to stand trial on consent, all the documents and evidence in the case are sent to the clerk of the court by which he will be tried, who, in effect, will be the Crown attorney or Crown prosecutor or other prosecuting official. It is now the clerk's task to draft the indictment.

Form of Indictment

The accused will have been ordered to stand trial for the specified offence. As we have seen, that offence can only be the one named in the information, or some other indictable offence in respect of the same transaction that is disclosed by the evidence taken at the preliminary inquiry. The Crown prosecutor knows, then, what offence should be alleged in the indictment — namely, the one for which the accused was committed. But drafting the indictment is not, in fact, as simple a matter as might

---

3 Since, if the appearance notice is confirmed, the accused is not notified and must appear, it would only be in rare cases that the accused would ever know whether s. 505 of the Code has been complied with or not until he actually gets to court.

first appear. In order to be able to plead intelligently and to make a defence in the event that he pleads Not Guilty, the accused must know precisely what it is he is charged with on what date and at what place he is alleged to have committed the offence in question; otherwise he will not have sufficient information to enable him to prepare to meet the charge.

If only one offence is alleged against the accused, the indictment will only contain one charge. If more than one offence is alleged against him, each offence must be separately listed as the separate charge in divisions known as "counts." The one count (or each count in the case of multiple charges) must specify the indictable offence with which the accused is charged, it must refer to only one transaction and it must give sufficient detail of the circumstances of the offence to give the accused reasonable information enabling him to identify the transaction referred to, but it does not have to list in detail all the circumstances of the allegation.

There is no special form of words that has to be used. The allegation may be in popular language (e.g., that the accused did murder the victim on a specified day at a specified place) or it may set out the words of the statute creating the offence (e.g., that the accused did cause the death of the victim meaning to cause his death on a specified day at a specified time). In fact, any words that are sufficient to give the accused notice of the offence with which he is charged will suffice. The allegation may, but does not have to, refer to the specific section (e.g., did commit murder contrary to Criminal Code, section 235).

The count must, in addition to setting out the offence, also identify the facts. This is usually done by specifying the victim, the date and the place, but sometimes this is not possible, in which case the count may read, "victim unknown," or "on or about a certain date," or "between the 1st day of January 1988 and the 1st day of February 1988," or "at or near the City of Regina," and so on.

Each count must refer to only one "transaction," but transaction is not necessarily the same as "incident" or "occasion." For example, if the conduct of the accused is one course of conduct spread over a period of time, then that may be one transaction — as, for example, incest committed with a daughter on a number of occasions over a six-month period, or a fraudulent scheme spread over a period of time.

However, if the count does refer to two separate offences rather than one, or if it refers to two separate occasions rather than one, the count is said to be "duplicitous" (or "multifarious" if the reference is to more than two) and, if it is truly duplicitous or multifarious, it is void and will not support a prosecution. But one has to be very careful in labelling a count duplicitous or multifarious. We have just seen that a count that refers to more than one occasion, may nevertheless only refer to one transaction and is not, thereby, rendered duplicitous. Similarly, what might superficially seem to be duplicitous as to the charge (or, duplicitous in law, as it is sometimes put) may, on analysis, be seen to be perfectly proper. For example, suppose a person is charged with driving at a specified place and at a specified time "while his ability to drive was impaired by alcohol or a drug." One might object that the accused would not be aware that he was being charged because he was under the influence of alcohol or under the influence of some other drug and thus the count was duplicitous in the sense that it contained an alternative allegation of two offences. But, in fact, the accused is being charged with one offence of impaired driving. If his ability to drive was impaired (which is all that the substance of the offence alleges), then so long as it was by reason of the ingestion of alcohol or a drug, he is guilty. In other words, it only charges one offence that can be committed in one of two ways — it does not charge two offences.

Similarly, if one is charged in a count alleging that he did discharge or cause to be discharged or permitted to be discharged or deposited pollutants into a water way, the essence of the offence is one of polluting water which can be committed in one or more various ways. There is nothing ambiguous or duplicitous about the charge, even though literally read, it may seem to charge one of several different offences in the alternative.

As one might well imagine, there can be differences of opinion between defence counsel and Crown counsel as to the validity or sufficiency of a count in an indictment. In the first place, the defence may complain that the count is not sufficiently detailed to give it reasonable information as to what is being alleged. It may, for example, object that the Crown has not sufficiently identified the place, or the victim, or even, in some cases, the means whereby the offence was supposed to have been committed. In such cases, the defence may move for what are called "particulars." It may ask the court[4] to order the prosecutor to furnish more details of the offence and the court will do so where it is satisfied that it is necessary for a fair trial. Once particulars are ordered, they are added to the indictment and the trial proceeds as if they had been originally included in the indictment.

In these cases, the trial judge must hold the balance between ordering the prosecution to produce excessive particulars (and thus requiring him to prove precisely what is alleged in all the details), and leaving a count so vague that the accused really does not have a fair idea of what it is he is charged with. On the one hand, the vaguer the count is, the freer the prosecution is to introduce any evidence that would support the charge no matter how it might be committed; on the other hand, the vaguer the count is, the more difficult it is to expect the accused to plead intelligently to the charge or to know what defence evidence would suffice to rebut it.

---

4 That is, the court trying the accused, or a judge of that court where it is not yet known who the actual judge will be.

Motion to Quash

If the objection of the accused pertains not to the sufficiency of the details, but rather to the validity of the count itself, this objection is taken by way of a procedure known as a motion to quash the indictment. A count may be invalid for one of two reasons. It may be invalid on its face — that is to say, one can see, merely by looking at it, that there is something wrong with it. It may, for example, be truly duplicitous, or it may fail to allege any offence or allege an offence that is not known in law — this is called a defect apparent on its face. On the other hand, the count may be invalid, not because of any defect apparent on its face, but because it alleges the wrong thing — for example, it may name John Smith as the victim whereas all the evidence shows that it was Bill Brown, or it may allege the offence of theft, whereas all the evidence shows that the offence was obtaining by false pretences.

In the case of the former type of defect, the motion to quash should be made before the accused has pleaded — in fact, if it is not, the judge's permission to move to quash will be required — since if the objection is valid, the count is a nullity and there is nothing to plead to or to be tried upon. If it is the other sort of defect, then, of course, the defence will not know about it until the evidence for the prosecution has been led, or at least has commenced to be led and thus cannot object until the trial has got under way.

At common law, there was little or no power to amend an indictment; either it was valid and the accused could be tried on it, or it was invalid and a nullity and there could be no trial on it. The Criminal Code, however, has provided (for the last 100 years) a very wide power of amendment. Even if the objection of the defence is upheld, the result will not necessarily be that the indictment will actually be quashed and the accused set free because the defence motion to quash will invariably be met by a prosecution request to amend the indictment if the objections are well founded. The application will usually, but not always, be granted. If the application is granted, then the necessary amendment is made; if it is not granted, however, the indictment will be quashed and the accused discharged.

While, therefore, it is true that in most cases even a successful motion to quash will not result in the discharge of the accused, the motion is still important for those cases in which an amendment will not be permitted. The key to the determination of whether to permit an amendment lies in fairness to the accused and whether he will be prejudiced by the proposed amendment. As can readily be seen, any relatively minor technical irregularity that a century ago would have resulted in the quashing of the indictment — such as a misspelled name or a misdescription of property which in no way misled the accused — will not now result in the indictment being quashed, but merely in its being amended. On the other hand, one can still have occasions when an amendment would not be appropriate, such as where the Crown seeks to change the offence charged to one of a totally different nature, or to substitute one victim for another, or where the indictment is a complete nullity from the beginning because it does not charge an offence known at law, or contain any facts at all.

The same principles we have discussed in relation to indictments also apply to an information. Each charge in the information must be listed in a separate count, each count must refer to one transaction and specify the offence charged and so on. There are similar provisions relating to motions to quash informations and similar powers to amend defective counts. In prosecutions for provincial offences, the same principles apply.

Substance of Indictment and Preferring Indictment

Assuming that the indictment is formally valid, we must now look at the substance of it. It will be recalled that when an accused is ordered to stand trial all the papers in the case are sent to the appropriate official who will draft the indictment. The offence charged in the indictment will, in almost all cases, be the identical offence for which the accused was ordered to stand trial. But difficulties can arise. The Crown attorney or other official will read the transcript of the preliminary inquiry and he may disagree with the finding of the judge presiding at that inquiry. He may feel that the evidence warrants trying the accused for a lesser offence than the one he was ordered to stand trial for, or for a more serious offence, or for a different offence or, indeed, even for added offences in addition to the one he was ordered to stand trial for. How much freedom does the Crown attorney have to indict the accused for an offence for which he was not ordered to stand trial or to vary the offence for which he was ordered to stand trial?

The preliminary inquiry exists so that a judicial officer can make the determination that there is a case to answer against the accused and thus prevent unnecessary or unfair prosecutions. As such, it is a necessary step in the process of the trial of indictable offences. But the judge at the preliminary inquiry has one role and the Attorney General (or his agent) has another. The latter is responsible for prosecutions and for drafting indictments. We have already seen that, at the preliminary inquiry, the judge may inquire into and order the accused to stand trial on, not only the offence charged in the indictment, but also any indictable offence arising out of the same transaction that is disclosed by the evidence.[5] In the same way, the Attorney General may prefer an indictment that not only charges the offence for which the accused was ordered to stand trial, but any indictable offence founded on the facts disclosed by the evidence

---

5 See Chapter 6, The Accused's Appearance in Court.

at the preliminary inquiry, in addition to or in substitution for the one on which the accused was ordered to stand trial.[6] Of course, there may arise a dispute as to whether the charge set out in the information is or is not one disclosed in the evidence, and the accused always has the right to move to quash the indictment on the ground that it has been improperly preferred under section 574, and it will be for the trial judge to rule whether this is so or not.

In addition to this normal procedure, the indictment may also charge the accused with any other indictable offence, even if not one for which he was ordered to stand trial or one that is disclosed by the evidence, if the accused consents to its inclusion. One might ask why an accused would consent to his being prosecuted for some additional offence when he was not originally charged with it, but, in fact, there may arise a situation where the accused is going to be tried anyway and if he feels that he is likely to be convicted, it may be in his own interest to have all other charges at the same time. If he knows that he will likely be prosecuted anyway he may thus get the benefit of what will probably be concurrent sentences rather than consecutive sentences.[7] It is not a particularly common practice, but far from rare.

There is, however, a third method of preferring an indictment which is applicable only to trials before a judge and jury and which is extremely important.[8] This is known as the preferring of a direct indictment and is provided for in section 577 of the Code. Where a preliminary inquiry has not been held at all, or where a preliminary inquiry has been held, but the accused has been discharged, an accused may still be indicted for an offence if the Crown attorney or other prosecuting official has the personal written consent of the Attorney General or Deputy Attorney General. This means that the Attorney General can, in effect, bypass the preliminary inquiry entirely and simply indict the accused directly (hence the name "direct indictment"), or disagree with the finding of the judge at the preliminary inquiry and indict the accused anyway, so long as he or his Deputy personally consents to this being done.[9]

It is also possible for a private prosecutor (as discussed in the previous chapter) to prefer an indictment directly against an accused person instead

---

6 Section 574.

7 If the outstanding offences which he wishes to have added to the indictment were committed in another province, he may still have them so added, but only if the accused pleads guilty to them and gets the consent of the Attorney General where the offences were committed (s. 478 of the Code).

8 Although the accused may elect trial by judge alone once the indictment is preferred. Section 571(7).

9 Alternatively, where, after a preliminary inquiry, the accused is discharged because of insufficient evidence, a new information could be laid charging the same offence because a discharge at this stage is not an acquittal, but even here the personal written consent of the Attorney General or his Deputy is required.

of proceeding by the more usual route of laying an information. But this can only be done if such private person first secures the written order of a judge of the court, before which the trial will proceed permitting it. This is a most exceptional proceeding and not likely to be encountered in practice.

A direct indictment by the Attorney General, however, is not all that uncommon. It may seem odd that the protection for an accused that we have built into the system can be simply short circuited by the Attorney General, but in fact what is substituted for the protection of a preliminary inquiry is the protection that the Attorney General must himself (or at least his Deputy) be satisfied that a prosecution is warranted and, of course, accept the political consequences if he is mistaken. Nevertheless, what is clear is that merely having an information dismissed at the preliminary hearing stage is not necessarily the end of the matter for the accused.

In sum, if the accused is charged with a summary conviction offence (or, in most cases, with a provincial offence) the document which will form the basis of the formal allegation against him is the information; once it is read to him, then, subject to any objections or motion to quash, and subject to any adjournments, he will be called upon to plead. If the accused is charged with an indictable offence which is triable by a provincial court judge, the information is again the written document upon which he is tried. There is no actual indictment in spite of the fact that it is an indictable offence and, once the information is read to the accused (again subject to objections and any adjournments and subject to the possibility that the provincial court judge may require the accused to be prosecuted on an indictment), he will be called upon to plead. If the accused is charged with an electable indictable offence, once the information is read to him, he must elect how he wishes to be tried. If he elects trial by a provincial court judge, again there is no actual indictment and the trial proceeds on the information; if he elects trial by judge, or trial by judge and jury, or if he must be tried by judge and jury, the information is not the basis of the trial, but the basis of the preliminary inquiry. If the accused is ordered to stand trial, then a formal indictment is drawn up and it is this that forms the basis of the trial. Once the indictment is read out to the accused then, again, subject to objections and adjournments, he is called upon to plead; in some exceptional cases, an indictment may be preferred against the accused even if there was no preliminary inquiry or, if there was one, the accused was discharged. This is possible at a trial before a judge sitting without a jury, only if the accused consents; if the trial is before a judge and jury, it is possible only either if the judge gives his written consent or if the Attorney General himself signs the indictment.

9

The Plea and the Verdict

It may seem odd to discuss the plea and the verdict in the same chapter since they come at the opposite end of the process — the plea at the beginning and the verdict near the end — but the reason is that it is not easy to understand the problem of making the proper plea without also understanding what verdicts are possible once an accused has been tried.

GENERAL PLEAS

Once the information or indictment, as the case may be, has been read out to the accused, he is, as we have seen, called upon to plead. If Not Guilty simply meant "I deny I did it," it would be an easy matter to discuss pleas, but in fact it is not that simple by any means.

In the case of summary conviction offences, the Code actually only gives the accused two choices of a plea of either Guilty or Not Guilty. In the case of indictable offences, the Code gives him five choices — Guilty, Not Guilty, Autrefois Acquit, Autrefois Convict and Pardon. In actual fact, nothing of substance turns on the technical difference between summary conviction offences and indictable offences since, whatever the form, these five possible pleas exist for all offences.

A plea of Guilty is a formal acknowledgement of what is charged against the accused and relieves the prosecution of the need to prove the case against him by the introduction of evidence. It constitutes an admission of the facts that would be necessary to support a conviction for that offence.[1] The plea of Guilty must be clear and unequivocal. Sometimes the accused (particularly if not represented by counsel) might wish to say "Guilty, but I have an explanation" or "Guilty, I suppose." Such pleas are not permitted (save in Ontario under the Provincial Offences Act for minor offences) and the trial judge may have to question the accused to make sure that he really understands the plea of Guilty and require him to plead Guilty unequivocally. Sometimes, he may feel that what the accused is really saying is that he has a defence to the charge, in which case he will enter a plea of Not Guilty and proceed to trial.

Even where the Guilty plea is entered, there can be complications. The accused will have to be sentenced and merely reading the information or the indictment does not give the trial judge very much information in which to assess the appropriate penalty. The prosecutor, therefore, will normally make a brief statement of the facts and any other information that will be useful to the judge. But at this point, the accused may intervene and object that the facts are wrong or that the prosecutor has been misinformed. Again, the trial judge will make some inquiry and if, in his view, the dispute is material to some issue in the case, he may permit (indeed, advise or, in an extreme case, require) the accused to withdraw his Guilty plea and substitute a Not Guilty plea, so that the issues may be resolved.

A plea of Not Guilty requires the prosecution to prove beyond any reasonable doubt all the facts necessary to support a conviction, but the accused may, during the trial, admit certain specific facts and so dispense with the necessity of proving them. Once a plea of Not Guilty is entered, the accused may then, under this general plea, raise any defence to rebut the charge, save the defences of autrefois acquit, autrefois convict or pardon, which we will discuss a little later. Thus, his defence may be simply that he did not do the act in question, or it may be that he did the act, but did not have the requisite intent. It may be that, in fact, he has no defence at all, but is simply relying on the fact that whether he did it or not, the prosecution will be unable to prove the necessary facts. Or he may raise some specific defence such as self-defence or provocation.

One defence that is often raised under the general plea of Not Guilty is that of mental disorder.[2] We shall discuss in Chapter 16 the substance

---

1 There used to be (though no longer in Canada) a plea called *Nolo Contendere* (I do not wish to contest) which is still found in some American jurisdictions. It is, in fact, a plea of Guilty without an admission of the facts. Not contesting something is not the same as admitting it. It is of no significance in the criminal process but it may affect any subsequent civil liability since a Guilty plea may be used in a civil case as an admission of liability whereas *Nolo Contendere* has no evidentiary value in a subsequent case.

2 In spite of what newspapers and T.V. insist on stating, there is no plea of insanity. The plea is Not Guilty and the defence is mental disorder.

of this defence, but at this stage it should be noted that this is the one defence where the burden of proof is on the person who raises it. In all other cases — for example, self-defence or provocation — once the accused has raised the issue by some evidence that makes such a defence at least a possible issue, the onus of proof then switches to the prosecution to prove beyond any reasonable doubt that the accused was not acting in self defence or was not provoked. Where the accused raises the defence of mental disorder, however, he is presumed not to be disordered unless he proves, on the balance of probabilities, that he was so disordered at the time he committed the offence.

SPECIAL PLEAS

The other possible pleas, of Autrefois Acquit, Autrefois Convict and Pardon, are known as special pleas and are actually pleas in bar — that is to say, if successful, they bar the prosecution. Unlike the general pleas, they are determined by the judge whether or not there is a jury, and if the matter is decided against the accused, he is then called upon to plead Guilty or Not Guilty, and the trial proceeds in the ordinary way.

Pardon

The easiest of the three to understand is the pardon. Under the Criminal Code,[3] the royal prerogative of mercy of Her Majesty is preserved, but there are also specific provisions relating to the grant of a pardon (either "free" — that is, absolute; or "conditional" — that is, upon some condition) by the Governor in Council (in effect, the federal cabinet) to any convicted person.[4] The effect of the pardon is that such a person is deemed never to have committed the offence in question and, obviously, if as a matter of law, he is deemed never to have committed the offence, then he cannot be subsequently prosecuted for it. Hence, the pardon prevents such a prosecution.

Autrefois Acquit and Autrefois Convict

The pleas of Autrefois Acquit (that is, "I was previously acquitted of this offence") or Autrefois Convict (that is, "I was previusly convicted of this offence") require more consideration since they are far from simple. The Charter of Rights and Freedoms now specifically provides that any person charged with an offence has the right, if finally acquitted of the offence, not to be tried for it again, or, if finally found guilty and punished

---

3 Section 571.
4 Section 749.

for the offence, not to be tried or punished for it again. This principle of "double jeopardy," however, is far older than the Charter and far more complex than would first appear.

Lesser or included offences

Some criminal offences are clearly less serious offences with some additional aggravating element attached to them — for example, an assault is, among other things, the intentional application of force to another person without his consent, but assault with a weapon is an assault, plus the additional factor that the accused was carrying a weapon at the time; or aggravated assault is an assault, plus the added factor that the accused also wounded the victim. Sexual assault is ordinary assault plus the added element that it is of a sexual nature.

Other offences are not those that, by the wording of the statute, are less serious offences plus some additional element, but are offences that must *necessarily* include the commission of a less serious offence if some requisite element is missing. For example, murder is, among other things, the causing of someone's death by means of an unlawful act intending to cause the death. But causing someone's death by means of an unlawful act is, itself, an offence — the offence of manslaughter. If, therefore, there is a death by means of an unlawful act and the Crown proves the intent to kill, then the result is murder; but if all that is proved except the intent to kill, then one is still left with the unlawful death and hence the offence of manslaughter.

In these two cases, a lesser included offence is either (i) one which, by the wording of the particular section involved, is an offence which must be committed as the more serious offence minus one of the aggravating elements; or (ii) one which, generally, must be part and parcel of the more serious offence, such as second degree murder being included in first degree murder, or manslaughter being included in murder. In these instances, really all one has to do is to look at the relevant section of the Code to determine whether there is an offence that can be labelled "an included offence" in the offence charged. One of the most obvious cases where an offence would necessarily be included in the more serious offence is that of an attempt. Where the accused is charged with the full offence — for example, obtaining by false pretences — there must be some time along the way to the commission of the full offence when, although the offence was not completed, the accused was in the process of trying to complete it. If, therefore, the Crown proves all the elements of the offence, except that it cannot prove that the accused actually succeeded in obtaining anything by the fraud, then it has proved sufficient facts for which a verdict of guilty of an attempt to obtain by fraud would be justified.

There is yet another way in which an included offence can be found and that is, not in the wording of the statute, but in the wording of the count of the indictment. We saw in the previous chapter what the basic minimum requirements were for a count in an indictment — a single transaction, alleging a specific offence and giving sufficient detail to enable the accused to identify the transaction involved. Suppose the accused strikes the victim over the head, saying, as he does, "I intend to kill you." The victim, however, survives the assault, so the accused is charged with attempted murder. The Crown could charge the accused in a count of an indictment that "the accused did on a specified day at a specified time and at a specified place attempt to murder the victim contrary to section 239 of the Criminal Code." This meets the minimum requirements for an indictment and, as such, is probably valid. The Crown could, however, on its own volition also include further details (or the accused could ask for, and the court order, further particulars so as to supply the details) specifying how the attempt was carried out — for example, it could add, "by striking him over the head with a baseball bat." If the count is in the short form and is left that way, then either the accused is guilty or he is not guilty because, as one reads the indictment, it is an all or nothing proposition — he either attempted to murder the victim or he did not. If, however, the count is in the longer form (or is ordered by the court to be amended to the longer form), then one can have a situation whereby the jury is satisfied that the accused struck the victim over the head with a baseball bat, but is not satisfied that he intended to kill him when he did so. Since the intent to kill is an essential element of attempted murder, they must acquit him of attempted murder. However, they have still found that he struck the victim on the head and this is, of course, itself an offence — it alleges, in popular language, the offence of assault or assault with a weapon. The Code provides that all counts are divisible — that is to say, can be divided up into parts so that if one part is proved, but another part is not proved, then the jury can find the accused guilty of the part that is proved — in this case, the assault or aggravated assault.

In these sorts of cases, it is only by looking at the actual words of the indictment that one can tell whether an offence is included as part of the offence charged or not. There are thus three ways to determine whether an offence is included in the charge of another offence — by a specific section so providing; by the wording of the section creating the offence in question; or by the wording of the count in the indictment charging the offence in question.

The importance of all of this is that a jury may always acquit of the offence charged, but find the accused guilty of another offence, if that offence is an included offence, in the sense that we have just discussed. As well an accused may plead Not Guilty to the offence charged but Guilty to an included offence and, if the prosecution agrees and the trial judge accepts that it is proper in the circumstances, the Guilty plea may be accepted and the accused found Not Guilty on the more serious charge.

The relevance of this to our discussion on double jeopardy is that when an accused is simply found Not Guilty, he is acquitted not only of the offence with which he was charged, but he is also acquitted of all offences for which he *could* have been convicted on that indictment, including, of course, all included offences. Not only that, but if the indictment is in law improper, but could have been amended, then he is acquitted of all offences for which he could have been convicted if all the proper amendments had been made. For example, the accused is charged with stealing something on May 4th but all the evidence shows the offence was committed on May 5th; the accused is therefore found not guilty of the offence charged. But this is one of those cases where the prosecution should have moved to amend the indictment and almost certainly, permission would have been granted since the accused was not misled or prejudiced. If the prosecution failed to move to amend, the accused obviously has to be acquitted; but he is acquitted not only of stealing on May 4th — he is also acquitted of stealing on May 5th.

Conversely, if the accused is convicted of the more serious offence, then he is also convicted, in that one conviction, of all the offences that are included in that offence for which he was convicted.

Accordingly, when an accused pleads Autrefois Acquit, he is asserting not only that he has been acquitted of the offence charged (because he was previously charged with that same offence and acquitted) but also that, although the offence now charged, is not, in form, the same as that previously charged, he could have been convicted of it the first time, but was not, and that therefore he must have been acquitted. Similarly, a plea of Autrefois Convict lies where the offence now charged was part and parcel of the first offence for which he was convicted, so that to convict him a second time for an offence that was included as part of the first offence, would be to convict him of the same offence twice.

It is often difficult to sort out whether a prior acquittal or conviction falls within these rules or not. It may require a great deal of legal expertise and a careful scrutiny of the record of the first trial and a comparison of that with the second charge, which is why such pleas are within the domain of the trial judge and not, as with other pleas, within the jury's function. It is a legal question whether the second trial is barred or not. If it is, then the accused cannot be tried and must be discharged; if it is not, then the trial may proceed and the accused be called upon to plead Guilty or Not Guilty.

Charging more serious offence

There are two other similar cases which are not really questions of double jeopardy, but which are obviously connected with this problem. The first is trying to charge an accused a second time, not with a lesser included offence, but with a *more serious* offence which amounts to the first offence plus some additional factor. If an accused is charged with common assault, clearly he cannot be convicted of assault causing bodily harm, even if the evidence discloses this to be the case. One can only be convicted of an *included* offence — not a more serious offence, which is why one usually talks of a "lesser included offence," although the term is slightly misleading since it means "lesser" only in the sense of fewer factual elements, not necessarily in the sense of a less serious penalty. Suppose, then, that in our case, the accused is convicted of common assault and the prosecutor then realizes that he should have been charged with assault causing bodily harm. Can he then charge the accused with the more serious offence?

Technically, this is not double jeopardy, since the accused was never in jeopardy of ever being convicted the first time of assault causing bodily harm, but there is something unfair about convicting the accused again when he has already been convicted once. (The same principle applies when he was acquitted the first time.) The Code therefore provides that where the second charge is substantially the same as the first, but adds a further element as to a specific intention or circumstances of aggravation tending to increase the punishment, then the second indictment is barred. To give a specific example, the Code provides that if a person is convicted (or acquitted) of manslaughter and the prosecution realizes that the accused actually intended to kill the victim and should have been charged with murder, it cannot subsequently charge the accused with murder for that same homicide.

Charging offences under different sections or statutes

A similar, but slightly different problem arises when an accused by one act, breaks two different sections of the Code (or other statute). For example, it is an offence to drive a motor vehicle while one's ability to drive is impaired by alcohol; it is a different offence to drive a motor vehicle when one's blood alcohol content exceeds .08 percent. Suppose an accused drives his car on a single occasion when his ability to drive is impaired by alcohol and his blood alcohol content is .10 percent. Can he be convicted of two separate offences for the one act?

Double jeopardy cannot possibly apply since the accused has not yet been convicted or acquitted of anything. Thus, there is no bar to his being *prosecuted* for both offences. In other words, he may be charged with two counts — one for driving while impaired and one for driving with more than .08 percent blood alcohol content. But it seems strange to say that he could be convicted of two different offences and, at least, in theory be sentenced to two consecutive sentences for just one act. And, indeed, the courts have held that while he can be charged with the two offences, he can only be convicted of one of them (or, of course, acquitted of both of them). The reason why this is so is not easy to understand, apart from one's instinctive feeling that it would be unfair to punish a person twice when he has only committed one act that results in one harm.

Basically, the reason lies in the juridical significance of an act and the harm caused by that act. If one act gives rise to one harm, then the combination of those two factors can only amount to one offence. If that offence is punishable under two different provisions as two differently labelled crimes, then the accused may be convicted under either, but not both. In our example, the driver of the car by committing the one act of driving while impaired and having more than .08 percent alcohol in his blood, can be convicted of only one offence — either impaired driving or "driving over," but not both. He is guilty of only one offence, even though it is punishable under two different sections of the Code. In other words, the mere fact that the offence is *procedurally* punishable under two sections, does not mean that, *in substance*, the accused commits two crimes.

This, however, only applies to prevent two convictions. The accused may still be *charged* for the two offences, as that is a procedural matter and procedurally he may be convicted of either. If he is convicted on the impaired driving count, then he must be acquitted on the "driving over" count. But if he is acquitted on the first count that does not necessarily mean that he must be acquitted on the second — a person may, in fact, have more than .08 percent alcohol in his blood, and yet not be proved to have an impaired ability to drive. Conversely, a person's ability to drive may be impaired even though he only has a blood alcohol level of .07 percent.

It is not always easy to ascertain when there has been one act and one harm, or two different acts or two different harms. If, for example, a person stabs a pregnant woman and causes the child to be borne prematurely and die of its injuries, then the accused is guilty of two offences — one involving the harm to the woman, and one involving the harm to the child because these are two different harms. Each case has to be decided upon its own particular facts and while the principle is easy to state, its application does cause considerable difficulties.

10

The Jury

If the accused pleads Guilty, nothing remains to be done at the trial and the court can proceed to the matter of sentencing which we will discuss in Chapter 18. If, on the other hand, the accused pleads Not Guilty, then the trial may get underway (we shall discuss the course of the trial and the process of proof in the next chapter). However, if the accused has elected trial by judge and jury, or if he is required to be tried by a judge and jury, then before the actual trial can commence, the jury must first be selected.

Trial by jury is now guaranteed by the Charter of Rights and Freedoms for all persons charged with an indictable offence punishable by five years' imprisonment or more.[1] This is not to say that he *must* be so tried since, as we have seen, the bulk of these offences are electable offences and the accused will probably not choose trial by judge and jury, but he at least has the right so to choose if he desires.

In Canada, a jury consists of 12 persons (in the Yukon and Northwest Territories, six persons[2] chosen at random from among residents of the

---

1 Canadian Charter of Rights and Freedoms, s. 11(f).

2 It has been decided under the Bill of Rights that a six-member jury panel does not violate the right to a jury trial, but some courts have held that s. 632, requiring a six-member jury in the Yukon and Northwest Territories, is unconstitutional as violating s. 15 of the Charter (equality before the law). *R. v. Emile*, 65 C.R. (3d) 135, [1988] 5 W.W.R. 481, 42 C.C.C. (3d) 408, [1988] N.W.T.R. 196 (C.A.).

locality where the trial is to take place. Since, as we have seen, the trial will normally take place in the locality (that is, county district or other division) where the offence was committed, the jury is normally drawn from residents of the place where the crime was committed. Before we consider the jury selection process, however, it will be as well to say a word about the application for change of venue.[3]

CHANGE OF VENUE

The concept of a jury trial necessarily includes the concept of an impartial jury and we shall discuss the procedural steps for ensuring impartiality. But it may sometimes happen that because of pre-trial publicity, or for some other reason, it is feared that it will not be possible to find 12 impartial persons to sit on the jury. Most often this arises where it is the accused who fears that any jury would be prejudiced against him, but it can sometimes happen that, for example, in a remote community, it is the prosecutor who fears that a jury would be subject to undue pressure from the accused and his friends and relatives. It may even be because the community is so small that an impartial jury simply cannot be found.

If the applicant, either the accused or the prosecutor, can show that a fair and impartial trial would likely not be possible in the present locality, then the judge (that is, the trial judge or a judge of the particular court in question) may order the trial to be held in some other locality in the same province, if it appears expedient to the ends of justice to do so, or if he is satisfied that a jury cannot be summoned for the trial.[4] Where the change of venue is ordered, there are various provisions for the transfer of all the documents in the case to be transferred to the new court and for ensuring that the accused appears for trial in the new place.

It is not easy to obtain a change of venue since the basic principle is that the trial ought to proceed where the offence was committed and the burden is on the applicant to demonstrate why a change should be ordered. It is not, in any case, possible to order a change to a place outside the province where the offence is committed since, save in only exceptional instances, one province has no jurisdiction to try an accused for an offence committed in another province.

SELECTION OF JURY

The Criminal Code picks up the process of the selection of jurymen from the time when the panel is present in court waiting to be chosen.

---

3 Actually, an application for change of venue may be made in a non-jury trial as well, but the problem, in practice, arises in the case of jury trials.

4 Section 599.

The panel is the whole group of potential jurymen from whom the actual jury will be picked. How the panel comes to be present in court waiting to decide whether they will be chosen or not, is governed not by the Criminal Code, but by the selection process of each province and territory. This process varies from province to province and is, in any case, highly technical and complicated. It is sufficient for our purposes to state that each year a guess is made (actually, based on previous years it tends to be a fairly good estimate) as to how many jurymen will be required for each district, county or other division for all the forthcoming trials in each locality and since allowances have to be made for jurymen being excused or found not acceptable, that number is increased by varying proportions. This number is then fairly divided among the local cities, towns, townships and so on in each district so that the burden falls as evenly as possible upon all the inhabitants. Names are then chosen from among all the qualified jurymen sufficient to make up enough prospective jurors that will be required. At the beginning of each of the court sessions the sheriff will choose by lot, in the presence of other people, enough jurors to make up each panel — that is to say, a body of prospective jurors that will be sufficient to provide for the required number of jurors, due allowance being made for objections or excuses and so on. These will then be summoned for jury duty at the appropriate time and will be the people sitting in court when the Criminal Code process takes over. The size of this panel will obviously depend upon the amount of business anticipated at each session and the number of juries that are likely to be needed and on the number of objections that are likely to be made. They can range from 40 or so up to three or four hundred or more.

The first thing that either the accused or the prosecutor may do is to object to the whole panel, but this he may do only, according to the Code, on the grounds of partiality, fraud or misconduct on the part of the sheriff in selecting it. In view of the checks and balances in the selection process, it is, in fact, virtually impossible for the sheriff ever to have the opportunity for fraud or misconduct, let alone exercise it if he did have the opportunity. What is more likely is that an objection will be made to the array on a constitutional basis. The sheriff can only select from those names given to him, and these names may have been discriminately picked — they may include no women, or no black person or only local farmers or something of this sort. It remains to be seen whether this sort of challenge to the panel — not based upon fraud on the part of the sheriff, but based on discrimination in the initial selection process — will succeed, but there would in any case be a heavy burden on the objector to demonstrate such discrimination and whether, if so, it would prevent a fair trial.

Assuming that the whole panel is not challenged, the next step is to choose those individuals who will end up as the 12 members of the jury.

Jurors may be excused by the judge on the basis of extreme hardship if they are required to serve. Jurors are obviously ineligible to serve on the jury if they are related to the accused or the complainant and, in the interests of saving time, it is not unusual for the judge to make a general inquiry of the whole panel as to whether this is the case or not, rather than waiting for each individual prospective juror to draw this to his attention and in those cases, the prospective juror will be excused. From those that are left, the jury must now be drawn.

The names of all the prospective jurors are placed in a box which is then shaken up and the clerk of the court then proceeds to draw out one name at a time until he has enough to find 12 jurymen after all the challenges and objections to individuals have been met.[5] At this stage, one tries to draw neither too few nor too many and somewhere between 20 and 40 or so will usually be drawn out.

Then each person's name is called out in the same order as it was drawn and that person then steps forward to be sworn in as a juror. But at that stage, before she is sworn, she may be challenged — that is, objected to by either the prosecutor or the accused. There are two kinds of challenge — the peremptory challenge, in which no reason need be assigned and which, once made, is conclusive (that is, the juryman must be excluded), and the challenge for cause, in which a reason for the challenge must be given and a determination be made whether the cause is made out or not.

Peremptory Challenges

The prosecutor is entitled, in any case, to four peremptory challenges only, while the accused is entitled to 20 peremptory challenges if charged with first degree murder, 12 peremptory challenges if charged with an offence punishable by more than five years' imprisonment, or four peremptory challenges in other cases. The reason why the prosecutor has the smallest number of peremptory challenges in all cases, is that he has another option available to him — the option of directing a prospective juror to stand by. When a prospective juror steps forward, and has not been challenged by the defence, the prosecutor may direct that that juror return to the panel which is still waiting and resume his place at the bottom of the list. He is not excused or challenged, but will not be called upon until all of the other members of the panel preceding him have been called upon and have been either sworn or excused. This the prosecutor can do up to 48 times (or more, with leave of the court), so that in any case where there is a large panel, it is unlikely that the panel will be exhausted

---

5 There may be more sophisticated methods of randomly selecting jurors from the panel, but the essence of randomness must be preserved.

with the result that the prosecutor will probably not have to use up any of his peremptory challenges in order to avoid having a juryman who he thinks is not suitable. Even with a smaller panel, a doubtful juror is put at the back of the list and will not be selected until all the others have been gone through.[6]

Challenges for Cause

With the limited number of peremptory challenges that either side has, one cannot afford to use them indiscriminately. Therefore, what will be done more in practice (by the accused more than the prosecutor since the latter has the right to direct a stand-by) is that a challenge for cause will be made, since there is no limit upon the number of permissible challenges for cause.

The possible causes are:

1. That the person called is not, in fact, a member of the panel constituting the array. This is clearly easy to determine and is done so merely by the judge inspecting the names on the panel and comparing it with the prospective juror. Slight variations of description or slight variations in the spelling of a name do not result in the objection being upheld, but a totally different person would suffice.
2. That the juror is not indifferent as between the Queen and the accused.
3. That the juror has been convicted of an offence for which he received a term of imprisonment exceeding 12 months.
4. That the juror is an alien.
5. That the juror is physically unable to perform jury duty.
6. That the juror cannot speak the official language of Canada in which the accused is required to be tried.[7]

The objector states that he is challenging for cause and he may be required to be more specific about what cause he is relying on and what reason he has for thinking that the cause is likely to be upheld. He may even be required to state this in writing, though this is not often the case. If the judge agrees that the issue should be investigated, as can be seen, while cause 1. is fairly easy to settle one way or the other, causes 2. to 6. may be disputed and not so easy to resolve. In these cases, the issue is decided, not by the judge, but by two fact-finders, who will be the last two members of the jury to have been sworn (if the challenge arises at

---

6 The Supreme Court has recently held in *R. v. Bain* (1992), 69 C.C.C. (3d) 481 (S.C.C.) that the stand-by provisions of the Code violate the Charter but it postponed putting its judgment into effect for six months to give the Government time to enact replacement legislation. As of the time of writing, this has not yet been done.

7 An accused, in some provinces, may apply for an order requiring him to be tried in either French or English as the case may be, subject to certain time limits and other constraints.

a time when there are some members of the jury already in place) or, if this is not the case, by any two persons present in the courtroom picked by the judge. They may be members of the panel already waiting, or two members of the news media or just two members of the public. These two people are then sworn to try the issue.

At this stage, unless the other side admits the validity of the challenge, there is a hearing to investigate whether the challenge should be upheld — that is, to determine whether the ground of the challenge is true. The prospective juror may be (in fact, invariably is) called and examined by both sides, other witnesses may be called, arguments may be heard and the two triers will be addressed. They then decide in favour of or against the challenge. If they are unable to agree, two new triers of fact are sworn in to make the determination.

In practice, the most difficult and most common ground for challenge is that the juror is not indifferent as between the Queen and the accused. What the accused is entitled to is an *indifferent* juror, not a favourable juror. Many accused (or their counsel) try, of course, to get as favourable a juror as possible. In some jurisdictions, the jury challenge has become a lengthy process of the accused attempting to assemble a jury that is predisposed to acquit, while the prosecution attempts to have selected jurors who are likely to convict. In Canada, the courts have avoided this excess by disallowing questions that are not relevant to showing partiality but are merely designed to embarrass the prospective juror or expose his weaknesses, by presuming that all prospective jurors will follow their oath and try the issues impartially unless it is clearly shown that they are unable to do so, and by limiting the right of either side to go on unwarranted "fishing expeditions" in the hope of coming up with something that will discredit the prospective juror. It is possible that the new Charter right might compel the courts to examine more closely in the future the limits they have placed on these rights to challenge for cause, but at the moment one can say that they have struck a satisfactory balance between ensuring an indifferent juror and preserving the privacy and dignity of prospective jurors.

If the two triers of fact find the ground for the challenge to be true, the juror is excused from that trial. If they reject the challenge, then the juror is sworn unless the person challenging him (or the other side) chooses to exercise his right to a peremptory challenge, if that option is still open to him.

In the normal case, when a prospective juror is called, the accused must first declare whether he is challenging him, either peremptorily or for cause, before the prosecutor is called upon to state whether he is going to direct him to stand by, or to challenge him, either peremptorily or for cause. This process is repeated each time a prospective juror is called.

As can be seen, one can easily have a case where the initial drawing of prospective jurors from the entire panel is exhausted, in which case the clerk again draws a suitable number and the process is repeated. This goes on until, of course, one reaches those jurors who have been directed by the prosecutor to stand by and then the process is repeated in respect of them. It is possible, though extremely rare, that the entire panel of prospective jurors is exhausted because of peremptory challenges and challenges for cause and still a full jury of 12 members has not been selected. In such cases, the court may, on the request of the prosecutor, direct the sheriff to summon as many people as are thought necessary by word of mouth (usually by going out to the street and summoning passers by) who then augment the panel and go through the selection process.

There are slight complications if the accused is charged with more than one count in the indictment or if there are co-accused. Where there are multiple counts, an accused does not have the accumulated total of all the peremptory challenges applicable to each count, but only to the number of peremptory challenges that the most serious count provides for. Where there are co-accused, each is entitled to the appropriate number of peremptory challenges and it is customary to alternate between them as to who goes first in his challenge so as to spread the challenges evenly. Similarly, in the case of challenges for cause, each accused is called upon alternatively, usually in alphabetical order. As each of the 12 members of the jury is chosen, he is sworn to try the issue as between the Queen and the accused on the evidence he shall hear. There is actually no set form of oath (or affirmation if the juror objects to swearing an oath). Once the 12 members are chosen, they become the jury. If, however, during the trial, a member of the jury dies or is discharged by the trial judge because of illness or some other reasonable cause, the trial may continue so long as there are at least 10 jurors left, but if the number is reduced below 10, then the whole jury must be discharged and the accused be arraigned again.

At one time it was almost the invariable practice to sequester the jury during the course of the trial — that is, to keep them together, usually in hotel rooms, under the supervision of the sheriff or his deputy, until they had delivered their verdict. This is still possible (and, indeed, not unknown) but, save in exceptional circumstances, it is more common to give the jurors permission to separate (that is, to return to their homes and report back when the trial resumes) except when they are actually in the course of their deliberations at the end of the trial. They are invariably warned not to discuss the case with anyone and to report whether anyone attempts to discuss it with them.

11

The Trial

We have now got to the stage when the trial is ready to begin. Whether it is a trial before a provincial court judge, before a federally appointed judge, or before a judge and jury, the principles we are about to discuss are common to all trials so, for the purposes of this chapter, it does not matter which offence the accused is charged with nor what his mode of trial is.

We have already seen that the Charter of Rights and Freedoms now controls certain aspects of the trial process — such as the right to be tried within a reasonable time and the right to a fair and public hearing by an independent and impartial tribunal — and these should be borne in mind when discussing the course of a criminal trial.

The purpose of a criminal trial is for the prosecution to prove, according to law, the guilt of the accused. What is required to be proved varies, of course, according to the offence with which the accused is charged, but, generally speaking, the prosecutor will be required to prove that the accused committed the *act* in question — for example that he caused the death of the victim — and that he had the requisite *mental* element when he did so — for example that he *meant* to cause his death, if the charge is murder, or that he was criminally negligent, if the charge is manslaughter. As we know, the *degree* of proof that is required is proof beyond reasonable doubt, so that it is not required of the accused to prove that he did *not* commit the act or have the requisite mental element. If the trier of fact (the judge or the jury, as the case may be) is in doubt about it, he must acquit.

FACT-FINDING PROCESS

The fact-finding process (that is, determining beyond reasonable doubt whether the accused committed the act, or whether he had the requisite mental element) is a process of inference-drawing. These inferences are drawn from data which are presented to the fact-finder and these data take the form of evidence which may consist of the testimony of witnesses or the presentation of documents, torn clothing, the murder weapon or other, what is called *real* evidence.

The law of evidence is that branch of the law that governs what data may be presented to the fact-finder and how and to what extent he may draw inferences from those data. The basic rule of evidence is that all evidence must be relevant to the issues in the case so that facts which are irrelevant to an issue are excluded. "Relevant" in this context means tending to prove or disprove the fact that must be determined, but, of course, relevance is not an absolute term — something can be highly relevant, probably relevant or only marginally relevant. For example, if on a murder trial a witness were to testify that he saw the accused shoot the deceased, that is clearly highly relevant in the determination of whether the accused *did* shoot the deceased. If the prosecutor were to show that the accused and the victim had a dispute over a girlfriend the day before, that may be relevant as showing a motive and, hence, that the accused *may* have shot the deceased, but it is not relevant to the same degree as the testimony of an eye-witness to the shooting. If the prosecution were to show that a month before the murder the victim had lost a $10 bet to the accused and refused to pay up, that may be vaguely relevant, but has only marginal relevance.

Evidence must be *sufficiently* relevant — that is to say, it must pass the test of materially assisting the fact-finder in the inference-drawing process. If it does not materially assist the fact-finder, it may do more harm than good. It may confuse the jury; it may prejudice the accused; it may divert the jury from their real task. The trial judge will, therefore, rule on whether any piece of evidence is sufficiently relevant before it is admitted, though, of course, in most instances its relevance is obvious and it is usually only where an objection is taken that the matter will have to be expressly ruled upon.

Even so, not all relevant evidence is admissible. The second basic rule of evidence is that even relevant evidence is only admissible if it is not excluded by some rule that excludes certain types of evidence. Some evidence, for example, is excluded on policy grounds on the basis that it would violate a "privilege" — such as the communications between a lawyer and his client or between a husband and wife. Some evidence is excluded because of its prejudicial nature, such as the bad character of an accused or his previous criminal record. Some may be excluded because of the manner in which it was obtained, such as an illegal wiretap or evidence obtained in violation of a Charter right. These are merely examples of a vast and rather technical list of rules that exclude relevant (even highly relevant) evidence from the fact-finding process.

The inference-drawing process depends not only upon the data which are available, but also on the weight that is going to be given to those data. Very often evidence is conflicting — a witness for the prosecution will say one thing and a witness for the accused will say the opposite. To draw any inference in such a case requires the fact-finder not only to receive the data but also to *weigh* them. He may convict the accused only if he is satisfied, beyond any reasonable doubt, that he should draw the inference favourable to the prosecution, but this requires him to determine which are the more credible witnesses. He may determine credibility on his own observation of the witnesses — whether they answer forthrightly or whether they prevaricate, or even whether they look honest and well-dressed or appear shifty and disreputable. Obviously each side will want to present its own witnesses in the best light possible, while trying to reduce the impact that opposing testimony may have. But evidence may also be called to assist in the assessment of a witness's testimony. There are rules, however, limiting how far one can go to introduce evidence that is not relevant directly to a fact that is in issue in the case, but only relevant to the assessment of weight or credibility, because as can be seen, the more the trial gets bogged down in arguing about whether a witness is, or is not, to be believed, the more the fact-finder may lose sight of the fact that his primary task is to determine whether the accused is guilty or not. While, therefore, the credibility of a witness can be attacked or supported, it is what is called a collateral issue and is subject to these limiting rules.

The fact-finding process is thus a process of receiving the data which are made available, weighing those data and then coming to a conclusion. The evidence which is presented may be either what is called direct evidence or what is called circumstantial evidence. If, to go back to our example, a witness testifies that he saw the accused shoot the deceased and if that witness is believed, then only one conclusion is possible and that is that the accused did shoot the deceased. With direct evidence of this nature, the problem is not what conclusion should be drawn, but whether it is believed or not. If, however, the issue is whether the accused shot the deceased, and a witness testifies that he saw the accused near the scene of the killing, even if that witness is believed, the conclusion that the accused shot the deceased is not the only possible one. With this sort of circumstantial evidence, the problem is twofold — whether one believes the witness in the first place and, if one does, whether the conclusion one is drawing from that testimony is the correct one. Since a finding of guilt requires the trier to be satisfied beyond any reasonable doubt, as can be seen, whether the fact-finder will draw the conclusion that the accused is guilty will depend upon the effect of the sum total of all the evidence, including the circumstantial evidence. One piece of circumstantial evidence in itself is unlikely to persuade the fact-finder, but an accumulation of pieces of circumstantial evidence, or circumstantial evidence in combination with some pieces of direct evidence, may well result in the fact-finder being satisfied, beyond any reasonable doubt, of the guilt of the accused.

CONDUCT OF TRIAL

One tends to think of the order of a criminal trial as the opening statement of the prosecutor followed by the calling of all the evidence for the prosecution; a statement by the defence followed by the calling of all the evidence for the defence; the addresses by the prosecutor and the defence to the jury; the summing up and directions to the jury (if there is one) by the trial judge and then the consideration of the verdict. Indeed, as a simple overview of the course of a trial, this is accurate enough, but to understand some of the complications that can arise, a more detailed analysis is required.

Competence of Witness

The prosecutor generally will make an opening statement in which he will outline the charge against the accused and how he hopes to prove it and then proceed to call his witnesses one by one. As each witness is called he will be required either to take the oath to swear to tell the truth or to make a solemn affirmation that he will tell the truth if he objects to taking an oath. All witnesses must be competent to testify, both in the sense that there is no legal impediment, such as the prosecution attempting to call the accused or his spouse, and in the sense that they are mentally competent — that is, able to tell the truth, answer intelligibly and to have perceived the events in question. Adult witnesses are presumed to be mentally competent and, usually, if there is any doubt about the matter, this will have been resolved beforehand and the witness will not be called, but it can arise at trial where, for example, the parties do not agree as to the competence of a witness. More often, this type of problem will arise where it is a child who is proffered as a witness.

Section 16 of the Canada Evidence Act provides that when the proposed witness is an adult whose mental capacity is challenged or is a child under the age of 14 years, the judge must conduct an inquiry to determine if that person is able to communicate the evidence and, if so, whether he or she understands the nature of an oath or solemn affirmation.

If that person cannot communicate the evidence at all in the sense of lacking the mental capacity to remember the events in question, to understand questions and respond to them intelligently, then he or she cannot testify at all. But also necessarily implicit in communicating evidence is that the witness understand what the truth is and be able to distinguish between the truth and a lie and recognize that he or she must tell the truth. This is what may be called the first hurdle. If that hurdle is passed, then the second hurdle is to determine whether he or she understands the nature of an oath or solemn affirmation. In the case of the oath, this means understanding that an oath binds the conscience of the witness. It is more than merely understanding the ordinary social and legal duty to tell the truth, though it is not necessary to believe that divine retribution will befall the oath-breaker. Presumably, though there have not, as yet, been any cases on it, an understanding of the solemn affirmation requires the witness to appreciate the solemnity of the occasion and the special responsibility to tell the truth that the affirmation imposes.

A witness who is able to communicate the evidence and understands the nature of an oath or solemn affirmation is fully competent to testify. However, if the witness passes the first hurdle but fails to pass the second, that is, is able to communicate the evidence but does not understand the nature of an oath or solemn affirmation, he or she may still testify upon a simple promise to tell the truth.

The inquiry into the testimonial competence of a witness takes place in the presence of the jury, if there is one. If the witness is ruled incompetent, no harm will have been done since no information will be elicited about the case itself during the inquiry. If, on the other hand, the witness is ruled competent, his or her credibility becomes very much a matter for the jury and they may derive considerable assistance in assessing credibility by listening to the inquiry as to competence. This is particularly true where the witness has been found able to communicate the evidence but unable to understand an oath and has given testimony merely on promising to tell the truth. It may even be that in some cases, the trial judge should warn the jury to be especially careful in assessing a witness's evidence, though there is no longer any legal requirement in criminal cases that unsworn evidence has to be corroborated by other evidence before an accused can be convicted.[1]

---

1 Although this requirement is still to be found in most provincial enactments and would thus still be applicable to prosecutions for provincial offences.

Examination-in-chief

The witness will first be questioned by the party that called him as a witness — in our case, the prosecution — and this is known as the examination-in-chief. In practice, of course, the party will have interviewed the witness before the trial, or the police will have done so, and one will have a pretty good idea of what that witness is going to say in the witness box. Indeed, there is a danger that counsel will, in fact, coach the witness and try to lead him through his evidence so that he gives the most favourable answers to the questions. This is why "leading questions," as they are called, are not generally permitted on an examination-in-chief, save for merely routine matters. A leading question is one that suggests to the witness what the answer should be — one that, in fact, "leads" the witness. For example, to ask a witness "what did you see then?" does not lead him, but to ask "Did you then see the accused shoot the deceased?" indicates that one expects the witness to agree. But the rule against asking leading questions is not really as rigid as is sometimes suggested. The danger lies more in counsel leading a witness to extract from him evidence than in the mere form of the question and most counsel would not object to what may technically be a leading question if it does no harm and expedites matters. In any case, a trial judge always has a discretion to relax the rule and permit leading questions when this seems to be the only way to get at the truth.

Cross-examination

When the party calling the witness has finished his examination-in-chief, the opposing party will then, if he wishes, question that witness — this is known as the cross-examination. Since the dangers that may arise when a party calls his own witness do not arise when it is an opposing witness, there is no bar to the use of leading questions during cross-examination. The purpose of the cross-examination is both to shake the weight and reliability of the evidence that the witness has given an examination-in-chief, and also to bring out new facts that are favourable to the cross-examiner.

This leads to an important difference in the scope of the examination-in-chief and that of the cross-examination. When the witness is being examined-in-chief he will be asked all those factual questions that are relevant to any particular issue in the case, but, except in the exceptional situation of the hostile witness that we will discuss in a moment, his trustworthiness as a witness is presumed so that no question may be asked of him, at that stage, which tends to prove that he is a *more* credible witness than anyone else. The reason for this is that if he is presumed to be credible anyway, it is unnecessary to attempt to show that he is credible, and thus such evidence is irrelevant to any issue since there is no issue as to his credibility. Nor, since that side has called that witness, can counsel *attack* the credibility of his own witness if he receives an answer he does not like. If one runs the risk of calling a potentially discreditable witness, then one only has oneself to blame if that witness later turns round and undermines one's case. (There are some exceptions to this rule that we will discuss in a moment.)

One purpose of the cross-examination is to show or attempt to show that the witness is *not* trustworthy and thus, on cross-examination, any question may be asked of him that is relevant to attack his credibility. So it is perfectly permissible to ask any question on cross-examination that is not relevant to any issue in the case but *is* relevant to attack the credibility or minimize the trustworthiness of that witness. The cross-examination may ask, for example, whether the witness has been convicted of criminal offences, whether he threatened to commit perjury, whether he has been involved in dubious financial dealings and so on.

Here, clearly, a line has to be drawn between questions that are honestly relevant to credibility and those that have no purpose save to harass or embarrass the witness. The presiding judge must protect the witness from insults and gratuitous attacks. They are, in any case, irrelevant, and he will prevent questions of this nature. On the other hand, if the question is honestly relevant to establishing that the witness is less trustworthy, then the cross-examiner is entitled to ask it. There is, however, a danger in asking these sorts of questions and the danger is that, generally speaking, the answers that are given to them are conclusive. The cross-examiner is stuck with the answer whether he likes it or not and cannot then go on to dispute the correctness of the answer by calling evidence to prove that it was wrong. The reason for this is that these questions relevant only to the trustworthiness of a witness are, as we have seen, called collateral issues — that is to say, it is not an issue directly relevant to something that has to be decided by the trier of fact; it is only relevant to something that the trier of fact may find helpful in the fact-finding process. Unless a halt is called to the exploration of such collateral matters, the trial might well degenerate into an inquiry as to the morals and character of a witness who is not on trial and the jury might well entirely lose sight of the fact that their real task is not passing judgment on the witness, but determining whether the accused is guilty or not.

As can be seen, if counsel asks a witness a question that he hopes will show that the witness is not trustworthy and then receives a reply that he does not expect, more harm than good has been done to his case. If one asks a witness, for example, "Is it not true that you failed to file your income tax return last year?" in the hope of showing that the witness is dishonest, but receives the reply, "That is not true, I did file my tax return," far from showing that that witness is dishonest, the jury is likely to feel more sympathetic towards him as the victim of an unwarranted attack and be likely to believe him more rather than less. In the result, counsel is well advised to ask such questions only when they are certain of what the answers will be and only when they are sure that the answers are not likely to prejudice the jury in his favour rather than against him.

To this rule of the conclusiveness of the answers to collateral questions, there are a few specific, but very important, exceptions. For example, if in answer to a question as to whether he has been convicted of a specific criminal offence, the witness denies it when he has been so convicted, the cross-examiner may prove the conviction. In other words, a denial of a conviction is *not* conclusive even though it only concerns a collateral issue. Another exception concerns what are called previous inconsistent statements. A witness testifies, for example, on examination-in-chief that when he saw the accused go through the intersection, the traffic light was red against him. On cross-examination he may be asked "Did you not tell the insurance investigator that the traffic light was green in favour of the accused?" If the answer is "yes," then clearly the witness is not very trustworthy, having said two different things on two occasions. If the witness denies making that statement, then the cross-examiner may call the insurance investigator to testify that that was what he was told. Obviously, the jury will have to decide who to believe, but at least counsel has made his point that here is a witness who is, if the jury believes the insurance investigator, at best, very unreliable if not a downright liar. Certainly, that witness's evidence is going to be treated with caution.

Re-examination

After the cross-examination is finished, the person who called that witness has the right of re-examination. The purpose of the re-examination is not to explore new issues (indeed, counsel will be stopped if he tries to open up new avenues that he could have explored on examination-in-chief), but to clear up ambiguities that may have arisen as a result of the examination-in-chief, or to attempt to counter any attack on the trust-worthiness of that witness that may have been made on the cross-examination. This is known as rehabilitating the witness. As we have already seen, a party calling a witness may not, in examination-in-chief, ask that witness any question that tends to show that he is a *more* credible witness because, *at that stage*, such a question is irrelevant. But, if the credibility of that witness has been *attacked* in cross-examination, then credibility *is* relevant and, hence, where a witness's credibility has been attacked on cross-examination, that witness's credibility may be supported on re-examination. If, for example, on cross-examination he has been asked about his previous convictions, he may, on re-examination, be asked about how good a citizen he has been since he got out of prison and so on.

The Adverse Witness

It sometimes happens that when a party calling his own witness asks him a question on examination-in-chief, he receives an answer he does not expect. This may range from the witness saying "I do not remember," to his giving an answer that is the complete opposite of what would help that side. Such a witness is not, whatever happens next, going to be a very satisfactory witness and, if his testimony is not very important, probably the best thing to do would be to stop questioning and obtain the substance of his testimony from other witnesses. But, if the party really needs his evidence, he may have no option but to try other measures.

In the case of the forgetful witness, it is always permissible to try to jog his memory, but one must remember the rule against asking leading questions on examination-in-chief. Thus, counsel might try rephrasing the question as a first step, but if this fails, he may try drawing his attention to statements he made before or to notes he may have taken. If, as a result of this, the witness's memory is jogged, then, of course, his evidence is receivable. Indeed, sometimes, it is unreasonable to expect a witness to remember details of events without referring to notes or records. This is quite permissible, though if the witness is merely reciting notes he has made in the past, rather than having his present memory jogged, it will have to be shown that these notes represent an accurate record of the events made by the witness at a time when they were fresh in his memory.

Even the witness who gives a totally contradictory reply to the one expected may be honest but forgetful and one should not jump to the conclusion that he is dishonest and antagonistic. It is, again, quite permissible, within the limits of the rule relating to leading questions, to attempt to get that witness to change his testimony to that expected (though the trustworthiness of such a witness is still somewhat dubious). This may be done by reminding him of what he said earlier or by rephrasing the question and so on.

If this fails and his expected testimony is really important, it might be necessary to take more drastic steps. If the witness demonstrates by what he says, and by the way he says it, that he is deliberately tailoring his testimony with a view to sabotaging the case for the party calling him, that party may ask the court to declare the witness hostile. If this occurs, then the party calling him has all the rights of a cross-examiner and is no longer limited to examining him in chief — in particular, of course, he now has the right to ask leading questions.

Nevertheless, it takes an extremely recalcitrant witness to be declared hostile. The trial judge has to be satisfied that such a witness is so antagonistic towards the party calling him that he would have scant regard for the truth in his efforts to see that party defeated. Most witnesses really do not demonstrate that degree of antagonism. Rather, they politely and almost apologetically give replies that are contrary to the interests of the party calling them without, by their demeanour, indicating that they hope that side will lose even to the point of lying. Such witnesses are not considered hostile and there is nothing that side can do about it short of contradicting them by other witnesses and hoping that not too much damage has been done — except in one case. The case in exception is where that witness has previously made a statement favourable to that side's case on the strength of which he has been called, only to find that he has changed his story by the time he gets on the witness stand. Here, that side is taken completely by surprise and it is not unfair to permit that side to do something about it.

What can be done is to ask the court to declare that witness "adverse." The court, in the absence of any jury, will look at the previous statement[2] and compare it with what the witness has just said, and if it finds that it is contradictory, it will conduct a hearing as to how the two divergent statements came to be made and why. If it is satisfied that all this shows the witness to be contrary in interest to that of the party calling him, the jury is called back and then that side is allowed to prove that the previous statement was made by the witness. Of course, this is not terribly helpful since the jury now knows that the witness said one thing on one occasion and a different thing on a previous occasion and is not likely to believe him very much anyway, but at least counsel has succeeded in undoing the harm the witness caused by the answer to his original question.

Occasionally, on re-examination, the party calling that witness will be allowed to explore a new issue which did not arise as a result of cross-examination because the subject matter was not foreseen or arose suddenly. In such cases, the opposing side must also be given permission to cross-examine on that issue as well. Sometimes, it will be necessary to recall a witness to explain some matter that has arisen as a result of the testimony of other witnesses.

Most of the evidence we see nowadays takes the form of oral testimony of witnesses, but there are other forms of testimony. Sometimes it can take the form of documents or records; often it may consist of objects such as the murder weapon or the narcotic drugs involved. These are admissible so long as their authenticity is proved — that is, so long as someone testifies that this weapon was the one found or that these drugs were those found on the accused. Another possibility is that the evidence may take the form of charts or diagrams or even demonstrations in the courtroom, or where that is not possible, by having the trier of fact going to the scene of the event in question and viewing it for himself.

---

2 If it is written, or reduced to writing. If it is only an oral statement, it will have to be proved by the person to whom the statement is alleged to have been made.

Ensuring Attendance of Witness

The procedure for ensuring that witnesses appear at the proper court at the proper time is fairly simple. Before the trial commences, both sides will have interviewed all the potential witnesses and will have decided which of them they wish to call. Each side then asks that an order (known as a subpoena[3] — i.e., "under penalty") be issued requiring that person to attend as a witness and, if it is required, to bring with him whatever he must produce in court, such as relevant documents or objects. In the vast majority of cases, that is all that is required and the witness will attend as required, though it is possible to order the arrest of a prospective witness if the court finds that he is evading service of the subpoena or he will not attend as required. Similarly, where he has been served with a subpoena, but has failed to show up or where, after having shown up, he later absconds, a warrant may also be issued for his arrest to compel his appearance.

If a witness does appear, but then refuses to be sworn as a witness or, having been sworn, refuses to answer the questions put to him, he is guilty of contempt of court and is liable to be punished under the general contempt powers of the court, or under particular sections of the Code dealing with specific types of proceedings. In fact, contempt of this nature is a serious offence and the punishment is likely to be severe.

Adjudication

The sum total of all of this evidence — by witnesses for both sides, all the documents or objects introduced and so on — constitutes the data from which the trier of fact will be required to draw his inferences. Defence counsel will then normally address the jury asking the trier of fact to give more credence to his side's view of the facts and to draw those inferences favourable to him. He will discuss the defence evidence and outline the case for the defence. The prosecutor will also address the jury, stress the evidence favourable to him and ask the trier of fact to draw inferences of guilt and try to minimize the case for the defence.

If there is no jury trial, the judge will then consider his verdict. If there is a jury, it is unreasonable to expect them, faced with a mass of conflicting evidence and possible inferences, and faced with the problem of reaching a verdict consistent with those inferences, to consider the matter without assistance. The trial judge will sum up for them, reviewing the evidence for the prosecution and discussing the theory of the prosecution, then reviewing the defence evidence and the theory of the defence. He will then instruct them on what the applicable law is and tell them that if they find certain facts, they will reach one decision and if they find

---

3 In some jurisdictions, the more modern term "summons" is used.

other facts, they will reach a different decision. Only then will he ask them to retire to consider their verdict.

12

Proof of Guilt

The course of the trial basically follows the route of the case for the prosecution, the case for the defence, the summing up and instructions to the jury, if there is one, and the consideration of the verdict. As we know, the burden on the prosecution is to prove the guilt of the accused beyond any reasonable doubt and that means essentially to prove all the necessary acts and all the necessary mental elements. If the jury or other fact-finder is, at the end of the case, left in any reasonable doubt as to one of the necessary items then they have to acquit — not because they are satisfied that the accused is "innocent," but because they are not satisfied that he is guilty.

As can be seen, if at the end of the case for the prosecution its case against the accused is so weak that no jury (or the judge where there is no jury) could possibly be satisfied beyond any reasonable doubt that the accused is guilty, there is no point in the defence putting in any evidence at all since the accused cannot be convicted anyway. If the course of the trial could be separated into neat self-contained packages of case for the prosecution and case for the defence, this would be obvious and cause no difficulty. But, in fact, the packages are not that neat. During the presentation of the case for the prosecution, its witnesses will be cross-examined by the defence, not only to weaken the effect of their testimony for the prosecution, but also to adduce testimony for the defence; similarly, during the presentation of the case for the defence, the prosecution will cross-examine both to weaken the effect of the defence testimony and also to bring out further evidence that supports the prosecution. The jury must reach its conclusion on the *totality* of the evidence, so one may well have a situation where the case against the accused is actually stronger at the close of the case for the defence than it was at the close of the case for the prosecution. This means that defence counsel may, in some cases, have a difficult choice to make — whether or not to call any evidence at all and risk a finding of Guilty,[1] or to proceed to put in a defence and risk making matters worse.

MOTION TO DISMISS

One way to avoid having to make such a decision is to make a motion to dismiss — as it is put where there is no jury — or to move for a directed verdict — as it is usually put when there is a jury. (Nothing turns on the different terminology since the effect is the same.)

If, at the close of the case for the prosecution, there is simply no possibility, as the evidence stands at that point, that a jury or other fact-finder *could* convict, then there is "no case to answer" since the accused must only answer (or risk conviction) when a sufficient case has been made out against him calling for some defence. But the defence argument must be that a jury *could* not convict, not that it probably will not convict. The former is a legal argument — that in law the evidence is insufficient to support a conviction. The latter is a factual argument — that, while in law, the evidence is sufficient, in fact no reasonable jury would be satisfied beyond any reasonable doubt. The rule is that if the prosecution does not, in law, adduce sufficient evidence for a reasonable jury to be able to convict by the time it closes the case for the prosecution, then the case will be dismissed and the defence will not be required to put in any defence evidence. If there is a jury, it is instructed to return a verdict of Not Guilty; if there is no jury, the judge himself will simply find the accused Not Guilty or dismiss the information.

If the motion is not granted, the trial judge is not saying that the accused *will* be convicted — rather, it is only that the accused is now at risk of being convicted. The defence will be called upon to make the decision as to whether to refrain from calling any evidence in the hope that, while the jury *may* convict, in fact, they will not be satisfied beyond any reasonable doubt and so will acquit or whether to put in defence evidence in the hope that it will increase the likelihood of an acquittal, but realizing that

---

1 One benefit arising from this course of action is that it entitles defence counsel to address the jury after the prosecutor. Normally, the defence counsel must go first and the prosecutor has the last word (except for the judge's instructions). This can be a considerable tactical advantage.

the tactics may backfire and, in effect, end up strengthening the case for the prosecution.

The motion to dismiss, while often made, is not often granted. Clearly it would mean poor preparation or poor presentation on the part of the prosecutor to have got to the stage of a trial without even having a sufficient case against the accused to pass this hurdle. It can, and does arise where, for instance, the prosecution assumes that a vital piece of evidence (such as a confession) is admissible against the accused, only to find that it is excluded, or where the prosecution has brought the wrong charge against the accused and that cannot be remedied by an amendment to the indictment or information. It can also arise where the prosecution, through an oversight, has omitted to prove one of the essential elements of the offence.

In this last case, however, even though the case for the prosecution has been closed, the trial judge has the discretion to permit the prosecution to reopen its case where to do so would cause no undue prejudice or hardship to the accused. If, for example, the accused is charged with the breach of a municipal by-law, the prosecutor may forget that by-laws of this nature have to be proved in evidence and fail to do so. At the close of the case for the prosecution, the defence may move for a dismissal on the ground that, since the relevant by-law has not been proved, there is no case to answer. This is true, but it would not be unfair (in the sense of putting him at a tactical disadvantage) to the accused, to allow the prosecution to remedy the oversight and the judge may allow him to do so. This right is discretionary on the part of the trial judge, so sometimes, even in these cases, this manoeuvre will be successful for the defence if the judge feels that the prosecution does not deserve the chance to reopen its case.

PRESUMPTIONS

The prosecution must, as we have seen, prove beyond any reasonable doubt, both the necessary act and the necessary mental element and it will do so by calling evidence in proof of them. Acts may be proved by eyewitnesses, by factual objects or by circumstantial evidence from which the act can be inferred. It might be objected that while acts are not too difficult to prove from the presentation of objective facts, no one can ever prove what was in the accused's mind — for example, whether the accused meant to cause death or whether he recklessly disregarded a consequence that he foresaw. However, this is not necessarily so. A mental element can be proved from objective facts in the same way that an act can be proved. For example, if a person is seen to pick up a loaded revolver, take careful aim at the victim and pull the trigger, it is not difficult to infer that he intended to kill the victim or, at the very least, to cause him serious bodily harm. If a person drives down a crowded main street at 90 m.p.h., it is not difficult to infer that he must have realized that he would likely kill or injure someone and was deliberately closing his mind to those consequences.

In other words, proof of what went on in the accused's mind is effected by exactly the same sort of inference-drawing process as is proof of what the accused *did*. It is more susceptible to dispute, of course, and hence more susceptible to the jury not being satisfied beyond any reasonable doubt that it existed, but the process is the same.

There are, however, cases where it would be difficult for the fact-finder to draw the inference of some necessary element from the data which would normally be available to the prosecution unless he had some assistance. In other words, in such cases, it would be difficult, if not impossible, for a prosecution normally to succeed. Of course, the accused may always admit that the necessary element was present, but in most cases, given that there is the high burden on the prosecution of proof beyond any reasonable doubt, a conviction would be unlikely. For example, the accused is found in possession of a stolen television set. It is an offence to be found in possession of stolen property, but only if the accused knew that it was stolen. In the absence of any other evidence or technique, it would be difficult to infer the requisite knowledge merely from possession. Or, to take another case, the accused breaks and enters a dwelling house. One might think that there is no difficulty in convicting him of the offence of break and enter, but that is only a criminal offence if the accused broke and entered with intent to commit an indictable offence therein.[2] How can the prosecution prove that he had that intent beyond any reasonable doubt?

There are many such offences and the way the problem is resolved is to enlist the assistance of what are called presumptions. A presumption states that if the prosecution proves beyond any reasonable doubt the required basic facts, then the trier of fact *must* draw the requisite inference, unless the *accused* demonstrates why that inference should not be drawn (or, as it is said, unless the accused rebuts the presumption).

There is a difference between a permissible inference and a presumption. In our two examples, for instance, if the prosecution proves that the television set was stolen and that it was stolen recently, then upon proof that the accused was found in possession of it, the jury (or judge, if there is no jury) may — not must — find that the accused knew it was stolen. This is a permissible inference from those facts, but it is not a required inference. Whether that inference will be drawn depends upon all the other evidence. On the other hand, in the break and enter case, the Code provides

---

2 Actually, the offence is somewhat broader than this, but this partial definition illustrates the point.

that proof that the accused broke and entered is, in itself, proof that he intended to commit an indictable offence therein, unless there is evidence to the contrary.[3] In this case, in the absence of evidence to the contrary, the inference of intent *must* be drawn.

There are many of these presumptions in the criminal law, some more drastic than others, but they all have the feature that, given proof of the basic fact or facts, the accused *will* be convicted unless he does something about it. What he must do in order to avoid having the inference drawn depends upon what the law or the particular section in question requires him to do so as to "rebut the presumption." In the case of break and enter, there must be evidence that he did not intend to commit an indictable offence (usually this will have to come from the accused himself, but not necessarily). Once the accused has done what is required of him he is said to have rebutted the presumption, but this does not *necessarily* mean that he will be acquitted. It is true that the presumption has gone so that the trier of fact no longer *must* draw the guilty inference, but if, at the end of the whole case, he is still satisfied beyond any reasonable doubt that the guilty inference *should* be drawn, then he will convict. Rebutting the presumption merely erases the presumption and the mandatory drawing of the guilty inference; it does not erase the discretionary drawing of the guilty inference where, on the totality of the evidence, there is proof beyond any reasonable doubt. Indeed, the explanation of the accused may be so ludicrous that it actually enhances the case for the prosecution. If the accused says he broke and entered a dwelling house on a bright sunny day in order to get out of the rain, it would not need any presumption for the jury to convict.

Onus-Shifting Presumption

A totally different presumption, and fortunately less common, is an onus-shifting presumption. It is an offence to obtain goods by means of a representation that is known to be false at the time it was made. A common false pretence is to give a worthless cheque — that is, a cheque that a person knows will bounce. But how does the prosecution prove that the accused knew the cheque would bounce when he will probably say that he thought he had sufficient funds in his account? The Code[4] provides that where the prosecution proves that the goods were obtained by means of a cheque that, if presented for payment within a reasonable time, was dishonoured on the ground that insufficient funds were in the accused's account, then a false pretence shall be presumed (that is, the requisite knowledge shall be presumed) unless the court is satisfied by evidence

---

3 Criminal Code, s. 348.
4 Section 362.

that the accused had reasonable grounds to believe that it would be honoured.

Or, to take another case, it is an offence to be in the care and control of a motor vehicle while one's ability to drive is impaired. Not uncommonly, a drunk person is found slumped over the steering wheel of a car, but he says he merely got in "to sleep it off." It is very difficult to prove that he was "in care or control of the vehicle." The Code, however, provides that where it is proved that the accused was in the driver's seat, he shall be presumed to have had care or control of the car unless he establishes that he did not enter the car for the purposes of setting it in motion.

There is a fundamental difference between these types of presumptions and those that we previously discussed. In these cases, the presumption is *not* rebutted unless the court is "satisfied" as to the opposite in the case of the worthless cheque or unless the accused "establishes" the opposite in the case of the drunk driver. These are called onus-shifting presumptions because they do more than merely require the accused to give a reasonable explanation or introduce some evidence to the contrary — they require him to prove the opposite. Where the onus of proof is on an accused in such cases, the degree of proof required of him is not proof beyond any reasonable doubt, but merely proof on the balance of probabilities. This only requires him to introduce enough evidence to make it more likely than not that his version is the correct one. Nevertheless, it does put an onus of proof on to the accused which it may be difficult for him to discharge.

It will immediately be seen that an onus-shifting presumption may be of dubious constitutional validity given section 11(*d*) of the Charter (the right to be presumed innocent) or section 7 (the right not to be deprived of liberty save in accordance with the principles of natural justice). If the Code sets out an offence in terms of the forbidden act and the forbidden intent or other mental element, but then provides that the only thing the Crown has to prove is the act, whereupon the intent will be presumed unless the accused proves that he did not have the intent, far from presuming the innocence of the accused, one is, in fact, presuming his guilt from mere proof of the act. It is therefore of critical importance to determine whether the provision is one that merely requires the accused to introduce some evidence to rebut the presumption or whether it is one that requires the accused to establish something in order to be acquitted.

If the provision creates a true onus-shifting presumption, it violates the Charter and is of no force and effect unless it can be saved by recourse to section 1.[5] If, on the other hand, the presumption merely requires the accused to introduce or point to some evidence to the contrary and if the presumption is one that can be rationally and logically drawn, then it does not violate the presumption of innocence.[6] But even if it does violate the Charter, it may still be upheld if it comes within section 1 of the Charter and constitutes a reasonable limit demonstrably justifiable in a free and democratic society. *Oakes*[7] held that in order to satisfy section 1, two central criteria must be met: first, the objectives sought to be met by the provision must be of sufficient importance to warrant overriding a constitutionally protected right and, second, the means chosen must be reasonable and demonstrably justified. In order to meet the second criterion, some form of proportionality test must be applied in which there are three elements. These are that the measure must be carefully designed to achieve the object in question; it must not be arbitrary, unfair or irrational; it must impair the right or freedom in question as little as reasonably possible in order to achieve the objective; and, lastly, there must be a proportionality between the *effects* of the measure and the objective in question. These are not easy criteria to apply and it is not surprising that there may be differences of opinion as to whether particular provisions satisfy them or not.

DEFENCES

Apart from these presumptions, the only burden of proof on the accused when defending a case, arises when he raises mental incompetence as a defence. (Since this issue involves a number of complications, it will be examined in a separate chapter.) In the case of any other defence, there is no burden on the accused. Rather, the burden is on the prosecution throughout to prove the guilt of the accused. As we have seen, "guilt" means proof of the requisite elements of the offence — that is, proof that the accused committed the act and proof that he had the requisite intent or other criminal state of mind. The theory of the defence, may, however, be a denial that one of the requisite elements was present because of some additional factor — that, for example, the accused did not intend to kill

---

5 *R. v. Keegstra*, [1990] 3 S.C.R. 697, 1 C.R. (4th) 129, [1991] 2 W.W.R. 1, 77 Alta. L.R. (2d) 193, 61 C.C.C. (3d) 1, 114 A.R. 81, 3 C.R.R. (2d) 193. It is not entirely clear whether the same holds true for "regulatory" offences as well as crimes in the "true" sense of the word, but the weight of authority supports the view that it should make no difference whether the accused is charged with, say, a Criminal Code offence or merely with some provincial regulatory offence — in either case, he is entitled to be presumed innocent. See *R. v. Wholesale Travel Group Inc.*, [1991] 3 S.C.R. 154, 4 O.R. (3d) 799 (note), 8 C.R. (4th) 145, 67 C.C.C. (3d) 193, 84 D.L.R. (4th) 161, 38 C.P.R. (3d) 451, 130 N.R. 1 for some differences of opinion.

6 *R. v. Oakes*, [1986] 1 S.C.R. 103, 53 O.R. (2d) 719 (headnote only), 50 C.R. (3d) 1, 24 C.C.C. (3d) 321, 19 C.R.R. 308, 26 D.L.R. (4th) 200, 14 O.A.C. 335, 65 N.R. 87.

7 *Ibid.*

because he was drunk at the time, or that he did not consciously strike the victim because he was in a state of shock when it happened. Or the theory of the defence may be that he admits the basic elements of the offence, but is raising a defence in spite of those elements — for example, he may admit that he killed the victim, and that he intended to kill him, but only in self-defence. Or that he was in a rage that was provoked by the wrongful act of the victim. Or he may admit that he stole property, but argue that he was under duress or compulsion at the time.

In these cases, one might well ask whether there is not some burden on the accused when he raises these issues and the answer is that indeed there is, but it is not a burden to *prove* these issues. The jury, or other fact-finder, is clearly the trier of fact — that is, they or she must infer what facts are to be found — but she is only the trier of those facts that are in issue. If there is no issue then there is no fact to be found. But a fact is only in issue if it is in dispute, and it can only be in dispute if there is some evidence that could support a finding one way or the other. When an accused pleads Not Guilty, he puts in issue all the facts necessary to support a conviction and this is why the burden is on the prosecution to prove all of the requisite elements. But *absence* of drunkenness or automatism, or self-defence, or provocation or duress is not one of the requisite elements of an offence — *unless the accused makes its presence one of the issues.* But he can only make it one of the issues by introducing sufficient evidence of its existence to make its presence a possible inference from the data.

When, therefore, the defence is dependent upon the finding of a fact to explain why the inference of guilt should not be drawn, there is what is called an evidentiary burden on the accused — not a burden of proving the facts upon which his defence rests, but a burden of introducing enough evidence which would make those facts a possible inference. Once he has done that, then there is a burden on the prosecution to prove beyond any reasonable doubt that they did *not* exist. Suppose, for example, that the accused is charged with murder and his defence is one of self-defence. At the commencement of the case, there is no initial onus on the prosecution to prove that there was no self-defence. If nothing is said about self-defence during the trial and in his address to the jury, the counsel for the defence suddenly mentions to them that the homicide might have resulted from self-defence, the trial judge will not even leave with the jury the possibility of acquitting on the ground of self-defence, since there is no evidence that could possibly support such a finding. If, however, during the course of the trial, prosecution witnesses were asked in cross-examination whether it is not true that the victim first attacked the accused or the accused gives evidence that he was attacked first and feared for his life, then the issue is supported by some evidence and the jury will be told to acquit unless they are satisfied, beyond any reasonable doubt, that the accused did not act within the rules relating to self-defence. The important factor is that if the jury has any reasonable doubt as to whether it was self-defence or not, they must *acquit* — not because they are satisfied that the accused was properly defending himself, but because they are not satisfied that he was *not* properly defending himself.

This burden of adducing evidence is only placed on the accused if the defence he is raising is dependent upon the establishing of additional facts. If the defence is merely a denial of the allegations sought to be proved by the prosecution, then, of course, there is no burden whatsoever on the accused because there is nothing for him to raise as an issue beyond denying the allegations against him. Thus, if his defence is that he was not the person who shot the deceased or that the shooting was accidental and not intended, then his very plea of Not Guilty immediately imposes upon the prosecution the burden of proving whatever is disputed.

There is, however, a complication. Some sections of the Code, and other statutes imposing criminal penalties, may purport to require the accused to "establish" a defence — common phrases are things like "without lawful justification or excuse, the proof of which lies upon him," or "unless he establishes" something. It was formerly argued that while a presumption that relieved the Crown of the burden of proving one of the constituent elements of an offence unless the accused disproved it violated the Charter, a provision that required the accused to prove a defence that did not constitute merely a denial of one of the constituent elements did not violate the presumption of innocence since it merely provided for proof of a positive defence. This argument has been decisively rejected by the Supreme Court.[8] The crux of the presumption of innocence is that no person should be convicted if the jury has any doubt about that person's guilt. It does not really matter whether that doubt arises because the jury has doubt about an element of the offence or about something that would constitute a defence. Any provision that requires the accused to establish or prove something that would, if so proved, constitute a defence means that if the jury is in doubt about its existence, the accused has *not* proved or established it and therefore requires the jury to convict. All such provisions, therefore, violate the Charter and are of no force and effect unless they meet the *Oakes* criteria of being saved under section 1.[9]

---

8 *R. v. Whyte*, [1988] 2 S.C.R. 3, 64 C.R. (3d) 123, [1988] 5 W.W.R. 26, 29 B.C.L.R. (2d) 273, 6 M.V.R. (2d) 138, 42 C.C.C. (3d) 97, 51 D.L.R. (4th) 481, 35 C.R.R. 1, 86 N.R. 328; and *R. v. Keegstra, supra,* note 5.

9 In *R. v. Schwartz*, [1988] 2 S.C.R. 443, 66 C.R. (3d) 251, [1989] 1 W.W.R. 289, 56 Man. R. (2d) 92, 45 C.C.C. (3d) 97, 55 D.L.R. (4th) 1, 34 C.R.R. 260, the Supreme Court, by a majority of 4:2, held that a provision requiring the accused to prove that he was the holder of a valid permit to carry firearms did not violate the Charter since, once the accused produced the permit, that was a conclusive defence. The case is difficult to reconcile with other authorities.

This leads to the final possibility, which is that Parliament could simply circumvent all these difficulties simply by removing any of these elements or defences from the offence, but that avenue, too, has been closed off by the Supreme Court by ruling that section 7 and the concept of fundamental justice necessarily imports certain minimal requirements of mental element, at least for the more serious offences, based upon some concept of moral blameworthiness that cannot be removed by Parliament[10] and by ruling that matters that would operate as valid defences cannot be removed either,[11] unless, of course, section 1 can be invoked.

PRESENCE OF ACCUSED

In addition to the presumption of innocence and all that it entails, the Charter requires that the trial itself be by way of a "fair and public hearing." "Fairness" is not a very specific concept that can easily be articulated. It has meaning only within the history and background of our common law traditions, chief of which may be the right of the accused to make full answer and defence, part of that being, as we have seen, the right to confront and cross-examine prosecution witnesses and to call his own witnesses. This may, in turn, demand the presence of the accused person throughout the trial, lest things go on in his absence that he is not given the opportunity to meet. But whether the *right* of the accused to be present is to be translated into a *requirement* that he be present may be doubted. In summary conviction proceedings an accused may be tried in his absence if, after having been given due notice of the proceeding, he fails to appear and, in prosecutions for provincial offences, the accused is very often tried in his absence.

In the case of indictable offences, generally speaking, the presence of the accused is not only a right, but also a prerequisite to jurisdiction to try him. Fears of secret trials and star chamber proceedings may have coloured our views on the necessity for the presence of the accused, but even this prerequisite is not absolute. An accused may be removed during his trial if he disrupts proceedings or if, on the trial of the issue of whether he is, on account of mental incompetence, unfit to stand trial, his presence would have an adverse effect on his mental health.[12] He may even be given permission by the court to be absent if he demonstrates a reasonable and proper cause for his absence. Finally, once the court does have jurisdiction over the accused by the fact that he was present at the start

---

10 *R. v. Vaillancourt*, [1987] 2 S.C.R. 636, 60 C.R. (3d) 289, 39 C.C.C. (3d) 118, 68 Nfld. & P.E.I.R. 281, 209 A.P.R. 281, 10 Q.A.C. 101, 47 D.L.R. (4th) 399, 32 C.R.R. 18, 81 N.R. 115, was the first case but several subsequent decisions have developed and refined this principle.

11 *Wholesale Travel Group Inc., supra*, note 5.

12 Section 650.

of the trial, jurisdiction is not lost if the accused absconds *during* the trial. The trial may proceed in his absence and convict him and pass sentence.[13]

---

13 Section 475.

13

Interrogation and Confessions

We must now look at some aspects of the case for the prosecution that need further examination and one that is particularly difficult is the question of the admissibility of any confession that the accused may have made.

The concept of the "suspect" is not known to law, though it is very popular in everyday usage. In law, a person is either someone in respect of whom there are no reasonable or probable grounds to believe that he has committed an offence (and hence not believed to be guilty), or someone who is reasonably and probably believed to have committed an offence (and hence who is subject to arrest or to having an information laid against him or other proceedings taken). Yet in practice, it is difficult to deny that there is also the person in between — the person who one believes may well have committed the offence, but in respect of whom this belief has not yet hardened into reasonable and probable grounds. He is what one might call a "suspect."

INTERROGATION

A suspect is not liable to arrest, but he, along with everyone else, is liable to be questioned by police during their investigations. Like everyone else, he is, of course, not required to answer any questions, but that does not mean that he may not be asked them; he, like everyone else, may be asked to come to the police station to assist the police in their inquiries; and he, like everyone else, may refuse the invitation, but he may still be invited.

Questions and invitations may have different appearances of persuasion and may be differently perceived by different people. While the responses to neither the questions nor the invitation can be compelled, they may be, and frequently are, given. Most people do cooperate with the police and even a guilty person may feel that he has more to gain by appearing to cooperate than by not cooperating. He may feel that his ability to lie or conceal facts may outweigh the ability of the police to discover the truth.

The first type of person, therefore, who may be subject to interrogation is the "suspect," the reason being that by these means he may be raised from the level of suspect to the level of the person in respect of whom there are now reasonable and probable grounds.

But there are other reasons why the police may seek to question a person. For one, they may already have reasonable and probable grounds against him sufficient to justify his arrest and to justify charging him. As we have seen, however, actually bringing the accused to trial is warranted only when there is admissible evidence against him sufficient, at least, to make a conviction reasonable. What may justify the police in their reasonable and probable grounds may not necessarily be admissible in a court of law. They may, for example, rely upon the evidence of the accused's wife, although she will not be a competent witness in his actual prosecution (save in exceptional circumstances); they may rely upon hearsay evidence or on privileged communications and so on. The second reason may, therefore, be in order to secure evidence against a person who is already arrested and charged, but in respect of whom a successful prosecution in the absence of such evidence, is unlikely.

A third reason may be to determine whether the accused had any accomplices who should also be charged. It may be that while the police know that he did have accomplices, they do not know their names or their whereabouts or their degree of participation in the offence.

Fourthly, even if there is enough evidence to convict the accused, the police may not know the location of, for example, the stolen property or proceeds of an offence. While convicting an accused may be the main objective of a prosecution, the recovery of property or other means of minimizing the harm caused is also desirable.

The fifth reason may be to determine whether the accused has been involved in offences other than the one with which he has been charged. When an accused has been arrested and is in custody charged with an indictable offence (but not a summary conviction offence) he is required to submit to being photographed and fingerprinted. This enables the police not only to check the identity of the accused, it also enables them, by means of telex apparatus, to check on his previous record, on any outstanding warrants against him and on whether he is suspected of other offences.[1] It may well be, that as a result of these inquiries, the police will wish to question the accused not only about the offence for which he has been charged but also about any other offences of which he may be suspected.

The last reason for questioning is perhaps the most common and understandable of all and that is the perfectly human tendency to want to be certain that one has the right person. An admissible confession bolsters the case for the prosecution, of course, but any confession which is believed by the person to whom it is made, whether legally admissible or not, reassures the police officer, in his own mind at any rate, that he has the right suspect. A police officer has no desire to accuse the wrong person and any lingering doubts he has may be resolved if the person arrested admits to committing the offence.

Whatever the reason, people are questioned. It is perfectly true that, as a general proposition, no one is compelled to reply and that silence, in the face of police questioning, is no evidence of guilt. Actually, there are a number of cases where an obligation to reply or to make a statement is imposed by statute, but they are of specific and limited application. For example, a person in control of a motor vehicle that is involved in an accident is required to give his name and address and, under several provincial statutes, must also give a statement regarding the circumstances of the accident. But the proposition that one is entitled to remain silent is generally true. It follows, that if one has the right to remain silent, then no adverse inference in law may be drawn from the exercise of that right, though whether, from a tactical point of view it is always advisable to exercise the right in this manner will depend upon the circumstances involved.

Remaining silent, however, is not the same as positively lying. If one does reply to a question from the police in a manner that can be proved from external objective circumstances to have been false, the fact of the lie may be evidence of what is called consciousness of guilt. Consciousness of guilt depends upon a deliberate falsehood designed to mislead the police

---

1 To digress slightly, the Identification of Criminals Act, which permits the photographing and fingerprinting of persons only applies where an accused is in custody charged with an indictable offence. This causes no difficulty if the accused is arrested and taken to a police station, but if an appearance notice or some other non-custodial pre-trial release mechanism has been employed, the accused is not in custody and therefore could not be fingerprinted or photographed. To meet this problem, the summons, appearance notice or promise to appear may also contain a provision requiring the accused to appear at a specified time and place for the purpose of being fingerprinted and photographed. Failure to appear as required is a criminal offence (if the process has been confirmed by a justice) but is, in any case, grounds for cancelling the pre-trial release mechanism and for issuing a warrant for the arrest of the accused.

— one may tell a lie unknowingly or forgetfully, or one may lie out of embarrassment or shame at the accusation. It is only if the jury or other fact-finder is satisfied that circumstances indicate that the lie shows a consciousness of guilt that he may so use it. If there is, or might be, some other reasonable explanation for the falsehood, then it is not evidence pointing towards guilt.

STATEMENTS

Exculpatory or Incriminating

When the suspect does reply to a question from the police or makes a statement to the police, what he says may be exculpatory — that is, tending to exonerate him from the offence. It may, on the other hand, be incriminating — that is, tending to involve him in the offence. If the statement (or reply) is totally exculpatory, both as to the content of the statement and as to the circumstances under which it was made, then clearly it will be of no use to the prosecution and the prosecutor will not seek to put it in evidence against the accused. If the prosecutor chooses not to put the statement in for that reason, then it is of crucial importance to understand that the accused *cannot put it in evidence for the defence.* One has a very clear, if one-sided and perhaps unsatisfactory, rule that if the statement is useful to the prosecution, the prosecutor may, subject to the rules we shall discuss, put that in as evidence *against* the accused, but if it is useful to the defence, then the accused *cannot* put that in as evidence in his favour.[2] The reason is that where it is beneficial to the accused, who is himself making the statement, its evidentiary value is minimal since it is self-serving evidence manufactured by the accused and adds nothing to what he could say on the witness stand. But if the accused says something that is *against* his interest, then it clearly is not self-serving and does have additional evidentiary value as part of the case for the prosecution.

Yet even an exculpatory statement may have incriminating ramifications. For one thing, as we have seen, if it can be proved to be a lie, then it may be admissible, not to prove that what was said was true (which it has been proved not to be), but to prove that it was a lie. The reasoning is that innocent people do not lie to the police, therefore the accused was showing that he was guilty by lying to the police.

Furthermore, the exculpatory statement may turn out to be inconsistent with other statements that the accused makes or be inconsistent with the story that he subsequently tells on the witness stand. When a person is

---

2 Under some limited circumstances, an accused may show that he did make an exculpatory statement to the police where it rebuts a prosecution allegation that the story he is telling on the witness stand is of recent fabrication.

questioned immediately after an offence has been committed, there may be a tendency, particularly if that person is, in fact, guilty, to say the first thing that comes into his head that will tend to exonerate him — it tends to be an immediate denial with a factual statement supporting that denial. After further police investigation (by which time the accused may have counsel to advise him), it becomes obvious that some of the facts he formerly told the police cannot possibly be true, so he changes his story to fit the new facts. Indeed, there may be further investigation and further changes.

One now has an accused person who has made two or more different and inconsistent statements on different occasions. Not uncommonly, the first statement is the one made to the police during the investigation and the second is the one made at trial when the accused is on the witness stand. One does not know which, if either, of those statements is true, but one does know that, in the absence of some explanation for the discrepancy, one is dealing with a person who cannot be believed — he either lied the first time or the second time, or on both occasions. The credibility of such a witness is considerably diminished and the jury is less likely to believe anything he says at the trial. Thus, what superficially appears to be an exculpatory statement can, in these circumstances, be an extremely useful weapon in the hands of the prosecutor, not as evidence relating directly to guilt, but as evidence attacking the credibility of the accused should be choose to testify.

In the result, while the prosecutor may wish to use statements that are clearly incriminating, he may also wish to use even those statements that appear to be exculpatory, but, because of the circumstances, are more useful to the prosecution than to the defence.

Very often, statements made by an accused are not as clearly divisible as being exculpatory or incriminating. Instead, they tend to be rather long rambling statements that contain elements that help the prosecution and elements that help the defence. In these circumstances, the prosecution must decide whether, on balance, it has more to gain by putting in the statement for its incriminating elements and letting the jury hear the exculpatory elements as well, or more to gain by choosing not to put in the statement at all, because the one fundamental thing the prosecution *cannot* do is edit the statement so that it only puts in the incriminating elements, but keeps out the exculpatory ones. If a statement goes in, then all of it must go in.

The reason for this is simple. If the statement were edited, the jury may end up with quite the wrong impression of what was said. If a person says "I killed him but it was in self-defence," it would clearly be totally unfair to tell the jury that he said "I killed him" without also telling them about the self-defence. So where the prosecutor decides to put in the statement, everything the accused says must be put before the jury.

In the same way, it often happens that what we call a "statement" is, in fact, a series of statements or a mixture of replies to questions and statements, sometimes spread over the course of several hours, days or even weeks. If this series is so connected that it can fairly be considered as part and parcel of one statement, then the whole series must be put in, if the prosecutor decides to put any of it in. Not only that, but generally speaking, the series should be presented to the jury in the same order as that in which they were made so that no false impression is given. If, however, it can clearly and fairly be said that each statement exists as an independent statement, then the prosecutor is not obliged to put in all of these separate statements, but may choose to put in only one or more of them. The reason for such a rule in the case of a series of statements is not only not to give the jury the wrong impression, but also to ensure that if there is a vitiating element that would render one statement inadmissible, that vitiating element will also carry through so as to make subsequent statements inadmissible, unless there is a clear break between the two statements that will terminate the effect of the vitiating element.

Voir dire

Let us therefore assume that the accused has made a statement to the police, either incriminating or exculpatory, that the prosecution wishes to introduce as part of its case against the accused. A cardinal rule of criminal evidence is that no statement made by an accused to the police[3] is admissible in evidence on behalf of the prosecution unless it is first shown to have been made voluntarily, and unless it was the product of his conscious operating mind.

When the prosecutor proposes to offer in evidence any statement made by the accused to the police, then a hearing, known as a voir dire[4] must be conducted, in the absence of the jury, in order to determine whether these conditions have been met. The hearing is conducted by the trial judge.

If this issue arises during the course of the trial, the prosecutor will ask that the jury withdraw without indicating the reason why he wishes the jury to leave. In practice, it will usually be known before the trial starts that an issue will arise as to the admissibility of a statement, and the voir dire may be held before the trial gets under way so as to obviate the disruption that occurs if the jury is asked to leave during the course of the trial.

The voluntariness of the statement is always in issue and the burden is on the prosecution to prove beyond any reasonable doubt that it was

---

3 The actual rule covers statements made to any "person in authority," which is wider than merely police officers, but there is no need to complicate the problem in this discussion.
4 This is Norman French — a corruption of the Latin *verum dicere*, to tell the truth.

made voluntarily. The accused may admit that it was voluntary or admit the facts that show it was voluntary, but this is merely evidence of the fact that it was voluntary and does not relieve the judge of making the determination. Indeed, there could be a case where, in spite of the admission of the accused, the judge is still not satisfied and he will have to rule the statement inadmissible.

Whether the statement was the product of the conscious operating mind of the accused is, however, not an issue unless there is evidence to indicate that it might be an issue. This may arise from the testimony of the police themselves, or it may arise from the testimony of the accused, but once there is evidence sufficient to raise the issue, then the burden is again on the prosecution to prove that the statement was the product of the conscious operating mind of the accused.

There may often be circumstances where this is not so. An accused may make a statement while he is drunk, or in a state of shock. He could even be under some form of hypnosis or under the influence of medication or drugs. In such cases, he may not be aware of what he is saying or even that he is saying anything. If this is so, it is difficult to call it "his" statement and thus it has no evidentiary value or, if it has some evidentiary value, it may be so slight that its value is outweighed by the opposing prejudicial effect. In these cases, the statement is excluded not because it is not voluntary, but because it cannot be regarded as the statement of the accused.

More frequently, the problem is not whether the statement was the product of the conscious operating mind of the accused, but whether it was "voluntary." In determining this on the voir dire, there is an obligation on the part of the prosecution to call as witnesses all those police officers who were present when the statement was made, unless, or course, a satisfactory reason is given why they are not called. The reason for this rule is that it is rather unfair to expect the accused to have to call them as his own witnesses when, in all probability, they are not going to be favourably disposed towards him, so that it is fairer to require the other side to call them and allow the accused to cross-examine. After the prosecution has called all of its witnesses on the voir dire and they have been cross-examined, the accused may then call his witnesses, though, frequently of course, he will be the only witness who can testify as to what went on during the taking of the statement.

The judge, having heard the evidence, must now determine whether the statement was made voluntarily. This has acquired something of a technical meaning, though, as we shall see in a moment, since the introduction of the Charter of Rights and Freedoms, these technicalities may be less significant than they once were. "Voluntary" means not induced by fear of prejudice or hope of advantage, a definition that has become something of a cliché. Basically, then, a statement is admissible only if the accused made it free from the fear, as a result of the police conduct or statements, that something bad would happen to him if he did not make the statement, or free from the hope that some benefit would accrue to him if he did make the statement. There is not much point in trying to set out the thousands of possible fact situations that might be caught by the rule — they range from the obvious ones of beating or threatening to beat the accused or of threatening to "throw the book at him" if he did not confess or telling him that he would get a lighter sentence or be allowed to see his wife if he did confess, to the less obvious ones such as threatening to deny him bail if he did not confess or promising bail if he did.

The reason given for the requirement of voluntariness was never entirely clear, but was assumed to be based on the fact that the evidentiary value of a confession depends upon the likelihood that it is true. If a person confesses in order to stop being tortured or in order to see his wife and children, it may well be that he makes the confession not because it is true, but because this is the only way to stop the torture or to see his family. It is not surprising that, given the history of judicial torture and the practices of the Inquisition, the common law should have rebelled against the admissibility of "involuntary" confessions in this sense, since only confessions that had some guarantee of being true had any evidentiary value.

But this rationale breaks down when it is applied to statements that are exculpatory yet useful to the prosecution — such as false statements to show consciousness of guilt or to show inconsistency of stories. In those cases, no one cares about the *truth* of the statement. Indeed, their whole evidentiary value lies in the fact that they are *not* true. So the feeling has been creeping into judicial reasoning that perhaps the reason why "involuntary" statements are inadmissible is not because of some fear that they are likely to be untrue, but simply because it is unfair for an accused to be subjected to threats or promises in order to induce him to talk.

If threats or promises are unfair, however, there may be many other things that might be considered equally unfair. Police officers know quite well what the rules regarding the admissibility of confessions are and, by and large, do not beat accused persons or threaten them or hold out promises, knowing quite well that if they do, the confession is going to be kept out anyway.[5] In any case, there are many ways of getting confessions short of brutality or promises. Trickery, in various forms, is

---

5 Of course, if they do not need the confession for evidentiary purposes, the rules of evidence do not matter. For instance, if they already have enough evidence to convict the accused without a confession, they may still want to recover the stolen property or find the names of accomplices. In these cases, it can only be their discipline and training or their own concept of fair play that can prevent abuses — or perhaps the fear of disciplinary action or civil or criminal liability.

often effective. An undercover policeman will be put in the same cell as the accused and boast of his criminal record. The accused, not to be outdone, then tells him about the offence he is charged with, only to find him as the prosecution's star witness at his trial. Or, where there are two accused, they are put in separate rooms and one is told that the other one has pinned all the blame on him, thus spurring the second accused to make a statement admitting guilt, but trying to pin most of the blame on his accomplice. There are many variations of this sort of trickery, but none of them fall within the definition of threats or inducements and are not, therefore, "involuntary" in the classical sense. If there is any objection to them, it is not because they were induced by threats or promises, but because, in some way, they are seen to be "unfair," and this raises the more important issue of the effect of the Charter on all of this.

Confessions and the Charter

The first and prime point to bear in mind is that even if there has been a Charter violation in the obtaining of a confession, section 24(2) does not necessarily exclude it from the trial; that evidence *shall* be excluded but only if it is established that "having regard to all the circumstances, the admission of it in proceedings would bring the administration of justice into disrepute." In fact, of course, since we are dealing with a confession emanating from the accused person himself and since that evidence would almost certainly constitute very strong evidence of guilt, it will almost certainly be excluded,[6] but it is still important to note that exclusion is not automatic.

The word "disrepute" necessarily involves a test of how the administration of justice is viewed in the eyes of people in general and the test that has emerged is whether the reasonable man, dispassionate and fully apprised of all the circumstances of the case, would regard the use of such evidence against the accused as something that would reflect adversely on his concept of the fair administration of justice. This will obviously depend upon many considerations quite apart from the *mere* violation of the Charter.[7]

---

6 The Supreme Court has drawn a distinction between cases where the Charter violation results in the accused being "conscripted" to provide evidence against himself, that is, where it results in the creation of evidence which otherwise would not have existed (as would be the case where it results in his making a confession), and cases where it merely results in the finding of evidence which already existed, as for instance, the finding of the murder weapon or some other piece of incriminating evidence. The former would almost invariably be excluded, but the latter not necessarily so. See *Collins v. R.*, [1987] 1 S.C.R. 265, 13 B.C.L.R. (2d) 1, 56 C.R. (3d) 193, [1987] 3 W.W.R. 699, 33 C.C.C. (3d) 1, 74 N.R. 276.

7 Some of these are set out in *Collins, supra*, note 6, but there is no closed list of matters that should be taken into consideration.

Some sections of the Charter clearly affect the admissibility of confessions, such as the right to retain and instruct counsel and to be informed of that right (section 10(*b*)), or the right to be informed of the reason for an arrest (section 10(*a*)), but it has still been necessary for the courts to interpret even these rights. Illustrative of the problems that the courts have been confronted with are the questions of waiver of the right to counsel, the effect of an accused being drunk or mentally incompetent at the time of arrest, whether an accused must be informed of the availability of legal aid, and whether there is some obligation on the part of the accused to exercise his right to counsel with reasonable diligence. It is also clear that the right to counsel is not the right to have counsel present at all times, merely to retain and instruct counsel, but once the accused has indicated that he wishes to avail himself of this right, no questioning or atempting to elicit further evidence may take place until he has been able to exercise that right.[8]

There are, however, other rights and freedoms guaranteed by the Charter that, less obviously, may affect the admissibility of confessions. One that may have profound repercussions is that contained in section 7 — the right not to be deprived of liberty save in accordance with the principles of fundamental justice. While, as we have seen, the common law managed to handle fairly well the exclusion of confessions not voluntarily given, because of its narrow interpretation of what "voluntarily" means, it did not handle very well the exclusion of confessions obtained in some manner that might be perceived to be in some way "unfair," such as the use of trickery by the police or the surreptitious taping of incriminating statements by undercover agents. This is because such statements, however much they might have been "tricked" out of the accused, are nevertheless voluntary since they were not obtained by means of threats or inducements.

The Supreme Court has how recognized that there is, at least in Canada, something called a "right to silence" which is protected by section 7 in the concept of fundamental justice. We shall see in the next chapter that, in some senses, a right to silence has long been recognized and enforced in the common law — the right of an accused not to be compelled to testify against himself or the right of a witness not to have any incriminating answers he may be compelled to give used against him in subsequent proceedings, but in *R. v. Hebert*[9] the Supreme Court extended the concept enormously. In that case, the accused had been arrested, told of his right to counsel, which he exercised, and had been advised to say

---

8 *R. v. Manninen*, [1987] 1 S.C.R. 1233, 61 O.R. (2d) 736 (note), 58 C.R. (3d) 97, 34 C.C.C. (3d) 385, 41 D.L.R. (4th) 301, 21 O.A.C. 192, 38 C.R.R. 37, 76 N.R. 198.

9 [1990] 2 S.C.R. 151, 77 C.R. (3d) 145, [1990] 5 W.W.R. 1, 47 B.C.L.R. (2d) 1, 57 C.C.C. (3d) 1, 49 C.R.R. 114, 110 N.R. 1.

nothing to the police. He informed the police that he did not wish to make any statement. He was then detained in a cell and an undercover police officer, posing as a fellow accused, was put into the cell with him. In the course of time, the undercover officer gained Hébert's confidence and succeeded in inducing him to make an incriminating statement. There is no doubt that at common law, such a statement would not have been inadmissible,[10] but the Supreme Court held that where an accused (or any person subject to the coercive power of the state) chooses not to speak, the "state" (here, represented by the police) could not subvert that freedom to remain silent by trickery or other means. While the accused is free to give up that right, or choose to speak, this can only be done where there is full awareness on his part as to what he is doing and the consequences of doing it.

Hebert represents a very significant step in the development of the law relating to the admissibility of incriminating statements obtained from accused persons. It, like the case of *Duarte*,[11] really represents a shift in emphasis from concentrating on the accused and how he perceives the situation to whether the conduct of the police is acceptable and in accordance with our concept of fundamental justice. The Charter, by guaranteeing certain rights and freedoms, has, by necessary corollary, imposed upon the state the duty to act in a manner that will uphold and protect those rights and freedoms.

Effect of Testimony by Accused

Leaving aside these unresolved difficulties, then, we can see that the voir dire has the very specific purpose of determining the circumstances in which the statement of the accused to the police was made. It is not concerned with the guilt or innocence of the accused, but only with whether the statement is to be admitted in evidence or not. If it is, then the jury will return to the courtroom, hear the confession and proceed with the trial; if it is not, the jury will return, will not hear the confession, and the trial will resume at the point it was broken off. The same principle applies where there is no jury and the trial judge is sitting alone, save that he does not, of course, physically remove himself from the courtroom and then return. But he, too, when presiding over the voir dire, is *not* presiding over the trial; if he rules the confession admissible, then he resumes the trial, hears the confession, and proceeds; if he rules it

---

10 Either because there was no threat or inducement or because, in any case, a disguised police officer, not perceived by the accused to be a police officer, would not constitute a person in authority so as to activate the confession rules.

11 Limiting the right of the police surreptitiously to tape conversations by the use of body packs on undercover agents. See Chapter 3, *supra*.

inadmissible, he resumes the trial, excises from his mind all reference to the confession and proceeds.

This, needless to say, can, at least superficially, cause difficulties. If an accused wishes to contest the admissibility of a confession, he is virtually (though not legally and not always) compelled to take the witness stand on the voir dire, since it is usually his word against that of the police. The only questions that are relevant on the voir dire are those pertaining to the voluntariness or consciousness of the statement. Questions that may be relevant to the trial as pertaining to guilt or innocence are not relevant on the voir dire, unless they also affect voluntariness or consciousness. Thus, generally speaking, an accused is entitled to testify on the voir dire, without running the risk of being compelled to answer questions relating directly to his guilt.

Unfortunately, it is not quite that straightforward, as it is not always easy to separate the two lines of questioning so clearly. Sometimes a question will be relevant on the voir dire that would also be relevant at the trial proper, and the accused's answer thereto may, in fact, be evidence of guilt.

If the trial is before a jury, this will not do any harm since the jury is not present during the voir dire and will not hear the incriminating answer. But the same thing applies to a trial without a jury where the judge, as a judge on the voir dire, is also the same person as the judge on the trial. Once the voir dire has ended, he must forget all about the evidence he heard on the voir dire and determine the case solely upon the evidence he hears at the trial proper — no matter how incriminating the voir dire evidence might have been, or how exculpatory for that matter.[12] This preserves the right of the accused to contest the admissibility of a statement by testifying freely at the voir dire without having that evidence come back to haunt him at the trial.

A confession which is admitted in evidence is not necessarily conclusive of guilt. Of course, defence counsel's main task is to attempt to keep out any incriminating statement, but even if it is admitted, it is still possible to attack the *weight* that should be given to it at the trial proper. The accused may, for example, have attempted to show on the voir dire, that the statement was obtained after he had been beaten by the police, but the judge did not believe him and ruled the statement admissible. There is nothing to stop the accused giving the same evidence before the jury at his trial. Indeed, the jury may come to a different conclusion from that of the trial judge and believe the accused. In that case, while they will have heard the confession, they may well discount it entirely and acquit the accused in spite of the confession.

---

12 Unless, for some special reason, evidence may be given at the trial as to what went on in the voir dire. This is very uncommon.

14

Self-Incrimination and Entrapment

We should now look more closely at something we have referred to a number of times previously: the so-called privilege against self-incrimination. Unfortunately, it has many aspects and it is not always clear in which sense it is being used.

PRIVILEGE AGAINST SELF-INCRIMINATION

In its first, original sense, the privilege against self-incrimination does not exist in Canada — that is the right of a witness, testifying at any proceeding, to refuse to answer a question on the ground that the answer may incriminate him. In Canada, as we saw in Chapter 2, this privilege has been replaced by the one afforded in section 13 of the Charter to a witness testifying in any proceeding not to have any incriminating evidence so given used to incriminate him in any other proceedings (except for a prosecution for perjury or the giving of contradictory evidence). It is a right enjoyed only by a witness and it is limited to any incriminating evidence so given. If section 13 is interpreted similarly to the statutory provisions in existence for a number of years, one would expect it to be of limited application. If the person involved is not a "witness" in any proceedings, the right does not arise. "Proceedings" are not limited to trials, either civil or criminal, but would include any judicial or quasi-judicial proceedings such as an inquest or a Royal Commission Inquiry. It would not, however, include merely police questioning or some informal inquiry. This right is only to have "any incriminating evidence so given" not used to incriminate. If the evidence is being used, not to incriminate, but for some other purpose, such as to impeach the credibility of that person in a subsequent case by proving that he made an inconsistent statement, then section 13 does not apply. More importantly, it is limited to "evidence so given," which, in essence, means the testimony and answers of that person. If real evidence is found as a result of that testimony (what is called derivative evidence), section 13 does not prevent that real evidence being introduced against him at a subsequent trial. But, although section 13 may have no application, it is possible that if the subsequent trial could result in the deprivation of liberty *and* if the use of that derivative evidence would render that subsequent trial not in accordance with the principles of fundamental justice, then section 7 might well be applicable and the evidence excluded on that basis.[1]

The second meaning that is sometimes given to the privilege against self-incrimination is the right of an accused person not to be compelled to be a witness at his own trial (now incorporated as section 11(c) of the Charter). In fact, this is not a very precise usage since, at least originally, it was not that an accused was not compellable as a witness at his own trial, but that he was incompetent to testify even if he wanted to. In the course of the 19th century, this restriction was lifted so as to make an accused person a competent witness for the defence, but not for the prosecution. Still, whatever the origin, section 11(c) now expressly enacts that an accused has a *right* not to be compelled to be a witness, either for the prosecution or for the defence. Obviously, the question of compelling an accused to testify for the defence would not usually arise, since it is the accused anyway who decides whether he is going to testify or not, but it could be significant where there are joint accused. Section 11(c) now makes it clear that one co-accused cannot be compelled to testify either for the prosecution or for the other co-accused if he does not wish to give evidence.[2]

---

1 See the judgments in the Supreme Court of Canada case of *Thomson Newspapers Ltd. v. Canada (Director of Investigation & Research)*, [1990] 1 S.C.R. 425, 72 O.R. (2d) 415 (note), 76 C.R. (3d) 129, 54 C.C.C. (3d) 417, 67 D.L.R. (4th) 161, 29 C.P.R. (3d) 97, 39 O.A.C. 161, 47 C.R.R. 1, 106 N.R. 161, in which the Court is clearly troubled by the possibility that a person who is compelled to testify, while having the s. 13 protection against having his answers used against him, has no clearly spelled out protection against having derivative evidence which he may have been forced to provide being used against him.

2 Nothing is said in the Charter about the spouse of an accused being compellable, but in most cases he or she is not a compellable witness for the prosecution. There are many important exceptions to this rule, however, in the case of specific offences such as sexual assault, offences with young children as victims, or where the accused is charged with an offence involving violence against the spouse herself or himself.

Quite apart from these two meanings, there is, as we saw in the previous chapter, a third way in which something that may be called the privilege against self-incrimination can be used, and that is in the connection with the developing "right to silence." We looked at this in connection with the interrogation of suspects and the investigation of offences and in connection with the surreptitious taping of conversations by undercover agents, but it may well be that the courts, having now clearly recognized the existence of a "right to silence," will develop its scope further. For example, a number of statutes, very often provincial, require, under penalty of fine or imprisonment, a person to make a statement if certain things occur. Under most provincial Highway Traffic Acts or Motor Vehicle Acts, for instance, a person involved in an automobile accident is required to give a statement to an investigating officer detailing the circumstances of the accident. That statement may be, and frequently is, introduced in evidence against him at his subsequent prosecution. It is a little difficult to argue that one has the right to silence when a statute provides that one can be fined or even sent to prison if one fails to make such a statement, and it is possible that the courts will find that such provisions are unconstitutional. On the other hand, perhaps a better argument would be that, while the statement can be compelled and while it would be an offence not to make the statement, if, at the time of any subsequent prosecution, it is found that to admit it would be contrary to the principles of fundamental justice, then it could be excluded at that subsequent prosecution, if, of course, to admit it would bring the administration of justice into disrepute. If this is true, it is not so much that there is, in this context, a right to silence as a right not to have a compelled statement used against oneself.

Attempts have been made to argue that the Criminal Code provisions requiring a person to provide, in some circumstances, a breath sample or blood sample to test for the presence of blood alcohol violate that person's privilege against self-incrimination, but the courts have consistently rejected that argument on the ground that section 13 is simply not applicable. This, as we have seen, is undoubtedly correct. Nor would it seem possible to argue that they offend against any right to silence since the person is not being compelled to say anything, but only to disclose matters already in existence. The use of the analysis result *may* possibly be said to violate the section 7 guarantee of trial in accordance with the principles of fundamental justice, but one would assume that section 1 would be invoked to declare it a reasonable limit and, in any case, its use would be unlikely to be characterized as bringing the administration of justice into disrepute. The same conclusions may be reached in connection with such matters as the compulsory fingerprinting and photographing of suspects or the use of identification parades and so on.

However, it must be admitted that the precise limits on what may be generally, if inaccurately, called the privilege against self-incrimination have yet to be fully worked out by the courts. The difficult line must be drawn between unduly hampering the police in their legitimate investigation of offences and prosecution of offenders and maintaining and making effective those rights guaranteed to the individual by the Charter.

POLICE ENTRAPMENT

An example of how the courts should control the legitimate limits to police investigation may be seen in the problem of those circumstances that may generally be grouped under the rubric of police entrapment. The fact situations can vary enormously, which is why, although the general principles are beginning to emerge, their application is not always easy and can lead to disagreement. At one extreme, we can have an accused, with no intention initially of committing an offence, who is befriended by an undercover officer and then persuaded, indeed, pressured, into committing an offence, whereupon he is then arrested. At the other, the police, being reliably informed that an accused is about to commit an offence, instead of stepping in to prevent it, lie in wait and permit the accused to commit an offence, which they could have prevented, in order to arrest him. In between, one can have an infinite number of variations.

The Supreme Court in *R. v. Mack*[3] has set out the general principles to be followed in such cases. Entrapment, in the legal sense, arises in two cases: when the police provide an opportunity to persons to commit offences without any prior reasonable suspicion that they are so engaged or without any *bona fide* motive relating to the investigation or repression of crime; or when, even though they have such reasonable suspicion or are acting *bona fide*, they go beyond merely providing an opportunity and actually induce the commission of an offence, "inducement" in this case being judged by the standard of the ordinary average person in the position of the accused. To the extent possible, the conduct of the police should be judged objectively in all the circumstances, and the predisposition of the accused to commit offences is irrelevant except insofar as it may go the justification of providing the accused with an opportunity to commit the offence.

On the question (which is the one that is most likely to arise) of whether the police have gone further than merely providing an opportunity for the accused to commit the offence and have actively induced the commission of the offence, the Court listed a number of factors that should be considered, such as the type of crime being investigated and whether other investigative techniques were available; whether the average person would

---

3 [1988] 2 S.C.R. 903, 67 C.R. (3d) 1, [1989] 1 W.W.R. 577, 44 C.C.C. (3d) 513, 37 C.R.R. 277, 90 N.R. 173.

succumb to the inducement; the persistence of the police opportuning and the type of inducement used, such as fraud, trickery or the offer of rewards; whether the conduct of the police exploited any particular vulnerability of the accused such as physical or mental handicap or exploited general human characteristics such as friendship or sympathy, and so on.

Entrapment is not, in law, a "defence" since it is hard to deny that even a person who has been induced to commit the offence nevertheless does commit it and intends to commit it. It is not so much that he is not guilty as that, because of the conduct of the police, there is something unfair about convicting him. The result is that this issue is tried, not by the jury, but by the trial judge only after the jury has determined that, apart from the entrapment issue, the accused would have been found guilty. At that stage, instead of recording the verdict of guilty, the trial judge will determine the entrapment issue.[4] Since what the accused is raising is not a "defence" but a procedural bar to his own prosecution, the onus is on the accused to establish (though, of course, only on the balance of probabilities) that the conduct of the police was such as to amount to "entrapment." If he succeeds, the remedy is not that he is acquitted but that a stay of proceedings is ordered by the trial judge and no verdict is recorded, which, while not an acquittal, from the accused's point of view amounts almost to the same thing.

It is, in fact, a very narrow principle and one that will be successful only in the clearest case of entrapment. For example, in one subsequent case,[5] the police, knowing that generally a particular area of Vancouver was frequented by drug dealers, were patrolling that area in civilian undercover clothing looking for young persons who fitted their own preconceived notions of what drug dealers looked like. They stopped one and eventually, after some persuasion, induced him to sell them drugs, whereupon they arrested him. The accused argued that the police were engaged in "random virtue testing," that is to say, having no prior reason to suspect the accused of committing an offence, they randomly stopped him to see if they could induce him to commit an offence. While the Court agreed that such random virtue testing was objectionable, it held (by a majority) that if the location were sufficiently well defined and if the police on reasonable grounds believed that such location was being used for the commission of offences of the nature under investigation, they may present any person associated with that area with an opportunity to commit the particular offence under investigation.

---

4 The same procedure, of course, applies, *mutatis mutandis,* when there is no jury, though it is rather more simple.
5 *R. v. Barnes,* [1991] 1 S.C.R. 449, 3 C.R. (4th) 1, [1991] 2 W.W.R. 673, 53 B.C.L.R. (2d) 129, 63 C.C.C. (3d) 1, 121 N.R. 267.

15

Illegally Obtained Evidence

One other aspect of the rules of evidence that can frequently be puzzling is the admissibility of evidence that has been obtained in some manner that is contrary to the law. It will be as well to distinguish cases where the illegality amounts to an infringement of a constitutional guarantee contained in the Charter, from cases where the illegality is a violation of the law, but is not an infringement of the Charter. Where a Charter right has been infringed, there are special provisions that must be considered.

We have already seen that, apart from a case where some special statutory provision applies, a legal search of premises requires the police to have a valid search warrant, and a legal search of a person requires that person to have been arrested on reasonable and probable grounds first. The Charter declares that everyone has the right to security of the person and the right not to be deprived thereof except in accordance with the principles of fundamental justice and the right to be secure against unreasonable search or seizure. One can have, therefore, a search that is unlawful, in the sense of not being sanctioned by law, without that search necessarily violating a provision of the Charter. For example, if the police search under the authority of a search warrant, the time limit on which has just shortly expired, that search (and any subsequent seizure) is illegal, but it is not necessarily unreasonable. On the other hand, were the police to stop a person on the street at random and forcibly search him, there would be little doubt that the search would be illegal in both senses.

Our discussion will be easier to follow if we deal firstly with the situation of illegal searches and seizures apart from the Charter provisions. Let us assume then that we are dealing with conduct that is not authorized by law yet is not a violation of the Charter.

ADMISSIBILITY

The admissibility of any piece of evidence depends first of all on its probative value — that is to say, upon whether it logically tends to prove the issue for which it is being introduced. If a person is illegally searched and narcotic drugs are found on him and he is charged with possession of narcotics, the relevance of the drugs is obvious and that relevance is not affected in the slightest by the fact that they were found illegally. They do prove that the accused was in possession of narcotics no matter how they came into the hands of the police. If one looks, therefore, at the question of the admissibility of illegally obtained evidence solely from the point of view of its *relevance*, one would have to conclude that such evidence is admissible unless, purely as part of the inference-drawing process, it was not material.

Indeed, that is precisely the view that has been taken by the courts in this jurisdiction. Apart from any special statutory provisions or the Charter, the rule that has been enunciated is that illegally obtained evidence is nonetheless admissible in evidence, unless, of course, factually it has no relevance. As we have seen, however, relevance is not a black and white concept and something can range from the highly relevant to the merely tenuously relevant. To this general rule of admissibility, there is, therefore, the slight exception that if the illegally obtained evidence is only tenuously probative and, at the same time, highly prejudicial to the accused (in the sense that it may lead to his conviction for the wrong reason), then the trial judge has the discretion to exclude it. Perhaps, indeed, he must exclude it, but when we are dealing with illegally obtained evidence, in the overwhelming majority of cases, the evidence is most unlikely to be tenuously probative. The whole point of such evidence (e.g., the murder weapon, the drugs, the counterfeit money) is that it is highly probative.

Some jurisdictions, however, notably those in the United States, have taken the view that relevance is not the sole criterion to determine admissibility. The Canadian courts have not been unmindful of the fact that the illegality in obtaining the evidence may give rise to other sanctions — to a civil action against the tortfeasor, to disciplinary proceedings or even to a criminal prosecution against the person acting illegally — but they have insisted that these have no bearing on the admissibility of the evidence at the trial of the accused. In contrast, other jurisdictions have taken the view that not only relevance, but "fairness" as well, must be considered. This approach has two aspects — firstly, the realization that alternative remedies are usually not very practical and, in any case, cannot undo the conviction of the accused. Secondly, that the courts, in admitting the evidence at the trial of the accused, may, by implication, at any rate, be seen to be sanctioning or at least condoning the illegality. Once it is accepted that relevance should not be the sole determinative factor, one can either opt for a rigid rule (as in the United States) that excludes all illegally obtained evidence and all evidence that is derived from the illegality, or one can opt for a rule (as in Australia or Scotland) that will give the courts either a discretion to exclude illegally obtained evidence (even though it is basically admissible) or a discretion to admit illegally obtained evidence (where the basic rule is that it is inadmissible), if certain criteria are met.

One can phrase the standards for the exercise of such discretion in various ways, but fundamentally they all have common basis in whether the use of such evidence, *in all the circumstances of the case*, would somehow bring the administration of justice into disrepute, thus reinforcing the second reason advanced above — that the courts cannot be seen to be condoning practices that strike at the very basis of what is perceived to be our system of justice.

In fact, Canada does adopt this position in one specific case, namely, the introduction of evidence obtained as a result of an illegal electronic interception (such as a wiretap) which, although admissible, may be rejected if its admission would bring the administration of justice into disrepute.[1]

Nevertheless, the general proposition remains that, in Canada, illegally obtained evidence is admissible against an accused and there is no discretion to exclude such evidence unless (a) it was obtained by means of an unlawful electronic interception, or (b) it is only tenuously probative and at the same time highly prejudicial.

EXCLUSION UNDER THE CHARTER

Now, however, what is most likely to arise is not the question of the admissibility of evidence under the common law rules regarding illegally obtained evidence, but the admissibility of evidence obtained after a Charter violation. Section 24 of the Charter is so important that it is worth setting out in full.

> 24(1) Anyone whose rights or freedoms, as guaranteed by this Charter, have been infringed or denied may apply to a court of competent jurisdiction to obtain such remedy as the court considers appropriate and just in the circumstances.

---

1 Criminal Code, s. 189.

(2) Where, in proceedings under subsection (1), a court concludes that evidence was obtained in a manner that infringed or denied any rights or freedoms guaranteed by this Charter, the evidence shall be excluded if it is established that, having regard to all the circumstances, the admission of it in the proceedings would bring the administration of justice into disrepute.

In this chapter, we are concerned with the application of subsection (2), since that is the one dealing with the exclusion of evidence, and it does give rise to several problems, not all of which have yet been resolved. A few preliminary matters of some importance should be noticed first.

The evidence must be obtained "in a manner" that infringed a Charter right. This is not the same as obtaining evidence *by* a Charter infringement and a strict causal connection between the infringement and the obtaining of the evidence is not required so long as the infringement took place in the course of the obtaining, although if the obtaining of the evidence merely follows a Charter infringement but is too remote from that infringement, it will not be within the provision.[2] In the second place, the court must "conclude" that evidence was obtained in a manner that infringed a Charter right. This does not impose any burden of proof on either side, but merely directs the court to inquire and come to a conclusion following the hearing of the evidence and listening to the arguments. Once that has been decided, however, there is a burden on the person seeking exclusion to "establish" that its admission would bring the administration of justice into disrepute. Normally, this will be an accused person in a criminal case and, of course, the burden is not to prove this beyond any reasonable doubt, but merely on the balance of probabilities. If, however, this is established, there is no discretion whether the evidence is received or excluded, since, if the court finds that its admission would bring the administration of justice into disrepute, the evidence *shall* be excluded.

The last preliminary point is that no guidance is given as to how or when this inquiry is to take place. The provision clearly envisages some sort of inquiry, quite apart from the trial on the issues in the case — a sort of *voir dire* to determine whether the evidence should be excluded. In most cases, this will cause no difficulties — the jury, if there is one, can be excluded and the proffered evidence examined, evidence received as to all the circumstances, arguments listened to and a decision made. If the evidence is admitted, the jury will return and hear it; if it is excluded, the jury will return and never hear about the excluded evidence. In practice, it may be that it will be known before the trial starts that a question arises as to the admissibility of a piece of evidence, and the matter can be decided before the trial actually gets under way. There may arise difficulties, however, in some cases, where it is not all that easy to keep distinct issues

---

2 See *R. v. Strachan*, [1988] 2 S.C.R. 980, 67 C.R. (3d) 87, [1989] 1 W.W.R. 385, 46 C.C.C. (3d) 479, 56 D.L.R. (4th) 673, 37 C.R.R. 335, 90 N.R. 273.

that are relevant to the obtaining of the evidence and issues that are relevant to guilt or innocence of the accused, and there may be problems in instructing the jury as to what is for them to decide and what is for the judge to decide. In fact, the courts have not yet worked out these procedural questions and, at the moment, practice seems to vary from jurisdiction to jurisdiction.

This is different from the question whether there can be, or should be, in Canada something along the lines of a pre-trial motion to exclude evidence, determined even before the case comes to trial, one advantage of which is that, if the evidence is ruled inadmissible and the case for the Crown collapses as a result, there is no need to go through all the process of bringing the accused to actual trial needlessly. Some judges are of the view that this would be the best way to handle these sorts of issues. But one thing is clear: Canadian criminal law does not, at least as yet, recognize what are called "interlocutory appeals," that is, appeals on procedural or evidentiary matters while the case is still pending. They do have the advantage that they may save useless trials and shorten the process in some cases. On the other hand, if a person appeals each individual ruling, the case itself may drag on interminably, and our courts have taken the view that it is better to delay the appeal until *all* matters that arise from it, from procedural issues to evidentiary matters to the substance of the actual trial and sentencing process, can be dealt with all at once.

These procedural problems aside, given that there has been a Charter violation and a finding that evidence was obtained in a manner that infringed one of the Charter rights, there must still be a decision made on whether the admission of that evidence would[3] bring the administration of justice into disrepute. The test favoured by the Supreme Court[4] is "would the admission of this evidence bring the administration of justice into disrepute in the eyes of a reasonable man, dispassionate and fully apprised of the circumstances of the case?" and this may well depend on the type of evidence involved. If the evidence is itself *created* as a result of the Charter violation, as a confession or some other statement, then the accused is, in effect, being conscripted to testify against himself and that would invariably bring the administration of justice into disrepute. If, on the other hand, the evidence was pre-existing and was only *found* as a result of the Charter violation, that would not necessarily bring the administration of justice into disrepute.

In this latter case, several factors would have to be taken into account in making this determination, and, while the list is not exhaustive, these

---

3 In French the words used are "*est susceptible de déconsidérer l'administration de la justice*," which has led the courts to construe "would" as "could."
4 In *Collins v. R.*, [1987] 1 S.C.R. 265, 13 B.C.L.R. (2d) 1, 56 C.R. (3d) 193, [1987] 3 W.W.R. 699, 33 C.C.C. (3d) 1, 74 N.R. 276.

would include the seriousness of the Charter breach, whether it was deliberate or inadvertent, whether circumstances of emergency were present, whether the police acted in good faith or whether other investigative techniques were available. It is even possible, of course, that if all these factors are decided in favour of the police, then to *exclude* the evidence would bring the administration of justice into disrepute.

In short, while it is not possible, nor desirable, to be categorical about when evidence will or will not be excluded under section 24(2), there have been enough cases decided under that section for us to see the thrust of how it has been interpreted and to see what a profound influence it has had on the law of evidence.

16

Mental Disorder* and Responsibility

UNFITNESS TO STAND TRIAL

One of the cardinal rights of an accused person is the right to make full answer and defence at his trial. If, therefore, a person, due to his mental condition, is unable to defend himself, it follows that he is unable to be tried so long as this mental condition remains.

A person who is unable to understand what is alleged against him, or is unable to understand the proceedings, or is unable to enter a defence or instruct counsel because of his mental condition, cannot be tried. This is not to say, however, that he is found Not Guilty — it is, rather, that no trial can be held and no verdict can be reached.

Today, there are so many opportunities for an accused who may be suspected of having mental problems to be subject to a psychiatric examination or at least observation, that it is unlikely that the issue of the fitness of the accused to stand trial would arise suddenly. But, in fact, it can arise, either at the beginning of the trial, before the accused has

---

* The defence of "mental disorder" (s. 16), which replaced the defence of insanity, was introduced into the Criminal Code together with the provisions of the new Part XX.1 on "Mental Disorder" by An act to amend the Criminal Code (mental disorder), S.C. 1991, c. 43, s. 2, re-enacting s. 16; s. 4, enacting Part XX.1.

pleaded (which happens most often), or it can arise after the accused has pleaded and during the course of the trial when suddenly it appears that the accused may be mentally unfit to stand trial. There are some procedural differences and practical difficulties in the latter case, so let us look first at the most common case — that is, where it is clear before the trial starts that the accused may have mental problems.

When an accused is arrested for an offence and either the accused appears to be acting in a strange way or the offence appears to be a peculiar one, it is usually in everyone's interest to see that he is examined as soon as possible. The police may themselves ask the accused to be seen by a doctor or the accused's counsel may ask to have arrangements made for his client to be examined. These "informal" examinations may be the first indication of the accused's state of mind. If such an accused is not arrested, but has been subject to some other form of pre-release mechanism, again, his counsel may make arrangements to have him examined.

If he is arrested and not released, there will, as we have seen, have to be some sort of bail hearing to determine whether he should be allowed judicial interim release. During that hearing, the presiding justice may adjourn the proceedings and remand the accused in custody for a period not exceeding three days. In some jurisdictions it is possible for such an accused to undergo some sort of brief psychiatric assessment within three days. Although it is not a very long time to make any definitive determination, it may be long enough to determine that there is nothing wrong with the accused or, conversely, to determine that further examination should be made.

One way or the other, though, by the time the preliminary inquiry starts (if there is one), or by the time the trial is ready to begin in other cases, there will usually be, in the appropriate cases, some evidence available as to the accused's mental state in the form of a medical diagnosis or a psychiatric report. The judge presiding at a preliminary inquiry or the judge presiding at a trial may remand the accused for psychiatric observation for a period of up to 30 days, or may order him to attend for psychiatric observation where there is evidence to support the belief that the accused may be mentally ill, or where both the accused and the prosecution agree and there is a written report to that effect. In exceptional cases the remand may be made without evidence or a written report if compelling reasons exist for so doing and in some instances the period for observation may be extended for up to 60 days.

Assuming that the report which will come back at the end of the 30 or 60 days does not clearly indicate that there is nothing wrong with the accused, it may then be necessary to determine whether the accused is fit to stand trial. It may be overwhelmingly clear that he is not (in which case the determination may be fairly easy) or it may be a question that could go either way. In either event, a fitness hearing will have to be held.

If the issue is dealt with at a preliminary inquiry, or at a trial where there is no jury, it is determined by the presiding judge after hearing all the evidence. He will determine whether the accused is "unfit" in the sense we have discussed of not being capable of understanding the proceedings or of instructing counsel. If the issue arises at a trial before a judge and jury and it arises, as will usually be the case, before the trial has commenced, then a special jury will be empanelled to determine whether the accused should be tried — if so, the jury will be selected according to the normal procedure and the trial will go on; if not, then there will be no trial. If the issue arises during the course of the trial, a special jury is *not* empanelled, but the same jury that is trying the case will also be instructed that they should now direct their attention to determining whether the accused is fit to stand trial.

If the accused is found to be unfit to stand trial, special provisions apply. If the judge is of the opinion that he can make a disposition readily and on the information then available to him, he may do so; if he decides that more information is necessary, then a Review Board[1] shall make a disposition within, normally, 45 days, pending which the accused's pre-trial terms of release (i.e., conditions of bail, appearance notice, promise to appear, etc.) continue in force unless the court orders him detained in a mental hospital. The disposition is made after a hearing, which, while informal in nature, nevertheless is subject to the usual safeguards of due process.[2]

That disposition may be a finding that the accused is now, at the time of the hearing, fit to stand trial, in which case the Board will order him returned to court for trial. If this is not the case, then the disposition ordered shall be the least onerous and least restrictive to the accused, taking into account the need to protect the public, the accused's mental condition and the needs of the accused, ranging from discharge subject to such conditions as the court or Board considers appropriate to detention in a mental hospital, subject to any appropriate conditions.[3]

After a finding that the accused is unfit to stand trial, there has not been any verdict one way or other and, as we have seen, he is ordered to be returned to court for trial when it is decided that he is now fit to stand trial. Whether or not he will actually stand trial is more a matter of discretion on the part of the prosecuting authorities. If the offence is not serious, it is unlikely that the prosecution will be pursued. If the accused

---

1 Each province has a Review Board, the duties of which are to make disposition and to review such disposition periodically. If it determines that the accused is fit to stand trial it shall order him or her to be sent back to court for trial.

2 The court may also direct the accused to undergo treatment for a period not to exceed 60 days, if some specific treatment is indicated to make that person fit to stand trial.

3 There are various provisions relating to procedural matters and appeals from disposition decisions that need not concern us here.

has been detained in a hospital for several years, it may be unfair to continue his prosecution and, in any case, witnesses may have forgotten the events or have died and a prosecution would be pointless. It is more accurate to say that an accused who has been found unfit to stand trial remains liable to be tried when he recovers, but whether he will actually be tried depends very much on all the surrounding circumstances.[4]

The result of this procedure is that a person who is found unfit to stand trial may end up spending years[5] detained in a hospital as a result of being charged with an offence of which he may, in fact, not be guilty, since if he is found unfit this is never actually determined. It may be that there is some disquiet at the prospect of using the criminal process to secure the custody — albeit therapeutic custody — of a person who is found mentally disordered when he might be quite innocent of any offence. Indeed, if the issue arises at the preliminary inquiry stage, it may never even have been resolved that there is a *prima facie* case against him.

To meet this disquiet, at least partially, it is now possible — indeed, common, particularly where the matter is disputed — to postpone the trial of the issue of fitness to stand trial until, in the case of the preliminary, the accused is called on to answer the charge, or, in the case of the trial, the opening of the defence (or even later on motion by the accused).[6] This enables the defence to move to dismiss (or move for a directed verdict of not guilty) when the prosecution has not even made out a case to answer. If successful, this means that the accused will be found Not Guilty (or have the information dismissed) without the issue of his fitness ever arising. While this technique does not absolutely protect a person who may actually be not guilty of the offence, it at least ensures[7] that the criminal process cannot be resorted to unless there is at least a *prima facie* case against him.

MENTAL DISORDER AT THE TIME OF THE OFFENCE

A totally different question from fitness to stand trial (which is procedural in nature) is the rule that a person who suffered from mental disorder at the time the offence was committed cannot be convicted of that offence. This is a question of substantive criminal law and really outside

---

4 In any case, s. 672.33 provides for a continuing examination of the evidence against the accused every two years, and where the court finds that there is no longer sufficient evidence to put the accused on trial, it shall enter a verdict of acquittal.

5 Though the time is subject to the "capping" provisions, discussed below.

6 In the case of hybrid or dual procedure offence, the trial of the issue *must* be postponed until the prosecution has, at least, elected whether to proceed by way of indictment or on summary conviction.

7 It is, of course, discretionary on the part of the court, so it does not "ensure" this, but it is the common practice.

the scope of this book, but to discuss unfitness to stand trial without discussing lack of responsibility on account of mental disorder would give a very incomplete picture.

This type of mental disorder has nothing whatever to do with fitness to stand trial. Section 16 of the Code states:

(1) No person is criminally responsible for an act committed or an omission made while suffering from a mental disorder that rendered the person incapable of appreciating the nature and quality of the act or omission or knowing that it was wrong.

(2) Every person is presumed not to suffer from a mental disorder so as to be exempt from criminal responsibility by virtue of subsection (1), until the contrary is proved on the balance of probabilities.

(3) The burden of proof that an accused was suffering from a mental disorder so as to be exempt from criminal responsibility is on the party that raises the issue.

While this type of mental disorder is often referred to as a defence and in the vast majority of cases is raised by an accused as an exemption from liability, it can, in rare cases, be raised by the prosecution even over the wishes of the accused, where the accused's own defence, while disavowing mental disorder as a defence, nevertheless puts the mental capacity of the accused in issue. It is therefore, strictly speaking, an "issue" in a criminal case, rather than a "defence."[8]

Exemption from responsibility on account of mental disorder only applies if the accused would otherwise have been guilty of the offence. If, of course, she did not commit the act anyway, then no question of her being "exempt" arises. This is why, under section 672.34, where the accused is found to be within the provisions of section 16, the jury or judge shall render the verdict "that the accused committed the act or made the omission but is not criminally responsible on account of mental disorder." This is not a verdict of Guilty or a conviction except for some limited procedural purposes.

Once that verdict has been rendered, then the effect, initially, is similar to that after a finding that the accused is unfit to stand trial. There will be a disposition hearing (either by the judge or, more usually in this case, by the Review Board), and a decision will be made about her, subject to the procedural safeguards and appeal processes. Again, the disposition shall be the least onerous and restrictive to the accused, ranging from, where the accused is not a significant threat to the safety of the public, an absolute discharge, through discharge on conditions to detention in custody in a

---

8 This is one reason why putting the onus on the accused to prove his mental disorder in order to be exempt does not violate the presumption of innocence, though the majority of the Supreme Court in *R. v. Chaulk*, [1990] 3 S.C.R. 1303, 2 C.R. (4th) 1, [1991] 2 W.W.R. 385, 69 Man. R. (2d) 161, 62 C.C.C. (3d) 193, 1 C.R.R. (2d) 1, 119 N.R. 161, held that this provision *did* violate the Charter but was saved by s. 1.

mental hospital. In this last case, however, there is an upper limit on the duration of the detention known as "capping." In general, the amount of time for which a person may be detained under these provisions may be no longer than the maximum term of imprisoment to which she should have been subject had she been found guilty, but if, at the end of that period, she is still unfit to be released then proceedings may be taken to have her detention continued under the provincial Mental Health Acts or their equivalent. In addition, after such a verdict, the Attorney General, where the accused has been charged with a specified sexual offence or with what is called a "designated"[9] offence that involve violence or conduct endangering the life or safety of others or that is likely to inflict severe psychological damage on another, may move to have the accused declared to be a dangerous mentally disordered offender. If such a declaration is made, then the cap may be removed and the detention may be for life.

The substantive issue is, of course, whether the accused comes within the provisions of section 16 in the first place, and the first matter that has to be shown is that the accused was suffering from a mental disorder, defined, in section 2, as a "disease of the mind." If a medical person were to object that there is no such thing, he may well be right from a medical point of view, but it is not that point of view that is relevant. What matters is that the accused must be shown to have been suffering from something that the law would categorize as a disease of the mind, and that means any abnormal malfunctioning of the mental processes brought about by some internal condition of the accused. If the cause of the malfunctioning is some external factor, such as a blow to the head or the consumption of drugs, then there is no basis for the finding that the accused was suffering from a mental disorder in this sense, though it may well be the basis for some other defence that may lead to an outright acquittal or a partial acquittal.

Furthermore, it is only if the malfunction was abnormal that there is a disease of the mind. If the malfunction was normal — that is to say, the sort of malfunction that any average person might undergo in the circumstances — then the accused would not need to rely on section 16 for a defence but, rather, might well have some other defence that leads to an acquittal. For example, if a mother were to walk into her house one evening and discover a man in the process of sexually assaulting her small son, as a result of which her mind "went blank" and, picking up the first object at hand, she struck him and killed him, it may well be that this a perfectly ordinary and expected reaction — not an abnormal one at all — and there would be no grounds for invoking section 16. Rather, on these facts, there should, as we shall see in the next chapter, be an

---

9 Listed in the Schedule to Part XX.I.

outright acquittal, or, at the very least, an acquittal of murder and a finding of Guilty of manslaughter only on the grounds of provocation.

It is not, however, any mental disorder that leads to the application of section 16. It must be such as to render the accused "incapable of appreciating the nature and quality of the act"[10] or "incapable of appreciating that the act was wrong." The inquiry is directed to the accused's capacity, not to what she actually appreciated or knew, though in most cases there is no practical difference, but it is essential that the jury be instructed as to *capacity*, not actual appreciation or knowledge, since it is possible that a person might have the capacity but not actually appreciate or know.

This incapacity must be directed to one of two things. It must be either an incapacity to appreciate the nature and quality or, if she did so appreciate, to know that the act was wrong. "Appreciate" is not the same as "know." The former requires not only the receiving of the information, but also an assessment of it; it means knowing and also understanding, rather than just knowing. That is to say, for example, she must not only know that she is stabbing someone in the heart, but understand that such stabbing will normally lead to death and comprehend what death entails. Alternatively, she must not be able to know that what she is doing is wrong and this means either wrong in the eyes of the law or wrong in the sense of being morally wrong — she must be unable to know that it is something that he ought not to do for either reason.

Fundamentally, this limitation on the *type* of mental disorder that will support a defence under section 16 means that it has to be one that affects the accused's *understanding* of what it is she is doing rather than one that affects her ability to control her actions, though in many cases the two will coincide and an ability to control one's actions may be evidence that those actions are not understood. But a person who is aware of what she is doing, appreciates her actions and knows that they are wrong but who, because of some inner impulse, is unable to stop herself or control her actions, is not within section 16. This is why, as it is sometimes said, an "irresistible impulse" is not a defence to a criminal charge, though this rather oversimplifies the problem.

Whether this should be the case or not has been the subject of countless discussions and the debate is still going on but, rightly or wrongly, it does mean that there are many people who are convicted and are in our penitentiaries who are mentally disordered but not within section 16. One reason for limiting the issue of mental disorder in law only to cases where the ability of the accused to understand is lacking is the concern that, if it were extended further, one may very well have serious difficulty in

---

10 Or omission, but it is easier merely to refer to "act" since very few cases under s. 16 involve an omission.

determining precisely where the line should be drawn between the mentally disordered offender and the ordinary offender. While the present definition may be limited, it may well be preferable to having such a defence so broad that responsibility ceases to have much meaning.

RAISING THE ISSUE OF MENTAL DISORDER

An accused, even though he may have a perfectly good defence of mental disorder, may choose not to raise it. If successful, it could possibly mean that he would be detained in custody (albeit in a mental hospital) for a long period of time, though no longer than the maximum term he could have got had he been found guilty. But most people, for most offences, are not sentenced to the maximum term, or anything like it, and an accused, rather than risk detention in a mental hospital for a lengthy term, may prefer either to plead Guilty, or to plead Not Guilty and not raise his mental disorder as an issue, thus risking being found Guilty, and take his chances that he will only receive a short prison sentence or even a lesser sentence such as probation or a fine.

Even better, for an accused, if it were possible, would be to argue that, because of his mental disorder, he lacked one of the essential ingredients of the offence that the prosecution has to prove and that, therefore, he should be acquitted outright not because of the mental disorder but because he lacked the necessary element for a conviction.

There is actually something a little illogical about the applicability of mental disorder as an exemption from criminal responsibility. Conviction for a criminal offence requires proof by the Crown of all the essential elements of the offence, *viz.*, the *act* by the accused[11] and the *intent*. In murder, for example, the Crown must prove that the accused caused the death of the victim and that the accused meant to cause his death.[12] "Act" in this context means a voluntary conscious act on the part of the accused and "intent" means with the purpose of bringing about the result. If, for instance, a person is unconscious when he stabs a victim, he is not guilty of doing the act, because there is no "act"; if he does not mean to cause the death of the victim he is not guilty of murder because he does not intend to cause death. But what if the lack of consciousness, in the first case, or lack of intent, in the second case, is the result of the accused's mental disorder? Can he argue that he should be acquitted outright because he lacks the essential element of the offence rather than only being found exempt from responsibility with its attendant consequences?

The answer is that he cannot if the mental disorder is sufficient to bring him within section 16, but he can if the mental disorder is not within

---

11 Or, in some cases, the omission.

12 Murder is actually slightly broader than this.

section 16 — that is to say, a disease of the mind affecting his relevant cognitive capacity. An accused who raises his mental state as a defence will, if it is to have any chance of succeeding, have to offer some explanation to support his claim that he was unconscious or lacked the requisite intent, otherwise the ordinary inference-drawing process will lead the fact-finder to conclude that he was conscious and did have the intent. This requires him to offer evidence as to the *reason* for the unconsciousness or lack of intent and, while medical evidence from experts is not, in law, a prerequisite, in practice this evidence is going to take the form of doctors and psychiatrists giving testimony as to the reason. If that reason is a "disease of the mind" in the sense that we have just discussed, then the judge will rule that what is being raised must be categorized as the defence of mental disorder and stand or fall on the applicability of section 16; if it is not a disease of the mind, then section 16 is inapplicable and the ordinary defences of lack of *actus reus* or lack of *mens rea*[13] will apply. While an accused is free to raise any facts that support any defence that is relevant, how those facts are categorized is not a question for the accused but for the trial judge, and if she categorizes them as raising the defence of mental disorder, she will instruct the jury (or herself) on the applicability of section 16. In other words, the accused may not rely on a mental disorder within section 16 to secure an acquittal but reject the consequences of being found to have been mentally disordered within section 16.

If, however, there is no evidence of mental disorder amounting to a "disease of the mind" in the sense discussed, or if the jury rejects the conclusion that the accused *was* mentally disordered, then section 16 ceases to be applicable and the jury must then decide, *on all the evidence*, including any medical evidence as to the state of mind of the accused, whether the Crown has proved beyond any reasonable doubt the necessary act and intent.[14] This does lead to some difficult and complicated cases. Suppose, for example, that an accused, charged with murder, simply defends himself on the basis that he did not intend to cause the death of the victim. There is medical evidence that he is suffering from some mental abnormality. In the opinion of some of the doctors, the reason why the accused did not intend to cause death was because he was, due to his mental disorder, incapable of appreciating that if he stabbed someone through the heart he would cause that person to die. In the opinion of other doctors, he was

---

13 These terms are merely legal jargon for the element constituting the act and the element constituting the intent.

14 This is why the phraseology of s. 672.34 cannot be quite accurate. It requires the jury first to find that the accused "committed the act" before ruling him to be criminally exempt. But if his form of mental disorder is such as to affect his conscious volition, he has not actually, in law, "committed the act" for which he is criminally exempt, but it is clear that the section merely is intended to make sure that the accused is the "right" person.

suffering from a mental disorder, but that did not affect his capacity to appreciate what he was doing. In the opinion of another doctor, he was not suffering from any mental abnormality. The accused merely says that, regardless of which of these doctors the jury believes, he simply did not intend to kill.[15]

The task for the jury (and for the judge, for that matter) in such a case is not easy. If they are not satisfied that the accused intended to kill (but not because of a "disease of the mind," upon which they will be instructed by the judge), then they must simply acquit.[16] If they find that the accused was suffering from what they have been instructed was a disease of the mind and that it was this that caused the lack of intent, then they must find the accused exempt on account of mental disorder. If they find that the accused intended to kill either because he was not suffering from a mental disorder or because, if he was, it did not affect his capacity to appreciate the nature and consequences of what he was doing, then they should convict of murder.

Perhaps surprisingly enough, this all works reasonably well. Whether some better scheme could be devised that meets all the social policy objectives as well as principles of fairness to the accused and due process, the plain fact of the matter is that criminal responsibility is not a medical problem but a legal one. Any test must be capable of being understood and applied by jurors who are not experts but ordinary laymen representing the public at large. The last thing one wants is for a criminal trial to degenerate into an unseemly squabble between psychiatrists, who practise, at best, an inexact science. The bottom line is that the common sense and experience of the members of the jury do, in practice, lead to the result that meets the social policy objectives while according fairness and due process to the accused.

As is apparent, there may be many offenders who are convicted and sentenced but who do suffer from some form of mental illness. This may be because their mental illness does not qualify as a mental disorder within section 16 or because they did not raise the issue in their defence even though they could have done so. There may also be many offenders who are convicted and sentenced whose mental condition deteriorates while they are serving their sentences. We shall discuss in Chapter 18 the whole question of punishment and consider what options are available for the diagnosis and treatment of such persons.

---

15 It can get even more complicated when, in addition, the accused says, supported by some evidence, that, in any case, he was drunk at the time, but this is best left to the next chapter.

16 At least of murder, but they may find the accused guilty of the lesser offence of manslaughter, if the facts warrant it.

17

Defences to Offences

This is a book on the criminal process, not a book on substantive criminal law, and it is not proposed to discuss substantive offences such as what constitutes the crime of murder or sexual assault or theft. Nor, therefore, as a general proposition, should we be concerned about what substantive defences may be available to a criminal charge. But we have discussed the specific defence of insanity because, as we have seen, it is really more of an issue rather than a defence and, as such, it has specific procedural problems.

However, since we have discussed mental disorder, the picture would be incomplete and misleading unless we also discussed those defences that have some relevance to the mental state of the offender and these are the defences of drunkenness, automatism, and provocation.

DRUNKENNESS

The excuse "I was drunk at the time" is very often put forward and is usually countered by the reply, "What difference does that make?" Indeed, one's immediate reaction may be that drunkenness only makes matters worse and far from being an excuse is more likely to be perceived as an aggravating factor. Merely pleading that one was drunk, in itself, has no effect whatsoever on criminal liability. There is no such thing as the defence of drunkenness.

If, however, one were to rephrase the excuse and say "I did not intend to do it, *because* I was drunk," then the defence becomes lack of intent while the *reason* is drunkenness, and lack of intent *is* a defence or, as we shall see, more accurately *may* be a defence. The first thing to realize, therefore, is that when drunkenness[1] is put forward as a defence, it is not the drunkenness itself that affects liability, but the mental state of the accused that is produced by that drunkenness that may affect liability.

We do not really know very much about the exact scientific effect that alcohol ingestion has upon the mental process, but it does not take a medical expert to know that it can range all the way from a hardly discernible relaxation to complete insensibility. At the former extreme it does not produce any diminished awareness, though only slightly beyond that it may produce a diminishing of reflexes or the lessening of one's inhibitions. One might, in this stage, be slower to react to situations or one might do things that otherwise one would not do, but one's awareness of what one is doing and the consequences of those acts remains. At this level, the drunkenness has no effect on liability, though it may affect what sentence is imposed. It may increase the gravity of the offence where it indicates a pattern of conduct on the part of the accused, or it may decrease it where, as it is sometimes put, the act "was totally out of character."

At the other extreme, continued excessive use of alcohol may produce in the accused a "disease of the mind" — that is to say, an actual degeneration of the brain cells leading to what would be categorized as mental disorder within section 16 of the Criminal Code. Here, then, it is not the drunkenness itself that is relevant, but the resultant disease of the mind affecting the capacity of the accused (the realm of the defence of mental disorder).

The problem arises when the accused is at neither extreme; when he is drunk in a manner that affects his awareness of what he is doing or of the consequences of what he is doing, or why he is doing it. If this lack of awareness is relevant to his criminal liability, then it should make no difference what its causes are. Except, however, that the issue of the effect of drunkenness raises not only strictly legal problems, but also social and policy problems. Quite apart from where rigid legal analysis would lead us, we must also ask ourselves whether, from a public policy point of view, we can afford to allow drunks to escape legal responsibility for their acts merely because they were drunk.

What the law has tried to do (perhaps not very logically) is to accept that impairment of awareness arising from drunkenness may be a defence, but at the same time to place upon such a defence socially acceptable limitations. It has, first of all, distinguished between what is called

---

1 Drunkenness is a convenient word to use, but precisely the same issues arise whether what is involved is impairment by alcohol or drug-induced intoxication.

involuntary drunkenness and voluntary drunkenness, though the terminology is not free from ambiguity. A person involuntarily drunk is one who is drunk through no fault of her own, either because she was unaware that she was consuming alcohol or drugs (as, for example, the person whose ginger ale is, unknown to her, spiked with vodka) or because the consumption was for *bona fide* medical reasons (more likely to arise, of course, in the case of drugs rather than alcohol). A person voluntarily drunk is one who is aware that she is consuming alcohol or drugs and does so for the purpose of achieving its effect — "for kicks" or "in order to get high." Perhaps somewhere in between is the young inexperienced person who knows she is consuming alcohol or drugs, but has been misled as to the effect of such consumption. It has not yet been decided into which category she falls, although one could argue for either.

Where a person is involuntarily drunk, there are, of course, no compelling reasons why she should not have all the defences that would normally be available to her. She is not likely to repeat the episode nor to be a danger in the future. If, therefore, while in this state, she acts unconsciously so as to be unaware of the fact that she is doing anything, there is no conscious voluntary act on her part and her defence is simply that she committed no criminal act. If while in this state, she knows that she is acting, but because of the intoxication, does not realize the consequences of her act, or does not intend these consequences or does not act for any unlawful purpose, then her defence is simply that she did not have the requisite mental element of intent or purpose or knowledge (whichever is required) and is therefore not guilty.

The voluntarily drunk person, however, poses a different problem. It is her own fault that she is in this state; she may, in all probability, repeat it again; and she may represent a considerable continuing danger to other people. One cannot simply apply to her the same principles that one applies to the person who is involuntarily drunk. On the other hand, one cannot merely convict her when, in fact, the necessary elements to make her guilty of the offence charged are not present.

The second thing that the courts have done, therefore, is to deny that, in the case of the voluntary drunk, drunkenness can be raised so as to negate the consciousness of the conduct of the accused. They have refused to accept that, unless the drunkenness has reached the extreme stage of mental disorder (in which case a verdict of not responsible on account of mental disorder with the ensuing consequences would be appropriate), a person could be so voluntarily drunk that she is not conscious of the fact that she is doing anything at all. This may not accord with the psychiatric realities of the effect of drunkenness, but, as we saw with mental disorder, we are dealing here with the *legal* problem of responsibility, not with the application of medical principles.

The third and, in many ways, the most difficult approach the courts have adopted to deal with the situation where the voluntary drunk claims that she lacked the necessary intent because of her drunkenness, is to distinguish between two different sorts of crimes. Some crimes require no more intent than the intent to do the act in question knowing that certain circumstances exist that render that act criminal. For example, manslaughter merely requires the causing of someone's death by criminal negligence or by an unlawful act; sexual assault merely requires the sexual touching of a person without that person's consent. Other crimes require not only the intent to do an act, but the doing of that act for the purpose of achieving some objective. For example, break and enter is only an offence if done for the purpose of committing an indictable offence in the place entered; murder requires the causing of death, with the intention of causing someone's death; theft requires not only the taking of something, but the intent to deprive the owner of what is taken.

The courts have accepted that drunkenness can be raised to negate the type of intent they call "specific" intent, but not to negate the mere awareness type of intent (what they call "general" or "basic" intent). In other words, they have accepted that a person can be so drunk as to not think rationally about what she is doing something for, but not so drunk that she cannot think rationally about the immediate circumstances of her act. Or, to put it a simple way, she is capable of thinking about the present, but too drunk to think about the future.

Whether it is all that logical or not, it is, in practice, a pretty good distinction because it does enable the courts to keep limits on the "defence of drunkenness." Because of the doctrine of lesser included offences that we discussed in a previous chapter, it means that in almost all cases, and in all cases that involve violence to a person, drunkenness is not a complete defence but only a partial one. If a person is charged with murder and successfully shows that, because of drunkenness, she lacked the intent to cause death, then she can be convicted of manslaughter, which is a crime of only basic intent, whereas murder is a crime of specific intent. If a person is charged with robbery — that is, an assault with intent to steal, which is a crime of specific intent — and she shows that she was so drunk that she did not have the intent to steal, she is still guilty of an assault, which is only a crime of basic intent.

One could actually reach substantially the same result by means of a different, but rather more logical route and there are signs that this route may be followed in the future. This route entails the recognition that, in addition to the requisites of an actual awareness that one is acting, or an actual desire to bring about the consequences, the mental element of many criminal offences may be satisfied by the accused being reckless as to whether she is going to act or going to bring about the consequences. If one can say that voluntarily getting drunk in the first place, under circumstances that make the commission of the act probable or the bringing about of the consequences likely, then an accused who does get drunk and who then acts or produces these consequences is reckless. Thus, drunkenness would only be a defence if it not only negated an actual awareness or intent, but if it also negated recklessness on her part.

AUTOMATISM

One essential element of all criminal offences is that the accused must have committed some act and that means that he must have consciously and voluntarily chosen to do the act. Thus, if a person is pushed into someone else, it is not his "act" and he is not guilty of an assault; or if someone is physically forced to do something, it cannot be said that that is his act. In the same way, if someone wanders naked down a street while sleepwalking, he is not consciously doing that act and thus cannot be guilty of any offence.

What has happened over the past 20 or so years is that we have realized that there are, in fact, an extraordinarily large number of conditions that may produce in a person a dissociative state during which he will go through the motions of doing something, but be totally unconscious of his acts at the time. We used to think that sleepwalking was the only example of this, but then we discovered that hypnosis can have the same effect. As medical knowledge grew, we realized that there were many other conditions. A blow to the head, for example, may produce a concussion, yet it may not affect the automatic or reflex actions in a person even though that person is totally unconscious at the time. We also know now that persons suffering from arteriosclerosis that affects the blood flow to the brain may act, but be unconscious at the time. An epileptic seizure may produce the same result, or a hypoglycemic episode in a diabetic. We also are beginning to realize that a sudden and extreme shock to one's nervous system may result in an unconscious physical reaction.

The criminal law developed at a time when we did not realize any of this and we were content to say that if a person acted, he must have been conscious of what he was doing unless he was sleepwalking or unless he was suffering from mental disorder. But we now have the problem of accommodating our increased knowledge within the structure of the criminal law that we have developed.

An easy solution would simply be to accept that any condition or event that produces a dissociative state can be raised as a defence to any crime. When, however, one bears in mind the problem of the onus of proof — that is, that the prosecution has to prove its case beyond any reasonable doubt and that the accused need do nothing beyond raising that doubt — the result of such a solution would be that it would be very difficult to convict anyone of anything. An accused might simply concoct some story about why he was in an unconscious state and thus stand a good chance of being acquitted. In any case, even if some limits could be devised to prevent that from happening, one would still be left with the utterly socially unacceptable result of having to acquit people who might, and probably would, do the same thing in the future and who may very well represent a considerable danger to the public. Just as the courts had to face up to their social responsibility in the case of drunkenness, so they have in the case of automatism — again, perhaps not logically, but the results may well justify the route taken.

While there is no burden of proof on the accused to prove that he was in an unconscious state, there is a practical requirement on him to introduce enough evidence to raise a reasonable doubt as to whether he was conscious at the time or not. Once he does that, the burden is on the prosecution to prove, beyond any reasonable doubt, that he *was* conscious. In practice, this requires the accused to do more than merely *say* that he was unconscious; it requires him to introduce some evidence of the *reason* why he was in this alleged unconscious state. The mere unsupported word of the accused is not going to cause the jury to have any reasonable doubt about his consciousness.

In virtually all cases this is going to require some form of medical testimony. The doctor is going to have to testify as to why it was that the accused went into a dissociative state. At this point, the courts have been able to distinguish between what they call insane automatism from non-insane automatism.[2] If the reason for the dissociative state is what can be labelled a "disease of the mind" then the accused's capacity to appreciate the nature and consequences of his act (or that he was acting at all) flows from a "disease of the mind" and what the accused is really saying is that he was mentally disorderedwithin section 16 of the Criminal Code. Thus, the proper verdict in such a case should not be an outright acquittal, but exemption from liability on account of mental disorder.

If, on the other hand, the accused was not suffering from a "disease of the mind," or, if he was, that that disease of the mind was not the cause of the dissociative state, then he cannot be within section 16 and the verdict of exemption on account of mental disorder is not possible. Thus, given that he was not conscious at the time of the event, the only proper verdict is a complete acquittal.

However, as we saw in the previous chapter, the courts have adopted a very wide meaning to the phrase "disease of the mind" — it is any abnormal condition impairing the functioning of the accused's mind that is internal to him. If the dissociative state is caused by any internal

---

2 Until now the distinction has been so called but that was because s. 16 referred to the defence of "insanity." Now that s. 16 no longer uses that word, replacing it with "mental disorder," it may be that the courts will now talk of "mentally disordered automatism" and "automatism not the product of mental disorder," but there is no reason to suppose that there will be any change in substance.

abnormality, then it is to be classified as "insane automatism" with the resultant verdict of exemption on account of mental disorder. It is only if the dissociative state is caused by external factors that this does not apply. If it is caused by self-induced intoxication by alcohol or drugs, then, as we have seen, the accused's defence, if any, would merely be whatever defence is afforded by his drunkenness. What we are, in fact, left with are very few cases of genuine non-insane automatism, such as a blow to the head that causes a concussion producing some unconscious reflex movement, or possibly some gross trauma produced by a violent sudden shock as might arise on seeing one's wife being raped by someone.

PROVOCATION

The third "mental disturbance" defence that frequently arises is known as the defence of provocation and is applicable only to the offence of murder. No one doubts that a person may be provoked into committing other offences — particularly assault — but in these cases the element of provocation can be taken into account by a reduced sentence. In murder, where the sentence is fixed by law at life imprisonment, the provocation element cannot be taken into account at the time of sentence and thus some other way has to be found to provide for the person who is provoked into killing another.

The defence of provocation, where it applies, has the effect of reducing what would otherwise be murder to the offence of manslaughter. It is a very old defence and was, in fact, in existence long before the courts had already analyzed the whole problem of intent and consciousness. The result is that there may be, as we shall see, some inconsistencies and overlapping with various other "defences."

The law recognizes that even the ordinary law-abiding person can be so provoked by someone else that he loses his temper and kills his tormentor. Provocation does not excuse the killing, but it does reduce that killing from murder to manslaughter.

Provocation is any wrongful act or insult that is sufficient to deprive an ordinary person of the power of self-control. This is to be judged by the jury on an ordinary objective standard. They must first be satisfied that whatever was said or done to the victim would have caused an ordinary person to lose his self-control, so that if the accused is unduly sensitive or more easily provoked than an ordinary person, the defence of provocation fails on this ground. This means that the ordinary person, in this context, means the ordinary person of the accused's age and background, but not with any susceptibilities or temperaments peculiar to the accused.

This is, however, only the first hurdle. Once that has been passed, the jury must then find that the accused was, in fact, deprived of the power of self control, or, to be more accurate, find that the prosecution has not proved, beyond any reasonable doubt, that the accused was not, in fact, deprived of his power of self-control. In other words, an accused cannot use the provocation defence as an excuse when he was not actually provoked, even if an ordinary person would have been provoked.

The third requirement is that the accused must have acted spontaneously before there was time for his passion to cool. If an accused is provoked but leaves the scene and, after brooding on the insult, decides to retaliate, he cannot plead provocation since provocation necessarily implies a sudden instinctive reaction — not revenge or getting even with the other person.

Provocation, however, only arises if the homicide would otherwise constitute murder. If the killing would not, in any case, be murder, the provocation has no relevance since its only relevance is to reduce murder to manslaughter. If the accused is, at most, only guilty of manslaughter anyway, then there is no point in even talking about provocation. But murder requires either an intent to kill or an intent to cause life-threatening bodily harm and a recklessness as to whether death ensues or not. If therefore a person was provoked and lashed out at the provoker, causing his death, but he did not intend to kill him or cause him life-threatening bodily harm, he is not guilty of murder — not because of the defence of provocation but because he lacked the necessary intent. He would, in any case, only be guilty of manslaughter.

The theory of the "defence" of provocation (and the only time it is needed), is that it is the provocation that produces the intent to kill or the intent to cause life-threatening bodily harm. It is precisely because one is provoked that one intends the consequences of one's reaction.

Suppose, however, that the provocation is so great that the accused is in such a blind rage that he loses all consciousness of what he is doing and lashes out automatically. Should he not then be entitled to raise a defence not of provocation, which would still make him guilty of manslaughter, but of lack of conscious act which would make him not guilty of anything? The answer to this is not entirely clear, but there are indications that the courts would be prepared to accept that such an extreme provocation would be a complete defence. If the accused went into the dissociative state because he was prone to black-outs when provoked, then presumably it could be held that his automatism was the result of some internal malfunctioning of his mental processes and that he was therefore suffering from a mental disorder. The result of this would be a finding that he was not responsible on account of mental disorder. If, however, the stress was so great that even an ordinary person would have blacked out, then one could not hold that the accused was suffering from any abnormal mental condition, and the result should be an outright acquittal.

18

Conviction and Punishment

If the accused pleads Guilty, or is found guilty, either of the offence charged, or of a lesser included offence, the judge is then faced with the problem of sentencing the offender. Whether there is a jury or not, it is the duty of the trial judge to pass sentence. In our system, the jury has no say in the sentencing process, save in the case of a conviction for second degree murder where they may make a recommendation to the judge that the period of non-eligibility for parole be increased from 10 years (which is the mandatory minimum) up to a maximum of 25 years, but even here this is only a recommendation and the judge is not bound to follow it.

Occasionally juries still add some sort of rider to their verdict of guilty such as "with a recommendation for mercy" or "with a recommendation for leniency." At the time when we had a mandatory death penalty such a recommendation could not be taken into account in the sentencing, but it was forwarded to the Minister of Justice for consideration by the Cabinet in deciding whether to commute the sentence or not. In cases other than those involving the death penalty, such a recommendation can be very confusing because if it indicates in the slightest that there may be some reservations as to the guilt of the accused, the trial judge, of course, will have to refuse to accept the verdict and send the jury back to reconsider, again emphasizing the principles of the burden of proof being on the Crown and what reasonable doubt means.

TYPES OF PUNISHMENT

Imprisonment

Determining the right sentence is far from easy. In some ways, it is the most difficult of all judicial functions, in spite of the fact that the range of different options is, in Canada, still rather limited. At the top of the scale is imprisonment. In most cases, where the Code or other statute provides for a term of imprisonment, it will do so by providing only for a maximum term — generally grouping offences into those where the maximum is life, 14 years, 10 years, seven years, five years, two years or six months, though there are a few sections that have odd terms of imprisonment as the maximum. In the case of murder, the punishment is fixed at life imprisonment — that is to say, the trial judge has no discretion other than to impose life imprisonment, though whereas in the case of first degree murder he must also impose a period of 25 years before the offender may be released on parole, in the case of second degree murder, he may impose a period of anywhere between 10 years and 25 years.[1] In some cases (though, comparatively speaking, not very many) there is not only a maximum period set, but also a minimum — for example, importing narcotics has a maximum of life, but a minimum of seven years;[2] second drunk driving offences have a maximum of one year and a minimum of 14 days.

Under the Canadian Constitution Act, the federal government has jurisdiction over "penitentiaries," while the provinces have jurisdiction over "reformatories," but these two expressions are not defined. By agreement, the arbitrary distinction has been adopted whereby a "penitentiary" is a place of detention for persons serving terms of imprisonment of two years or more, while a "reformatory" is a place of detention for persons serving terms of less than two years. Penitentiaries are therefore under the control of the central administration set up by the Penitentiaries Act, while reformatories are under the control of each provincial authority, though the terms and conditions of imprisonment of inmates in reformatories who are serving sentences after being convicted of *federal* offences are governed by a federal statute. While the programmes offered and methods of incarceration in federal penitentiaries are, therefore, fairly uniform throughout Canada, the programmes and methods in provincial reformatories may vary from province to province. If a trial judge decides upon a term of imprisonment as punishment, one consideration in deciding upon the *length*

---

1 This does not mean that the prisoner will be released after the period of ineligibility for parole. It merely means that he cannot be released before that period has elapsed.

2 Though the Supreme Court of Canada has held this provision to be a violation of the Charter guaranteeing freedom from cruel and unusual punishment. *R. v. Smith*, [1987] 1 S.C.R. 1045, 58 C.R. (3d) 193, [1987] 5 W.W.R. 1, 15 B.C.L.R. (2d) 273, 34 C.C.C. (3d) 97, 40 D.L.R. (4th) 435, 31 C.R.R. 193, 75 N.R. 321.

of the term will have to be whether it should be served in a provincial institution (in which case the term will have to be less than two years — indeed, two years less a day is not uncommon) or in a federal institution.[3] He may also order an offender to be detained in a mental hospital for up to 60 days as the initial part of any custodial sentence he has imposed where he finds that the offender is suffering from some acute mental disorder (though not, of course, one that would result in a finding of exemption from criminal responsibility on account of mental disorder) and is satisfied that immediate and urgent treatment is required to prevent further deterioration. At the end of the period specified in the order, the offender is then transferred to a prison or penitentiary to serve the rest of his sentence.[4]

Fines

The second type of punishment is the fine — that is, a monetary penalty. Unless the offence is one for which a fixed or minimum term of imprisonment is prescribed, a fine may be imposed in addition to, or in lieu of, a term of imprisonment where the maximum penalty is imprisonment for five years or less. If the maximum is more than five years' imprisonment, a fine may be imposed only *in addition* to a term of imprisonment, though that term may be quite short. If the fine is not paid, as ordered,[5] a term of imprisonment may be imposed, but may not exceed two years in the case of offences punishable by less than five years, or five years in the case of offences punishable by more than five years.[6] Generally, where both a fine and a term of imprisonment are imposed, an extra term for failure to pay the fine may not exceed the term of imprisonment imposed.

Probation

The third type of disposition is the suspending of the passing of sentence and the imposition of a probation order, which is possible in any offence not having a proscribed minimum. Generally, a probation order

---

3 It can get rather complicated where the offender is convicted of two offences and sentenced to two consecutive sentences or where he is already serving a term of imprisonment and a second term is then added to the first. All these variations are provided for in the Criminal Code, s. 717.

4 This provision requires the cooperation of the provincial authorities who will have to provide the facilities and has not, in consequence, yet been proclaimed in force. As provinces announce that they now have arrangements in place, it will be proclaimed.

5 There are several provisions relating to the right of a convicted person to apply for time to pay a fine, which, in some cases must be granted (see s. 718 of Criminal Code).

6 Part payment of a fine results in a *pro rata* reduction of a term of imprisonment imposed for default.

may not exceed three years in duration and will contain a number of conditions respecting the conduct of the offender while he is on probation. These may include standard conditions such as being on good behaviour, reporting to a probation officer and so on, and specific conditions such as abstaining from alcohol or performing some community service work. If the probation is successfully completed without breach of conditions, then no further sentence is imposed and the offender is discharged. If, however, the offender breaches the probation order, he is guilty of the specific offence of failing to comply with a probation order and he may, in some circumstances, be returned to court and be sentenced for the offence of which he was originally convicted.

Where an offender has been fined in lieu of imprisonment, or has been sentenced to a term of imprisonment not exceeding two years, or has been sentenced to an intermittent term of imprisonment not exceeding 90 days — that is, one that is ordered to be served, for example, on weekends — then a probation order not to exceed two years in duration may also be imposed.

Absolute or Conditional Discharge

If the offence is not one with a minimum penalty, nor one punishable by imprisonment for 14 years or life, the offender may, in spite of the conviction, be given an absolute or conditional discharge. The effect of the discharge is that no conviction is recorded against that person. Where an absolute discharge is given it is effective immediately; where the discharge is conditional, the offender is under a probation order for the requisite period and must comply with the conditions. At the end of the term, if he has not violated the conditions, he will be deemed not to have been convicted of the offence; if the order is breached, he may be charged with the offence of failing to comply and, under some conditions, be brought to court and sentenced for the original criminal offence. The crucial distinction between a suspended sentence and probation order and a conditional discharge and probation order is that, in the case of the former, successful completion of the probation still results in a conviction, whereas in the case of the latter, successful completion of the probation means that there is no conviction against the offender. This is why a discharge, either absolute or conditional, may only be given if the judge considers it to be in the best interests of the accused and not contrary to the public interest.

In general, these are the only options available to the judge,[7] though there may be other consequences of conviction for certain offences. Forfeiture, for example, may be ordered of things such as illegal drugs, weapons, obscene materials and so on. In some circumstances, the offender may be ordered to make restitution to the owner or be ordered to make recompense to the victim. Sometimes loss of certain rights may follow, such as the suspension of a driving licence or the inability to sit as a member of the House of Commons or of a Legislature.

PRINCIPLES OF SENTENCING

Given these options, how does a judge choose one over another? Of course, he is limited by the maximum penalty provided and sometimes by a minimum or fixed penalty, but more often than not, these do not help a great deal. The question can only be resolved by determining the purpose of punishment — by asking why we impose any punishment at all.

Punishment is not vengeance or retribution and by and large our judges start with the proposition that they should impose the least serious penalty on the offender that will achieve (or may be seen to achieve) the objectives of punishment. All punishment exists to protect society, but this, in itself, does not advance matters much because one must then ask how is society protected by the imposition of punishment?

Punishment may have a moral, educative effect on the community. For example, if a substantial segment of the population inclines towards making light of the offence of drunk driving, then they may have to be informed of its seriousness and one way of doing that is by imposing more severe punishment on such offenders. Eventually, one hopes, the seriousness of the offence will be brought home to them and hence drunk driving will be minimized.

Deterrence

Closely allied to this is the concept of general deterrence. If there are members of the community who cannot, or will not, accept the fact that drunk driving is socially harmful (or hate propaganda, or discriminatory offences, or income tax evasion or any other offence), then perhaps they will be deterred from committing the offence when they see punishment meted out to other offenders. Whereas the moral, educative

---

7 The same sort of options are available after conviction for a provincial offence, but the penalties are likely to be less serious. Most commonly, fines are imposed with a short term of imprisonment in default, but some provincial offences can result in fairly substantial fines or terms of imprisonment.

effect of punishment hopes to see people stop committing offences because they are taught not to, deterrence hopes to prevent those offences by threats of what will happen if they do.

Deterrence only works, of course, if people rationally stop to consider what might happen if they commit an offence. It requires them to realize that there is a good chance they will be caught and a good chance that such a punishment will be imposed on them. It also requires that they be made aware of the threat and this requires publicity.

While such aspects of punishment are directed towards having an effect on *other* people, punishment, of course, is also directed for its purpose towards the offender himself. It may deter *him* from committing a similar (or any) offence again — this is called specific (as opposed to general) deterrence. It may also *isolate* the offender from the general community so that, at least for the period of his incarceration, he is incapable of inflicting any harm on society in general, though he may harm the specific prison community of which he is a member.

Imprisonment for the purposes of isolation has its problems. It is expensive,[8] and may result in the individual's spouse and children becoming dependent upon the taxpayer during the incarceration. The inmate is taken out of the work force for what could be a very productive period of time and, in most cases, the offender will eventually be returned to society where he may represent an equal, or even more serious danger, than when he went in.

Rehabilitation

On the other hand, imprisonment may be for the purpose of educating or reforming the offender. By offering him a chance to further his education or his skills, or to alter his way of life, he may not wish to commit further offences when he is released. In this event, the purpose of imprisonment is not deterrence by threat, but by reform or rehabilitation.

Discretion of Trial Judge

No one purpose of punishment can be singled out as the sole factor. Either expressly or intuitively, every judge will consider the offence and the offender — that is, the objective circumstances of the offence, its seriousness, the harm caused, the degree of violence used, the effect on the victim and so on, and the objective circumstances of the offender, his age and sex, his criminal record, his family and personal history, his medical and mental problems and so on. He will then mesh those considerations with all the purposes of punishing the offender for the offence and decide

---

8 It costs about $50,000 a year to keep one person in prison.

what is appropriate. He will usually hear representations from the prosecutor and from the accused and may receive any evidence that is relevant to the process. He may require a pre-sentence report to be prepared by a probation officer to assist him. Sometimes it is a short and simple task (a trial judge is not likely to spend much time deciding on a sentence for someone convicted of failing to stop at a stop sign) and sometimes a trial judge will spend days agonizing over the appropriate sentence.

This may lead to what is perceived as disparity in sentencing. In Canada we do not have a tariff system — that is, fixed penalties for each offence — though in some provincial offences (usually of a minor nature) there will be a set fine for each offence (though even there, there are usually provisions for varying the fixed amount). Murder and high treason have fixed penalties, of course, but generally speaking, all sentences are geared to the individual who committed the offence. One may have two offences that, objectively, are identical — for example, two offences of theft of $500 — yet one offender may be given a sentence of six months' imprisonment and the other a conditional discharge. The sentences are disparate, but not the principles according to which the sentences were arrived at. One offender may be a 30-year-old man with a record of 10 similar convictions; the other may be an 18-year-old youth with no prior convictions. It is perfectly justifiable that the sentences *are* disparate.

Dangerous Offenders

There is one special part of the Code that deserves particular mention with regard to sentencing and that is that dealing with dangerous offenders. As was mentioned earlier, one trouble with imprisonment is that the offender will one day come out of prison and he may represent more of a danger than when he went in. Yet if his sentence has expired, he must be released. Only the person sentenced to life imprisonment may be incarcerated for life.

When a person has been convicted of what is called a serious personal injury offence — that is, one involving the use of violence against another, or one that endangers the life or safety or mental health of another that is punishable by 10 years' imprisonment or more, or when he has been convicted of one of the more serious sexual offences — then an application may be made to the judge to have that person declared a dangerous offender. The application requires the consent of the Attorney General and then there must be a due hearing, with evidence called for both sides, after which, if the court is satisfied that the offender constitutes a threat to the life, safety or physical or mental well being of other persons (based on the evidence as to the personality of the offender) or, if he is a sexual offender, that he is likely to cause pain, injury or other evil to other persons because of his failure in the future to control his sexual impulses, then the court, in lieu of sentencing him for the offence of which he was convicted, may declare him to be a dangerous offender and impose a sentence of detention for an indeterminate period. Whether such an offender is actually released, and if so, when, depends not on the sentencing judge, but upon the Parole Board.

RELEASE FROM PRISON

Remission

Any inmate serving a fixed term custodial sentence for a federal offence may be entitled to what is called earned remission, which may actually reduce the time spent in prison by one-third. Remission is earned basically by satisfactory participation in some rehabilitation programme and by satisfactory conduct generally while a prisoner. This is assessed monthly and the inmate is notified each three months of the amount of remission earned. However, remission can also be lost for a variety of reasons, ranging from unsatisfactory performance in a programme, to a serious offence against discipline. In practice, most inmates earn (and keep) all of the remission for which they are eligible, and few lose more than a few days of the accumulated total. Thus, generally speaking, an inmate will know that he is due for release, not at the end of the period of time for which he was sentenced, but after only serving two-thirds of that time. When he is released, however, he is subject to what is called mandatory supervision for the remaining one-third of his sentence. We shall return to this in a moment.

Parole

In addition to remission, an inmate may be released from an institution long before the expiration of his actual sentence by action of the National Parole Board. This Board has jurisdiction over all inmates serving sentences for federal offences.[9]

An inmate generally is eligible to be granted parole after serving one-third of his sentence or seven years, whichever is the less, except where there is a statutory limitation (as in the case of inmates convicted of first or second degree murder) or where some special statutory conditions apply (as in the case of a person serving preventive detention as a dangerous offender). Of course, being eligible for parole does not necessarily mean that parole will be granted. Parole is not a reduction of the *quantum* of the sentence — it is merely release under supervision. In other words, the sentence remains, but instead of being served in the institution, it is served

---

9 Some provinces also have their own provincial Parole Boards.

in the community. The conditions of release under the supervision of a parole officer tend to be fairly strict to begin with, tapering off to a "parole reduced" standard, until finally the parole is successfully completed at the end of what would be the time limit imposed by the original sentence. In the case of persons sentenced to life imprisonment or preventive detention, that means, of course, that some form of supervision — even the most minimal — remains in effect for the rest of the offender's life.

If the conditions of the parole are breached, then the parolee may be returned to the institution to serve what remained of his sentence — in which case his parole is said to be revoked, or it may be suspended for a period of time.

Some form of partial parole may also be granted (eligibility for which normally occurs after serving only one-sixth of the sentence in custody) through what is called "day parole" — though this term is very flexible in meaning. It may enable the inmate to work in the community during the day and return to some form of custody at night, or it may enable him to live in some place other than a penal institution (such as a "half-way house" or even in private accommodation) and report periodically to a social worker or parole officer. It is particularly useful in enabling an institutionalized person to acclimatize himself to living in the community by giving him a chance to adjust gradually.

In addition to day and full parole, when an inmate who has not received, or has rejected, parole has served two-thirds of his sentence, he will, as we have seen, normally be entitled to be released by virtue of his earned remission. When he is so released he is subject to what is called mandatory supervision — that is to say, release on conditions that closely resemble those applied to paroled offenders.[10]

The parole process is an integral part of the sentencing process. If some of the purposes of incarceration are deterrence and rehabilitation, there may come a time when these objectives are fulfilled (or can be better fulfilled) on parole, and when further incarceration is not only unnecessary, but may also be counterproductive. If so, it is to everyone's interest — both the inmate's and the public's — that the offender be released. Of course, not every inmate is a fit subject for parole (indeed, some prefer to remain in prison rather than be released under supervision and wait until their sentence has fully expired) and many parolees fail and are returned to custody. Nevertheless, as a programme, it is clear that parole plays an important role in the overall sentencing structure.

---

10 The Parole Board may also grant temporary absence enabling an inmate to leave the institution for a short period of time for medical, humanitarian or rehabilitation reasons.

PARDON

The National Parole Board also administers the provisions of the Criminal Records Act. One serious disadvantage to being convicted of a criminal offence is that it results in what is popularly called a "criminal record," though, in law, that really does not have much meaning. Certainly, the conviction will be filed away and may be used subsequently for a variety of purposes, but, quite apart from that, many occupations and applications for various things require that a person not have a criminal conviction. Thus, the effect of a criminal conviction — even a relatively minor one — may continue long after the offender has served his sentence and has been fully reintegrated into society.

To meet this problem, the Criminal Records Act allows a person who has successfully completed his sentence (after a period of time which depends upon the gravity of the offence[11]) to apply to the Solicitor General for a pardon. He will then refer the application to the Parole Board who will investigate. If it is satisfied that the applicant has been of good behaviour and that the conviction should no longer reflect adversely on his character, it will recommend that a pardon be granted. The effect of this is that, unless the pardon is subsequently revoked (e.g., where the person commits another criminal offence) the conviction is "vacated" and removes any disqualification that any federal statute may have imposed.

This procedure, welcome as it is, is not entirely satisfactory. It is a federal statute and may not affect any provincial disqualification, though this largely depends upon what "the conviction being vacated" means. It cannot mean that the conviction is totally expunged, since it is capable of being revived if the pardon is revoked, and it remains in some record or other even if that record is not generally available. Whether it entitles the person to answer "No" if asked whether he has been convicted of an offence seems to be a moot question, though if he cannot, the whole point of the Criminal Records Act is dubious.

MENTALLY DISORDERED OFFENDER

One final problem concerns the mentally disordered offender. As we have seen, many such persons are not within the scope of section 16 of the Code and are thus convicted, yet it is clear that they are in need of treatment. If the offence for which they are convicted is not too serious, one possibility is to impose a term of probation on condition that the offender take psychiatric treatment, but with any more serious offence

---

11 Generally, two years after the completion of a sentence for a summary conviction offence and five years in the case of an indictable offence. The actual time limits are a little more complicated.

there is little that can be done except impose a term of imprisonment and hope that some treatment can be provided in the institution.[12]

Custodial psychiatric facilities are not, in general, good in this country, though they vary from province to province and from provincial institutions to federal institutions. A sentencing judge has no power to order in which institution an inmate must serve his sentence, since that is a matter for the prison authorities, though he does know that if the term is less than two years it will be served in a reformatory and, if it is two years or more, that it will be served in a penitentiary. He must first, then, make the decision as to whether the offender should serve his time in a provincial institution (in which case the maximum must be two years less a day) or in a federal institution (in which case it must be two years or more). He is then perfectly entitled to recommend to the appropriate prison authority that the offender receive psychiatric treatment or serve his time in a particular institution which has the required facilities. Some provinces have good facilities, but others are lacking in adequate facilities. The federal system, on the other hand, is so crowded that, even with the best will in the world, treatment is likely to be rudimentary at best.

Finally, there are provisions enabling an inmate serving a custodial sentence to be transferred from the penitentiary or prison to a mental hospital for treatment where his condition is such that treatment and care in the penitentiary or prison is inadequate. He is returned to penitentiary or prison on the conclusion of such treatment to serve the remainder of his sentence, though, if still dangerous, the provincial Mental Health Acts may be invoked to retain him in custody if the term of his sentence expires before a cure is effected.

---

12 Except for the hospital order, discussed above, which, being at most for 60 days, can do little more than stabilize an acute problem.

19

Appeals and Other Remedies

Subject to the conditions we are about to discuss, a convicted person may appeal against his conviction, against the sentence passed, against being found not criminally responsible on account of mental disorder, or against being found unfit to stand trial, in both summary conviction offences and indictable offences. In the case of indictable offences, the Attorney General may appeal against an acquittal, against a finding of lack of criminal responsibility on account of mental disorder, against sentence or against a finding that the accused is unfit to stand trial. In summary conviction offences, the informant or the Attorney General (or his agent) may appeal against a dismissal or against sentence. It should be noted that the real effect of these provisions is that, in those rare cases where there has been a private prosecution of an indictable offence, the private prosecutor has no right of appeal — only the Attorney General (or his counsel) may bring an appeal in such proceedings. The position in Ontario, under the Provincial Offences Act, is somewhat different and will be considered separately.

INDICTABLE OFFENCES

Whether the trial was before a provincial judge or a federally appointed judge sitting without a jury, or a judge and jury, the appeal is taken to the Court of Appeal in the province concerned, though the actual name of that court varies from province to province.

A convicted person may appeal against his conviction, as of right, on any ground that involves solely a point of law, or, with leave of the Court of Appeal,[1] on any ground involving a question of fact or of mixed fact and law or some other issue. He may, with leave of the Court of Appeal, appeal his sentence, unless that sentence is fixed by law (though he may appeal against the discretionary portion of any period set for non-eligibility for parole after conviction for second degree murder as of right). In the same way (that is, as of right, if only a question of law is involved; with leave in other cases), he may appeal a finding that he was not criminally responsible on account of mental disorder or the finding that he was unfit to stand trial.

The Attorney General may appeal an acquittal as of right on any ground that involves solely a question of law against a finding of not criminally responsible on account of mental disorder or against a finding that the accused is unfit to stand trial. He may appeal against the sentence imposed only with the leave of the Court of Appeal (except for the discretionary portion of non-eligibility for parole after conviction for second degree murder for which no leave is required). The Attorney General *cannot* appeal an acquittal if the grounds for the appeal involve only a question of fact or of mixed fact and law.

What is a question of law as opposed to a question of fact or a question of mixed fact and law can become rather complicated, but, in essence, if the trial judge has made an incorrect legal ruling (by, for example, wrongly interpreting the meaning of a statute or by wrongly admitting a piece of evidence that was inadmissible), then a question of law is involved. If the trial judge has applied the law correctly, but has drawn the wrong inference from the facts (for example, where the appellant argues that the alleged eye-witness should not have been believed), then a question of fact is involved. Sometimes, it can be partly one and partly the other as, for example, where the appellant argues that the case was not proved beyond any reasonable doubt, which may involve both legal and factual issues.

There are time limits within which notice of an appeal must be made, but there are provisions for extending that time for proper reasons. Pending the appeal, the convicted person may be released on terms similar to those applicable for the pre-trial release mechanism. Once the appeal process is underway, the Court of Appeal will receive all the relevant documents in the case, including a transcript of the trial proceedings and each side will have all of the material available. The Court of Appeal may, in addition, order the production of any other material it considers relevant and may

---

1 Leave may also be given by a single judge of the Court of Appeal or by the trial judge. In any case, the appellant must receive permission before he can appeal in these cases.

hear the testimony of any further witnesses, though usually the appeal will consist merely of arguments of counsel based on material already before the court.

If the accused is appealing his conviction or other adverse verdict, the Court of Appeal may allow the appeal if it is of the opinion that the trial judge made an error in law, or that the verdict was unreasonable and cannot be supported by the evidence, or that there has been a miscarriage of justice. In such cases it may either direct that the accused be acquitted or it may order a new trial. Generally speaking, if, with the error corrected, it is apparent that there is no evidence left that would support a conviction, it will direct an acquittal, but if, with the error corrected, there still remains a case for the accused to answer, it will order a new trial. A successful appeal does not, therefore, necessarily mean that the accused will go free — in most cases, he will merely be entitled to a new trial.

If there is no merit in the accused's appeal then, of course, the court will dismiss the appeal, but it may also dismiss the appeal if it is of the opinion that, in spite of the error, no substantial wrong or miscarriage of justice has occurred. In other words, if there was an error, but no reasonable jury could have failed to convict even without the error, then it may dismiss the appeal.[2]

If the Attorney General is successful in his appeal against an acquittal, then the court may either order a new trial (which it will usually do) or, except where the trial was before a judge and jury, enter a conviction and pass sentence. It will only do this in those cases where, if it were not for the error, the accused must have been convicted on the evidence properly before the judge.

If the appeal is against sentence, the Court of Appeal may either dismiss the appeal or vary the sentence in accordance with the legal limits. But this does not necessarily mean reduce the sentence when the accused appeals or increase it when the Attorney General appeals, though this is usually the case. The court may, on the contrary, allow an appeal and increase the sentence when the accused appeals or decrease the sentence when the Attorney General appeals.

In addition to these general appeal provisions, the Minister of Justice may, upon application by a convicted person or a person sentenced to preventive detention, refer any matter to the Court of Appeal to hear as though it were a regular appeal, or advise him on any matter on which he requires its assistance, or even by-pass the Court of Appeal and simply

---

2 The court also has the power to substitute a conviction for an included offence where that would have been the correct verdict (e.g., manslaughter for murder), and to substitute a finding of not responsible on account of mental disorder or find the accused unfit to stand trial.

direct a new trial or a new hearing. This last procedure is virtually obsolete, though the Minister's power to refer a case to the Court of Appeal, while not common, is still exercised.

From the Court of Appeal there is a limited right of appeal to the Supreme Court of Canada, but this requires the leave of the Supreme Court itself.[3] Generally, the Supreme Court will only hear appeals against convictions by the accused or against acquittals by the Attorney General that involve questions of law and, even then, only if some important issue is involved.

Under the Supreme Court Act, the Minister of Justice has a similar right to refer a matter to the Supreme Court of Canada as he has under the Code to refer a matter to the Court of Appeal.

SUMMARY CONVICTION OFFENCES

Oddly enough, the appeal procedure in summary conviction cases seem rather more complicated than those for indictable offences, but that is only because there are alternative ways of proceeding.

There are two forms of appeal in summary conviction offences that may be used in the alternative, but they cannot both be used. The first method, the ordinary route, enables a defendant to appeal his conviction or sentence, or the informant (or Attorney General or his agent where he has prosecuted) to appeal a dismissal of or order staying the information or sentence passed on a convicted defendant to what is called the appeal court. This is not the Court of Appeal, but a single federally appointed judge — a judge of the Supreme Court or court of equivalent jurisdiction. No leave to appeal is required and the appeal may be brought on any question, whether of fact, or law or mixed law and fact. There are provisions for the interim release of a defendant pending an appeal that are similar to those given to the Court of Appeal in the case of indictable offences, and the procedure, in general, is not too different from that case. It may sometimes happen, however, that the transcript of the original trial before the summary conviction court is missing or defective and there is a provision in section 822 for the appeal court, instead of hearing the appeal based on the papers before it, to order the appeal to proceed by way of "trial de novo" — that is to say, a new hearing by re-trying the defendant all over again.

A second method is to proceed by way of what is called a summary appeal on the transcript or on an agreed statement of facts. If there is no dispute as to the facts and the only point in issue is a question of whether

---

3 Though leave is not required if one judge dissents in the Court of Appeal and the appeal is taken on the point of law on which he dissents. The right to appeal without leave is actually a little more complicated than this, but this is the provision usually invoked.

the trial judge made an error in law, or as to his jurisdiction (by exercising it when he had no jurisdiction or by refusing to exercise it when he has jurisdiction), then either side (or the Attorney General) may appeal the conviction, judgment, acquittal or any other final determination to what is also called the appeal court, but for this purpose "appeal court" means and must be the superior court for the province involved. This means, in practice, a single judge of the superior court of the province, though since the Court of Appeal is also the superior court, it could mean the Court of Appeal.

The appeal is argued on the basis of either the transcript of the trial or on the basis of a short statement of the facts that the parties are agreed upon. Since no argument is permitted on the facts under this method of appeal, and since both parties are in agreement as to the facts, the actual transcript of the trial proceedings are not all that important. Having heard the argument, the appeal court will then deliver its judgment, affirming, reversing or modifying the decision of the trial court or send the matter back to the trial court for the trial judge to deal with it in accordance with the opinion of the appeal court. It is a simple and convenient way of appealing a summary conviction matter when there is only a legal or jurisdictional issue involved.

From a judgment of the appeal court if the first method was adopted, or a judgment from the superior court if the second method was adopted (save where the superior court in question is itself the Court of Appeal), an appeal may be taken by either party (or the Attorney General) to the Court of Appeal of the province, but only on a question of law and only with the leave of the Court of Appeal.

While the Code does not provide for an appeal to the Supreme Court of Canada from a court of appeal involving a summary conviction offence, the Supreme Court Act does itself provide for an appeal on a question of law with leave of the Supreme Court from any final judgment of a provincial Court of Appeal. Such Supreme Court appeals in summary conviction matters are not very common, but when they do arise they tend to involve some matter of high public importance, such as a constitutional question or a question involving some fundamental legal issue.

PROVINCIAL OFFENCES

Since most provinces adopt the same procedure as is provided in the Code for summary conviction offences, it is not necessary to deal with them separately. Ontario, however, as we have seen, has its own Provincial Offences Act procedure and should be at least noted. If the trial court was presided over by a justice of the peace, then an appeal lies, in the first instance, to the provincial court judge, but if the trial court was itself presided over by a provincial court judge, then the appeal is taken to a judge of the Ontario Court of Justice (General Division). The appeal lies as of right against a conviction or dismissal.[4] That appeal court has similar powers to those of an appeal court under the Code and the procedure is similar and need not be further discussed.

From that decision, a further appeal may be taken to the Court of Appeal, but leave of a judge of that court is required (which will not be given unless special grounds are made out) and the appeal may only be on a question of law alone, or in some cases, as to sentence.

REMEDIES OTHER THAN APPEAL

As will be seen, appeals generally lie only in respect of convictions, acquittals or sentence (or their equivalents), yet there are many other things done in the course of the criminal process that do not come within "convictions, acquittals, or sentence." For example, search warrants or arrest warrants are issued, accused people are committed for trials, a judge may refuse to proceed or an inmate may be detained, and all of these things may be done without justification. But if no appeal lies in respect of any of these things, what remedy does an aggrieved person have? The answer is that he may, depending on the circumstances, be able to benefit from what is called an extraordinary remedy by applying for one of four possible prerogative writs.[5] They are called prerogative writs because they stem from the inherent power of the sovereign, acting through her superior court judges, to remedy any injustice for which no other adequate remedy is available. They have a long and colourful history, as is shown by their rather quaint titles — *mandamus*, prohibition, *certiorari* and *habeas corpus*.

Mandamus[6]

This is an order that is issued by a superior court ordering an inferior court or tribunal to perform a duty that is imposed upon it and which it has refused to perform. If, for example, a justice of the peace refuses to receive an information (which he *must* do, though what he does with it once he has received it, is within his discretion), *mandamus* may issue to order him to receive it; if a provincial court judge refuses to hear a case, he may be ordered to do so.

The writ only lies against an inferior court or tribunal — that is, in the criminal context, against a justice of the peace or a provincially appointed judge. *Mandamus* generally only lies if there is no other adequate remedy; if there is an appeal process which will serve equally as well,

---

4 Or a finding of unfitness to stand trial, but this would not often arise in provincial offences.
5 There are actually more than four, but the others rarely arise in the criminal process.
6 Literally, "we order."

then there is no room to invoke *mandamus*. Thus *mandamus* only lies against these inferior courts to compel the performance of such duties as are not susceptible to the appeal process.

Mandamus also lies against "tribunals" — that is to say, administrative bodies that perform some decision-making process affecting the applicant. There are too many of these in the criminal law context to enumerate them all, but they include bodies such as the Parole Board or the Commissioner of Penitentiaries. However, if *mandamus* is being sought against a *federal* body of that nature, the application must be brought in the Federal Court of Canada, which has exclusive jurisdiction. If it is being sought against a *provincial* body of that nature (such as a *provincial* parole board), then the application must be brought in the appropriate provincial superior court. For example, if the National Parole Board has refused even to hear an eligible inmate's application for parole, *mandamus* will lie in the Federal Court of Canada; if a provincial parole board refuses to do so, the application is brought in the provincial superior court.

It might be thought that *mandamus* is of limited use in the criminal process — a provincial court judge will not very often simply refuse to hear a case or a justice of the peace not very often refuse to receive an information. But the writ is actually very useful as a means of determining some legal or jurisdictional issue. If, for example, a provincial judge determines that a legal point should be resolved in favour of the accused and for that reason refuses to hear the case, *mandamus* may be a way of reviewing the legal decision.

Mandamus only lies to enforce a duty, not to order a person to exercise a discretion in a particular way. As we saw earlier, many of the functions that are performed in the criminal process are discretionary not mandatory. For example, whether the Attorney General should order a stay of proceedings, whether a person should be prosecuted and if so, for what, or whether criminal process should be issued after an information is received are all discretionary matters. *Mandamus* will not lie in such cases because there is no *duty* to do anything — only a discretion whether something should be done or not.

Prohibition

Prohibition is, in many ways, the opposite of *mandamus*. It lies against any inferior court or tribunal to prohibit it from doing something that it has no jurisdiction to do. It is essentially an order from the superior court preventing the lower court or tribunal from exceeding its jurisdiction. Again, this may occur in an obvious case that really is not very likely to arise in practice (e.g., a provincial court judge proceeding to try an accused for first degree murder which would be a complete nullity). But more likely, in practice, it, like *mandamus*, will be used to get a ruling of a superior court on some legal issue to test the validity of what the lower court is about to do. For example, a provincial judge rules that a particular statute or section of a statute is constitutionally valid and proposes to try the accused for an offence under it. Prohibition will lie, but, of course, the point of seeking the order is really to test the constitutional validity of the statute.

Prohibition requires some diligence on the part of the applicant. It will not lie *before* the lower court has made a ruling, since it cannot be presumed that that court will rule incorrectly. On the other hand, if the lower court has already completed the proceedings, it cannot be prevented, after the event, from proceeding — some other remedy will have to be sought. It, therefore, must be sought *after* the ruling, but *before* or *during* the exercise of the allegedly illegal jurisdiction. It is not, actually, as common as *mandamus*, but still useful within its limits.

Certiorari

Perhaps the most common of all the prerogative writs is *certiorari*,[7] which is, in fact, a motion to quash a decision that has already been made on the grounds that the lower court or tribunal had no jurisdiction to make that decision. What, in effect, it does, is to remove the proceedings from the lower court or tribunal to the superior court, so that the superior court may review the proceedings below and determine their validity. Like the other writs, it only lies if there is no other adequate remedy and, indeed, the Code provides that it will not lie if an appeal was taken or could have been taken. It is thus of limited value in quashing *convictions* since an appeal is available in such cases, but it is nevertheless of immense value in other parts of the criminal process.

Essentially, it only lies to quash something done without jurisdiction. It does not lie if the lower court or tribunal acted within its jurisdiction but the applicant does not like the decision that was reached. For example, where a provincial judge is conducting a preliminary inquiry, his powers are limited to those set out in the Code. If he exceeds those powers, then *certiorari* will lie to quash a committal for trial. If, however, he acts within those powers, but the applicant just does not think that he ought to have been committed for trial, then *certiorari* will not lie.

Certiorari lies to review a large number of the processes in criminal law — to quash an arrest or search warrant where there was no jurisdiction to issue it, to quash an unlawful committal for trial, to quash an illegal decision of the Parole Board, to quash a decision based on a constitutionally invalid statute and so on.

---

7 Literally, "to be made certain." In many provinces the actual process has been simplified into a "motion to quash," but the essential elements remain.

Habeas Corpus

Probably the best known of all the prerogative writs is that of *habeas corpus*[8] though, in fact, it is of limited use in the criminal law since there are usually alternative remedies open to an aggrieved person. But where it is available, it is of great importance. It is the only writ that is now enshrined in the Charter of Rights and Freedoms which gives some indication of the esteem in which it is held.

Essentially, *habeas corpus* is a writ to review the legality of the detention of someone who alleges that he is being unlawfully confined. It is brought either by that person or by someone on his behalf. It has obvious uses — such as where a person is being locked up by someone else with no justification whatsoever — but in the criminal law context its use is rather more subtle. It may be used, for instance, to determine the release date of an inmate who has been convicted and sentenced to a term of imprisonment. This may actually be a rather complex problem where the inmate is serving three or four terms of imprisonment, some imposed concurrently and some consecutively.

One might have thought that after so many centuries during which *habeas corpus* applications have been heard, the scope and limitations of the remedy would, by now, have been fairly well established. In fact, however, *habeas corpus* is still developing. At one time it used to be asserted that *habeas corpus* would only be issued to order the release of a person, the illegality of whose detention was apparent on the face — that is to say, detention not justified by any warrant of committal at all or by a warrant that was manifestly unlawful, where, for instance, the time of legal detention had obviously expired or where the warrant was not signed. But, it was said it could not be used to go behind the warrant to examine the lawfulness of the proceedings that result in the warrant.

For example, if a person had been found guilty of an offence and committed to prison by a warrant of committal, he could bring *habeas corpus* if the warrant itself was defective. But suppose his complaint was not as to the superficial validity of the warrant, but as to the fact that the trial proceedings themselves were illegal. A number of older cases and authorities would say that *habeas corpus* would not be used in such a case because his remedy should have been to appeal the conviction or bring some other remedy to erase the conviction rather than *habeas corpus* to secure his release.

To circumvent that possible limitation, it was, and still is, common to bring two writs together in what is usually called *habeas corpus* with *certiorari* in aid. The writ of *habeas corpus* is to enable the detainee to secure his release, while the writ of *certiorari* is to enable the superior

---

8 Literally, "that you have the body."

court to examine the record and quash a conviction where it is justified. However, it will be recalled that the *certiorari* part of this two-writ application is subject to two limitations — first, it will only be against inferior courts or tribunals and second, it could not be brought if an appeal was or could have been brought. However, subject to these two limitations, the combination of *habeas corpus* and *certiorari* is a useful device to secure one's release and, at the same time, examine the jurisdictional basis for making the order for detention in the first place.

In fact, there are indications that the courts in Canada will be willing, in the future, to abandon the historical limitation that has been put on the writ of *habeas corpus* and permit it to be used even if the attack on the validity of the detention extends beyond the apparent invalidity of the warrant into an attack on the proceedings leading up to the detention.

WRIT OF *HABEAS CORPUS*

IN THE SUPREME COURT OF (PROVINCE)

IN THE MATTER OF A.B. of the City of (Name) in the County of (Name), confined or restrained of his liberty at (Insert place of confinement).

ELIZABETH THE SECOND, by the Grace of God, of the United Kingdom, Canada and Her other Realms and Territories, **QUEEN,** Head of the Commonwealth, Defender of the Faith.

TO: (Insert name or designation of person having custody — e.g., Superintendent of institution, etc.) at (Insert address).

GREETING:

WE COMMAND YOU, that you bring A.B. in person before the Presiding judge in Chambers at (Name and address of court house), on (Date and hour), together with this writ, so that such judge of our Court may then and there cause to be done with A.B. what is right and just according to law.

WE DO FURTHER COMMAND YOU to send forthwith to the Registrar's Office at (Court house) all orders, warrants, committals or other documents pursuant to which the said A.B. is confined or restrained of his liberty and which are in your possession or control, together with your certificate that the documents listed in such certificate are all of the documents pursuant to which the said A.B. is confined or restrained as aforesaid.

(signed) **REGISTRAR,**
(COURT).

ISSUED from the Registrar's Office of the Supreme Court of (Province) in the (County), pursuant to the Order of the Honourable Mr. (Madam) Justice -------- dated this (Date).

(signed) **REGISTRAR**.

20

Young Offenders and Corporations

YOUNG OFFENDERS

A child under the age of 12[1] cannot be convicted of a criminal offence in any proceedings. An adult, on the other hand, is liable to be prosecuted for any offence he commits in accordance with the processes we have discussed in this book. Between the child under 12 and the adult are those people who are called "young persons" and in respect of whom very different rules are applicable. A young person is someone who is over the age of 12 but under the age of 18.

Such people are subject to the provisions of the Young Offenders Act, which contains its own procedural and substantive rules. The Act establishes a special court known as a Youth Court which has exclusive jurisdiction to deal with any person charged with committing any federal offence while he was a young person. However, the Act encourages alternative methods of disposition by informal processes and envisages formal Youth Court proceedings only as a last resort. It leaves the decision up to the provinces how best to establish informal methods of dealing with young offenders, but, generally, if a young person accepts responsibility for the offence and is willing to participate in some rehabilitation programme and is successful therein, formal court proceedings are dropped. If he is partially successful, then formal court proceedings may also be

---

1 Or who appears to be such, but these days definite proof of age is not difficult to obtain.

dropped. It is hoped, in this way, to divert from the judicial process, those young offenders in respect of whom the social objectives may be reached without a court appearance. Thus, the Youth Court will, in practice, be dealing with young persons who have committed fairly serious offences, or who dispute the charge against them or who have shown that they are not appropriate for some other diversion scheme. At the moment not all provinces have opted to join such diversion schemes.

The preliminary steps in the process — such as the laying of an information and the issuing of a summons or arrest warrant — in general apply to offences involving young offenders in the same way as they do to those involving adults, but the young offender has rather more protection from detention in custody before trial and more protection while in custody if it is ordered. The parents (or guardians) of the offender are to be notified as soon as possible (as they must be even if only a summons or an appearance notice has been issued) so as to enable them to attend the hearing. Indeed, even if they choose not to attend, they may be ordered to do so at any stage of the proceedings, where the court considers it necessary or in the best interests of the young person involved.

There are special rules regarding the admissibility of any written statement that the young person makes to investigating officers. Such a statement is not admissible against him unless it is explained to him what the consequences of making such a statement may be and he must be given the opportunity to consult with a lawyer or his parents, or failing that, some responsible adult. Although the actual trial proceeds along the lines of an ordinary adult court with, of course, the young offender having the right to counsel and all the other constitutional and legal guarantees, there are some special provisions relating to the obtaining of medical reports, the exclusion of the public from young offender trials and restrictions on the reporting of the names of offenders.

One of the most fundamental differences between the adult system and the Youth Court is the sentencing process or, as it is called in the case of young offenders, the disposition process. The court may call for a "pre-disposition report" to examine and report on the background of the young offender and his previous history and prognostications for the future. This is to enable the court to choose the best from the large number of various dispositions that are available to it. These range from an absolute discharge to a period of secure custody in the most serious cases, not to exceed three years in duration.

In between these two extremes lies a fine or an order to pay compensation of up to $1,000, but regard must be had to the offender's ability to pay or to earn such amount through employment. The young offender may be ordered to perform some appropriate community service that does not interfere with his normal work or education for some period of time between 40 hours and 240 hours. The judge may also impose a term of probation with appropriate conditions not to exceed a period of three years. Finally, the Act provides "open" (as opposed to "secure") custody — that is, required residence in some place such as a residential centre, group home or wilderness camp, where the young person lives under supervision and is subject to control, but it is not kept in close confinement. While detention in "secure custody" is possible, it is to be used only as a last resort.

However, where the offender was over the age of 14 years, but under the upper age limit at the time of the commission of the offence, either the offender himself or the Attorney General may make application to have the proceedings transferred to the ordinary adult court if the offence that is alleged to have been committed is an indictable offence more serious than those that are within the absolute jurisdiction of a provincial judge.[2] The application may be made at any time before an adjudication is made.

The transfer may be ordered if the court thinks that it is in the interests of society, having regard to the needs of the young person involved, that he be tried in ordinary adult court. This will require the court to consider the seriousness and circumstances of the alleged offence and the history and background of the offender himself, as well as the question of whether the Young Offenders Act is the most appropriate way of proceeding. The reasons for ordering the transfer or for refusing the application must be given and various rights of appeal from the order or the refusal are provided.

Like that of the former Juvenile Delinquents Act, the purpose of the Young Offenders Act is to combine what is in the interests of the community as a whole with the special needs of young offenders. The trial process, once the trial gets under way, is similar to the process of adult court, which was not the case under the Juvenile Delinquents Act. Indeed, any other scheme would probably conflict with the Charter of Rights and Freedoms. It may be that, even now, some of its provisions will be tested for their constitutionality. One hopes that with the wide range of dispositions now available, more appropriate methods of dealing with young offenders will result in fewer of them developing into adult criminals.

Since the federal provisions are limited to young persons who commit what, in the case of an adult, would be a federal criminal offence — either an indictable offence or a summary conviction offence — it is not applicable if what is alleged against the young person would be a provincial offence. All provinces now have their own provisions for dealing with such offenders which, by and large, try to echo the objectives of the federal Act.

CORPORATIONS

Hitherto, we have assumed that the "accused" is an individual, but

---

2 This refers to those offences discussed in Chapter 11, The Trial.

there is one final point that must be noticed. Many crimes of an economic or regulatory nature (such as fraud or pollution) may be committed by a "person," but the advantage or profits that are hoped to be gained by the crime accrue not to the individual committing the offence, but to the company or corporation that employs him. For example, if a retail chain store advertises some merchandise fraudulently — say "diamond rings worth $500 each, on sale for $250," when the rings are, in fact, only worth $50 each — it is not "the store" that actually places the advertisement, but someone such as the manager on its behalf. However, the profits that are expected to accrue from the fraud go not to the manager, but to "the store."

But what is "the store"? It is an operation of an incorporated company, consisting of all of the shareholders constituting that company. When a group of individuals decide to enter into a business association they may create a "corporation" — that is, a business entity[3] that has an independent existence. One ends up with the individuals that join in creating the corporation — the directors and the shareholders — and the corporation itself.

In the case of our fraudulent advertising, one could, of course, prosecute the manager for the fraud, but it is the corporation treasury that is gaining the illegal profits and through the corporate treasury, ultimately the shareholders. If one really wishes to get at the source of the illegality, one has to go after the "corporation," not the individual. But, of course, a "corporation" cannot act — or can only act and think through the persons who run the corporation.

There are two ways in which a corporation may be criminally liable.[4] One is by making the corporation directly liable for the acts of its directing officers when they act in their capacity as the directors of the corporate affairs of the company. Under this principle whenever someone who "runs" the corporation (e.g., the president, chairman, board of directors, managing director) commits a criminal offence in his capacity as a directing mind of the corporation, then not only is he personally liable, but the "corporation" itself is also liable.

The second way is through the principle of what is called "vicarious liability."[5] When a corporation undertakes an operation (such as running a store) and delegates to someone else the managerial functions of actually running that operation, it cannot take the profits and at the same time

---

3 In fact, it need not be a "business" entity, as it may be a charitable organization or a public corporation such as a municipality or a government corporation, but it is easier if we just deal with business corporations.

4 One cannot, of course, imprison a corporation or put it on probation, but one can certainly fine a corporation — a very common penalty.

5 An individual may be liable vicariously for someone else's criminal act on the same principle.

avoid responsibility for any offences which its manager has committed on its behalf. So long as the manager is acting for the corporation and within the general scope of its delegated authority, then the corporation will be held liable for the acts of its manager.

Thus, to revert to our example of the fraudulent advertising of the diamond ring, if the advertisement is placed by the managing director of the company (or some such "directing" person), then the company is directly liable for the acts of its "director"; if it is placed by someone to whom the general management of the store has been delegated (but who is not himself part of the overall directorship of the company), then the company is vicariously liable, but liable anyway. It is only if the advertisement is placed by a mere employee who has no delegated authority that the corporation would not be liable either directly or vicariously.

The result is that where, under these principles, a corporation is held liable for the commission of an offence, in general, the procedures discussed in this book will apply to the prosecution of it for that offence. Of course, there will be differences in detail — a corporation cannot "appear" personally to answer a charge, for example — but the scheme of the prosecutorial process remains the same.

Glossary

Appearance Notice. A notice issued to an accused, in lieu of arrest, requiring him to attend at court on a specified date and time. It must be followed by the laying of the information as soon as practicable in order that it may be confirmed or cancelled.

Arrest. Compulsory restraint of an accused person in order to secure his appearance for trial, either without a warrant or under the authority of an arrest warrant.

Attorney General. The chief Law Officer of the Crown ultimately responsible for the prosecution of accused persons, the Attorney General of the Province in the case of Criminal Code offences and provincial offences, the Attorney General of Canada (the Minister of Justice) in the case of non-Criminal Code federal offences.

Certiorari. A writ issued by a superior court to review the decisions of a lower court.

Committal. The former term for an order that an accused person stand trial made by a judge after a preliminary inquiry.

Direct Indictment. An indictment preferred directly by the Crown against an accused before the court trying him, either without any preliminary inquiry or in spite of the dismissal of an information at the preliminary inquiry.

Election. The right of an accused to choose his method of trial in the case of most indictable offences. May also refer to the Crown's right to choose whether to proceed by way of indictable offence or summary conviction offence in the case of "hybrid" offences.

Habeas Corpus. A writ issued by a superior court to examine the legality of a person's detention and secure his release if the detention is illegal.

Hybrid Offence. An offence punishable either as an indictable offence or as a summary conviction offence at the option of the Crown.

In Camera. A trial or hearing from which the public is excluded.

Indictable Offence. An offence in respect of which (apart from a few of the more minor ones) the accused either must, or has the right to choose to be, tried on indictment by a judge and jury.

Indictment. A formal written allegation that the accused has committed a specified offence set out therein. Replaces the information as the document forming the basis of the prosecution.

Information. A sworn written statement before a justice alleging that the person named therein has committed a particular offence, or, in the case of a search warrant information, that there is evidence that would justify the issuing of a search warrant.

Joint Trial. A trial at which there is more than one accused person.

Judicial Interim Release. The release of an accused person from custody by a justice or judge pending his trial.

Mandamus. An order from a superior court requiring an inferior court or tribunal to proceed to perform its duty.

Peace Officer. The Criminal Code term that includes, but is not limited to, a police officer.

Preliminary Inquiry. An inquiry made by a judge in the case of indictable offences where the accused has elected to be tried by a judge alone, or by a judge and jury, to determine whether the evidence justifies ordering the accused to stand trial.

Prohibition. An order by a superior court prohibiting an inferior court or tribunal from acting in excess of its jurisdiction.

Promise to Appear. A written and signed promise to appear in court on a specified date and time given in return for being released from custody.

Prosecutor. Initially, the person who swears out the information before the justice, replaced by the Attorney General or his agent once he intervenes.

Recognizance. An acknowledgement of a debt that will be owed to the Crown in the event that certain conditions are breached.

Search Warrant. An authorization for police officers to search specified premises or other places.

Stay of Proceedings. A direction by the Attorney General to suspend proceedings against an accused person; also an order by a court that proceedings against an accused are not to be taken or not to be continued.

Summary Appeal. An appeal in summary conviction offences to the appeal court on an agreed statement of fact.

Summary Conviction Offences. The more minor offences tried on the information without further pre-trial formalities.

Summons. An order by a court ordering the appearance of an accused or witness before it.

Warrant. An authorization (usually judicial, but sometimes executive, as in a Lieutenant-Governor's warrant) empowering a person to do what is set out in the warrant — e.g., to arrest someone, to search premises, to commit someone to prison.

Index